DIGNITY IN CHANGE
EXPLORING THE CONSTITUTIONAL POTENTIAL OF EU GENDER AND ANTI-DISCRIMINATION LAW

Contributions by:

Gianluca Bascherini, Antonello Ciervo, Yolanda Gómez Sánchez,
Catherine Hoskyns, Anna Lorenzetti, Silvia Niccolai,
Giorgio Repetto, Ilenia Ruggiu, Theresa Wobbe

Edited by
Silvia Niccolai and Ilenia Ruggiu

EUROPEAN PRESS ACADEMIC PUBLISHING

This publication was funded by the Fondazione Banco di Sardegna and by the Università degli Studi di Cagliari and it is the result of the activities promoted by the Jean Monnet Chair "European Gender Policies: Building a New Menschenbild"

Fondazione
Banco di Sardegna

Education and Culture DG

Lifelong Learning Programme

ISBN 978-88-8398-062-6

Contents

6

Acknowledgments

The idea of this book emerged from the Jean Monnet Conference "Anti-Discrimination in Europe" which was held at the University of Cagliari, Political Science Department, in May 2008, with the support of the EACEA-European Commission Jean Monnet, Erasmus Programme, as one of the initiatives of the Jean Monnet Chair entitled "European Policies on Gender: Building a New European Menschenbild". We are indebted to all the students and scholars who participated in that debate: this book is one of the results of the many links and new collaborations that originated from the conference.

All authors who participated in this project owe a debt of gratitude to the people and places that accompanied them through their research. In particular, we would like to mention the Museums and the Artists (as Darlene Gait, http://www.onemoon.ca and Chemanious and Duncan anonymous Artists) that allowed us to publish pictures of their work in this book for no financial recompense.

We are grateful to the Jean Monnet-Erasmus Programme for having enabled us to establish all the connections and relationships on which this book rests; to the University of Cagliari and the Bank of Sardinia Foundation for covering the costs involved in publishing this book; to Pietro Sorrentino of the Department of Public Law and Social Studies of the University of Cagliari for administrative support; to Chiara Francesconi for her patience in the troubling phase of editing and to Alice Adams and Eric Steven Dennis for their help in revising the English version of some of the texts.

Cagliari, May 2010

Silvia Niccolai and Ilenia Ruggiu

List of Contributors

Gianluca Bascherini holds a PhD in Public and Constitutional Law, University of Rome "La Sapienza". He is Lecturer in Constitutional Law, University of Rome "La Sapienza" and Adjunct Professor of Comparative Immigration Law at the University of Perugia. His principal research interests concern Comparative and Constitutional Law, Immigration Law, Law and Literature, Emergency Powers, and Colonial Law. His main works in these areas include: "Immigrazione e diritti fondamentali. L'esperienza italiana tra storia costituzionale e prospettive europee", Jovene, 2007; "Las políticas migratorias en Europa: una visión comparada", in *Revista de Derecho Constitucional Europeo* n. 10, July/December 2008; "L'emergenza e i diritti. Un'ipotesi di lettura", in *Rivista di diritto costituzionale* 2003; *The contribution of literature to identity building: The case of European constitutional transition*, co-author with G. Repetto, paper presented at the 10th International Conference of International Society for the Study of European Ideas: "The European Mind: Narrative and Identity", University of Malta, 24–29 July 2006; "*Ex oblivione malum*. Appunti per uno studio sul diritto coloniale italiano", forthcoming in A. Cerri et al. (eds.), *Scritti in onore di Angel Antonio Cervati*. Email: gianlucabascherini@gmail.com.

Antonello Ciervo, holds a PhD in Public Law, University of Perugia (Italy), Faculty of Law. He is a lawyer in Rome. His research interests cover Legal interpretivism, Bioethics & Constitutional law, Critical legal studies, Law & Literature. Email: anto.ciervo@hotmail.it.

Yolanda Gómez Sánchez is Professor of Constitutional Law at the Faculty of Law of the National University of Distance Education (Madrid, Spain). She holds the Jean Monnet Chair on "European Constitutional Law" at the same University. She is Member of the Spanish Legal Group (FRALEX) in the Fundamental Rights Agency of the European Union; Member of the Bioethics Committee of Spain, and Director of the Official Master on European Union and PhD Programs on Fundamental Rights in the European Union. Her research interests cover European law, fundamental rights, specifically equality and gender equality, theory of legal argumentation and interpretation, and biotechnology, biomedicine and biolaw in Europe. Email: ygomez@der.uned.es

Catherine Hoskyns is Professor Emerita in European Studies and Gender Politics at Coventry University, UK. She is also a Visiting Fellow at the

Centre for the Study of Globalisation and Regionalisation (CSGR) in the University of Warwick. She is the author of *Integrating Gender – Women, Law and Politics in the European Union* (Verso, 1996) and is currently researching various aspects of gender and macroeconomics. Her most recent publication (with Professor Shirin M. Rai) is 'Recasting the Global Political Economy: Counting Women's Unpaid Work' *New Political Economy* 12/3, September 2007. Email: c.hoskyns@coventry.ac.uk

Anna Lorenzetti is a PhD candidate in "European public and Tax law" at the University of Bergamo, Italy. Her thesis will examine the European Council Directive which implements the principle of equal treatment between men and women in the access to and supply of goods and services (2004/113) and the evolution of the European antidiscrimination law. Her main interest is the study of the European antidiscrimination law. Email: anna.lorenzetti@unibg.it.

Silvia Niccolai is Professor of Constitutional Law and Jean Monnet Chair for European Law at the University of Cagliari, Italy, Political Science Department. Adopting a historical and rhetorical approach to law, her research focus on legal interpretation as a vehicle for transforming values of the living togheter. She has written extensively on European Anti-Discrimination Law and the ECJ's case law. Her recent works include: "Framing the Lisbon Strategy within the History of European Policies on Gender: a Post-Modern Vision of Human Dignity in the Making", in L. Jesién (ed.), *European Union Policies in the Making*, Kraków, Tischner University, 2008; "Derecho Anti-Discriminatorio, Nuevos Valores de Convivencia y Argumentación Constitucional, Comentario de la Sentencia Coleman vs Attrige Law del Tribunal de Justicia de la Unión Europea", in *Revista de Derecho Constitucional Europeo*, n. 11/2009. Email: niccolai@unica.it.

Giorgio Repetto is lecturer in Public Law at the Faculty of Law, University of Perugia (Italy), S.J.D. in Public and Constitutional Law, Rome, Italy. He has been visiting scholar in the Universities of Berlin (Humboldt Universität), Hamburg and Freiburg i. B.
His research interests cover comparative constitutional law, European law, human rights adjudication, comparative methodology, history and theory of legal argumentation. He recently published "I diritti all'identità sessuale e il ruolo della morale pubblica" in A. Vespaziani (ed), *Diritti fondamentali europei. Casi e problemi di diritto costituzionale europeo*, Torino, Giappichelli, 2009. His principal work concerns the use of comparative legal arguments in ECJ and ECHR case law and the

historical background thereof, with the forthcoming title: *Argomentazione comparativa e diritti fondamentali: da Vico al diritto costituzionale europeo.* Email: giorgiorepetto@yahoo.it.

Ilenia Ruggiu is lecturer at the Department of Public law and Social studies-University of Cagliari-Italy where she teaches constitutional law and local government law. She is the author of *Contro la Camera delle Regioni. Istituzioni e prassi della rappresentanza territoriale* (Jovene, 2006) in which she develops a critic of Regional Chambers. She taught Human Rights in the International Master programme in Derecho Constitucional at the University of Seville. She benefited of grants from Italian, Spanish, Canadian governments, and from Scottish and Sardinian institutions to study identity related subjects. Her research interests are: federalism; cooperative institutions between state and regions; regional identity; comparative methodology; dynamics of recognition of cultural identity in juridical texts and in courts; cultural identity of aboriginal people and the Roma people. Email: iruggiu@unica.it.

Theresa Wobbe is Professor of Sociology of Gender at the University of Potsdam, Germany. She is the author of *Von Rom nach Amsterdam. Die Metamorphosen des Geschlechts in der Europäischen Union* (Verlag für Sozialwissenshaften, 2009) (with I.Biermann). Her research focus on the shifting modes of gender equality while relating EU-gender politics to deeper structures of societal inclusion and solidarity. From a sociological perspective, she explores the profound shift to including individuals as "gendered persons" in the more broadly historical context of European modernity. Together with B. Berrebi-Hoffmann and M. Lallement (CNRS, Paris), she is currently researching national notions of gender equality during the 19th and early 20th century. Her recent publication is "Vom 'nation-building' zum 'market-building'. Der Wandel von Vergesellscafttungsformen im Europäischen Integrationsprozess", *Mittelweg,* 36, 3-16. http://www.eurozine.com/pdf/2009-06-23-wobbe-de.pdf. Email: twobbe@uni-potsdam.de.

Introduction

Silvia Niccolai and Ilenia Ruggiu

1. Dignity as an object of legal research

This book discusses dignity without attempting to rigidly define this somewhat awe-inspiring European postwar constitutional concept, now considered, following the entry into force of the European Charter of Fundamental Rights, as one of the cardinal values of the EU legal order. After all, assigning a normative content to dignity is impossible (for a resume of the plurality of meanings: Ceccherini 2008). As its often noted "generality" (Schefold 2007 and 2008) demonstrates, the principle of dignity is a recapitulatory clause to a series of qualities, considered absolute essentials, pertaining to the individual and to the relationships between individuals and groups (there is no dignity without equality, there is no dignity without integrity, there is no dignity where someone or something dominates someone else). To agree, philosophically, that dignity opposes the human person being used for the values and interests of others (Habermas 2004) does not avoid, at the juridical level, facing a qualitative value judgement (Giuliani 1966), one that is historically situated (Caiani 1954) and basically comparative (Repetto 2009a), every time it is required to ascertain, in order to solve a concrete controversy, where exploitation and undue subordination begin, and where instead there is a normal and tolerable, or even just and appropriate, relationship between concrete human beings, their lives and their relevant contexts. These latter elements are in turn many and changing: if dignity was born to defend individuals against the assaults of political regimes and economic systems, today science and technology as well as the family and the various communities to which a person belongs, including cultural minorities, are perceived as possible threats to human dignity (as well as components of it), and the list goes on. Since legal reasoning is nothing but the never-ending dialectic effort to find, to practical ends, a provisional consensus among the meaning of expressions destined to remain obscure and that for this reason are leading (Perelman 1980), dignity is thus a quintessential legal "topos". That is, it assumes a practical content only as reflection, applied to concrete controversies, of shared opinions about what a normal and worthy life consists of. When an image of human beings and their relationships, in a given time and context, takes enough form to assume a certain capability of being recognized and accepted and is thereby referred to in deciding between conflicting interests, then the principle of dignity reflects it.

Dignity is thus a highly emancipatory principle that protects liberty, and that is rooted in common sense. It is from this that the many paradoxes of dignity originate: there is always the risk of dignity being invoked to justify the majority's will to condition, limit and, to borrow a word from Michel Foucault, discipline the ways through which other people try to signify their personality (Gómez Sánchez 2005). Such a risk is counterbalanced only by keeping as open and pluralistic as possible the variety of the communicative means and forms of representation which are able to influence the views about what is fair and reasonable (and thereby corresponding to the principle of dignity).

In fact, in order for an image of normal and worthy life to take shape, evolve and change, a number of factors come into play. These make dignity evidence of the cultural character of law (Häberle 2003) and stimulate the jurist to carry out broad and multifaceted research. Among the many factors influencing and shaping the idea of dignity, the choices or preferences that a given legal order expresses are certainly included (from the normative acts it adopts to the interpretative traditions it cultivates; from the services it provides to the constitutional values it proclaims). Others factors can be traced at the social, economic and symbolic levels, the various and changing trends which become perceptible through many different paths and with the intervention of many different players (ranging from political parties and movements to novels, films and the arts: Cervati 2009a). Often the demands for justice, which pose new and challenging questions, are revealing. They signal changes in what is considered fundamental to the human being.

2. Contents: investigating EU gender and anti-discrimination policies as signs of a change in values in contemporary living togheter

This book looks at the European integration process as one of the main factors that in Europe, over the last 50 years, has contributed to the transformation of views about normality and value, justice and reasonability, of which the principle of dignity is a vehicle. EU gender and anti-discrimination policies are seen as the main components and key elements with which to decipher the EU contribution to the contemporary idea of a normal and worthy life. The book stresses that these policies are based on a characteristic balance between economic and social concerns, which makes them 'new' in comparison with the traditional, state-based, approach to rights. From this angle, the book analyses how the idea of normality is changing regarding work and care labour, the heterosexual and homosexual paradigm and how values such as equality are tranforming in order to recognise and promote diversity.

In the first section, the book starts by arguing that the EU contribution to a renewed idea of a normal and worthy life basically operates in a very specific and highly relevant field: the acceptable and desirable relationship between life and the economy, society and the market, or, in other words, between the productive and the re-productive spheres. The book stresses that this contribution comes mainly from EU Gender Policies, given that, as Catherine Hoskyns explains in her chapter, this is the field where the Economic and the Social intertwine, urgently questioning the value of care and unpaid work (reproductive activities). According to Silvia Niccolai, the idea of the exchangeability of gender roles – flowing from the anti-discrimination principle - inspires EU gender policies, and features the shifting boundaries between production and reproduction generated by the entry of women into the market place. Controversial and challenging, this idea proves the capability of the European integration process to produce constitutional change by applying the hermeneutic potential linked to its characteristic economic sensitivity, which has allowed the European Union – as Theresa Wobbe argues – to develop towards the idea of a Community based on proper feelings of recognition and belonging.

The ECJ's case law and the process of EU law's national implementation are two crucial instances where the needs, ideas and points of view that emerge from the national and sub-national levels have an influence on the EU discourse. The book's second section explores this process of circulation and mutual exchange, which is particularly revealing with regard to investigating the values in the construction of post-patriarchal society. In this process, the EU gender acquis, surely based on the rhetorical strength of the equality principle (explored by Antonello Ciervo in his chapter), provokes reactions that enrich its fabric. This is significantly mirrored by two examples presented. The first, that reported by Yolanda Gómez Sánchez, of the Spanish "effective equality" Act of 2007, which takes inspiration from the EU gender equality acquis and adds much to it, not least a differing qualification of the crime of sexual violence if committed by a man or by a woman. The second, that of the implementation process of the Goods and Service's directive, is the earliest step in the search for a new balance between the Economic and the Social, which has been studied by Anna Lorenzetti.

The book's third section broadens the scope by analysing issues surrounding other non-majority identities. Homosexual, immigrant, and cultural difference are at stake here along with their potential to pluralize our view of meaningful life. In exploring the legal reasoning adopted by the ECJ in its early sexual orientation-case law, Giorgio Repetto notes that the Court's use of the anti-discrimination principle abandons the dichotomist visions of reality (such as those supported by the male/female pair of comparators adopted by more formal and traditional approaches to anti-discrimination) that gender has originally promoted. Ilenia Ruggiu perceives the European discourse concerning minorities and cultural diversity as going beyond a mere perspective of protection of minority rights and towards an understanding of diversity as a public good, which implies "the insertion of new meanings in the juridical universe, the capacity to problematize points of views and to enrich the constitutional conversation". Migrants' rights at the EU level are put on the table by Gianluca Bascherini as the testing ground of the coherence of the EU approach to rights issues, of the values they actively promote, of the society they are able to depict and as revealing signals of the limits potentially affecting an evolving notion of dignity, that is however still provincially fenced around European women and men.

3. Proposal: pluralizing the concept of meaningful life

The point of view the book supports is that there is a change in values (and thereby a transformed idea of dignity) at stake in European gender policies and, more broadly, in anti-discrimination policies. What was initiated by the gender equality issue is an event, the success of which, in terms of the concrete transformation of cultural paradigms and mentalities, is linked to its capability to promote the decentring of majority and unanimistic views and to favour, instead, more porous and problematic visions of what defines a meaningful life both at the individual and the collective level.
As such, this book is far from identifying gender equality in itself as the value these policies should lead to recognizing, and the reason why they are innovative, interesting and challenging. What this book proposes seeing as at stake within EU gender policies is the possible change in the value attributed to what women have been connected to in the past (care

and reproductive activities; the physical and the sexual; an understanding of difference as a disadvantage or liability or, at least, as special attributes deserving protection). Given that women have fully entered the public arena, all these activities and conditions are now waiting to be recognized as the elements of a transformed living together, that is, to be re-valued in comparison to what has been traditionally considered superior to them (productive activities; social control of sexuality; uniformity or universalism). The book thus proposes reading EU gender policies – their permutations included - as the components of a notion-in-flux of dignity "rooted in the specificity and variety of human desires" (Repetto).

4. Method: legal experience in context

Even if a lawyer in a court room makes different uses of them, in shaping the idea of normality, worth and justice which is summarized by dignity, and which judges apply, a written legal text contributes as much as an artistic creation like sculpture. The legal experience, after all, is basically language (Cervati 2009a), and languages are many. For this reason, the chapters of this book present different materials, ranging from statutory laws to photographs; and they approach them from various angles (for example considering a controversy once for the ruling on it and once for the story the case tells, or reading a legal text as a source either of norms or of narratives), and includes insights from different disciplines. A vision of law in context is the main reason for the need of the interdisciplinary approach followed by this volume. Contributions from sociologist and political science scholars (Hoskyns and Wobbe) are not perceived merely as "other" perspectives of the same problem, but are examples of the knowledge without which law cannot proceed.

Consequential to this vision of "law in context", norms and judicial rulings are not perceived in the book in an ontological sense as autonomous entities (Vespaziani 2004; Ruggiu 2006). On the contrary norms are perceived in constant relation to concrete needs and demands for justice. Similarly, judgments are not perceived as strict applications of norms but as a dialogue between the judicial reasoning and the changing values of society.
In order to better discover these changing values and in to participate in this never-ending constitutional conversation about the concept of normal and meaningful life, legal scholars in the book give attention to insights that come from other sciences. For example: psychology (see the

reflections by Repetto on the heterosexual paradigm such as the taboo underlying the accommodation of gay, lesbian, bisexual and transexual identities), and anthropology (see Ruggiu's report on the legal translations of the concept of ethno-sphere).

The book also pays attention to comparative methodology: materials offered by different legal orders – international, European, and national (in Europe and transatlantic) – are analysed and compared as they all participate in the circulation and formation of new images of dignity.

The book owes a debt to many current philosophical or legal theories and particularly to critical theories of law (feminism, postmodernism, cultural studies, identity politics) and hermeneutic and rhetoric conceptions of law. It tries nevertheless to avoid some critical aspects of these conceptual horizons.

Critical studies, and particularly the post-modern attention to identity and culture have been accused of neglecting redistributive aspects, resulting in a lack of attention toward the material conditions of justice/injustice (Cromptom 2006). This is true in feminism, which arose to give more rights to women and to question the constituted order and started to miss some of its aims when the "cultural" entered the debate (Fraser 2009); and it is also true regarding other identities that some times receive a symbolic recognition that avoids removing the true cause of oppression (e.g. distribution of land and resources for aboriginal people).

Even when the distributive question is kept in mind, the claim for recognition of neglected identity, which finds one of its higher expressions in anti-discrimination policies, has sometimes been accused of reducing minority identity by way of an imprisoning "vulnerability".

In their turn, hermeneutical conceptions have been accused of reducing law to a linguistic game, in which law is seen only as a super-structure, which hides practices of domination and oppression.

The book tries to overcome the criticisms connected to these perceptions.

Firstly, the book pays attention to the redistributive aspects and adopts a pluralistic vision of identity. In this sense the book refuses to assume a fixed definition of gender or any other identity analysed, and goes further in the need to recognize neglected identities, sustaining the idea of coexistence of different identities in the public sphere as a source of increased dignity for everybody.

Secondly, if the book pays attention to what happens within the legal experience, to what kind of interests and questions arise in case law, what kind of reasoning and narratives are used, and what kind of ethical commitments law follows, this has not had the aim of de-structuring law. On the contrary, our aim is to re-discover law as a practical space in the search for a more equitable balance among competing interests.

PART I

LINKING THE ECONOMIC AND THE SOCIAL
IN A NEW IMAGE OF DIGNITY

The Economic and the Social
in EU Gender Policies

Catherine Hoskyns

Synopsis. This chapter examines how the economic and the social interact at the level of the EU and how this affects and is affected by gender politics and gender policy making. Using frame analysis and multi-level governance as theoretical starting points, the chapter illustrates this interaction at three key moments. These are: 1957 the adoption of Article 119 (now A 141EC) on equal pay and the follow up; 1992 before and after the adoption of the Maastricht Treaty; the present – focussing particularly on developments in EU economic and social policy and the implications for gender.
These are all points at which the economic and the social interact in particular ways at the EU level providing opportunities and challenges for the adoption of gender sensitive instruments and anti-discrimination policies more broadly. The chapter will look not only at how these issues play out with respect to labour and employment but also what attention is given to unpaid household and community work and the effects of the greater involvement of women in employment on provisioning in these areas. The main argument of the chapter is that at EU level the economic and the social are now more visibly intertwined. The economic is already deeply embedded in the social. The challenge is to bring the social, and with it gender, into the economic.
Keywords: Economic, Social, Gender Mainstreaming, European Union.

1. Introduction

This chapter asks a basic question: how do the economic and the social interact in EU policy making? The findings are crucial to an understanding of EU gender policy – they underlie the possibilities and help to explain the limitations. One point needs clarification from the beginning. In a material sense the economic and the social are always inextricably linked. Economic activity rests and relies on its social base and the social is deeply affected by prevailing forms of economic activity. However, the precise nature of these links varies and policy makers have a tendency to separate the policy making in these areas - and deny or minimise the links between the two. This is particularly true at the level of the EU. Indeed, one could argue that one of the reasons for the formation of the European Community in the 1950s was to make easier the separation of issues to do with economic management and the creation of the common market, and deal with them at European level, while leaving the social to be dealt with for the most part by the individual member states. This creates a false duality which as we shall see is constantly broken into by need and material reality.

What are the economic and the social and how are they defined and given function at the level of the EU? Fundamental to the EU's common and now single market are the free movement of goods, services, capital and labour – the four freedoms as they are commonly known. Establishing, maintaining, and regulating an integrated market on this basis is the main function of macroeconomic policy within the EU institutions. This involves a direct concern with general economic policy, fiscal and monetary policy (including managing the common currency) trade policy and labour market policy. The EU Commission has varying powers in these fields: it is the main player in trade and competition policy, but can only advise governments on issues to do with direct taxation and broad economic policy. To carry out these functions the EU has developed a widespread and diffuse interstate bureaucracy interacting with highly specialised professional networks to set standards and administer and advise on complex policy areas. Most of this activity is bureaucratic and distant from everyday life, although its impact is extensive.

The social involves everyday life and all the issues to do with the way people live both as individuals and in communities. Social policy is a form of management which deals with problems as they arise in these spheres and devises measures to remedy and control them. It also in some areas sets objectives. As far as the EU is concerned there has been a continuing debate over to what extent the EC/EU requires a 'social dimension' alongside its economic policy. The effect of this would be to harmonise objectives, standards and provision and to some extent values. Overall, the approach has been to downplay the social dimension and reduce it to the minimum required to facilitate economic integration (Hantrais 1995). Crucial here have been the different values and cultural traditions present in the member states which help to determine the kind of social policies developed. Thus by and large the policy reflects the strategy of 'embedded liberalism', the model developed by John Ruggie to explain the situation after the Second World War when certain aspects of international economics were liberalised, while the management of the consequences and social policy was primarily left to the nation state (Ruggie 1982).

Generally, in the social field policies to do with labour, which is anyway regarded as an economic category, have been most strongly developed at the European level, particularly those which encourage free movement and the right to benefits of EU internal migrants. In addition, as we shall see, the EU has developed some strong policies on equality and rights, including those on gender. The issue of unpaid work and its measurement, which could play a key role in bringing together the economic and the social, has never been taken up as a core issue. Unpaid work as a factor in the economy has been taken for granted and not dealt with centrally in either economic or social policy at EU level (Hoskyns and Rai 2007).

Keeping the social and the economic separate has the effect of separating the decision-making in a way that makes it easier (so the argument goes) to take the necessary economic steps without populations being alarmed and delaying implementation. On the other hand, it distances economic decision makers from the social consequences of their actions and makes it hard for social actors to intervene. Nevertheless, there are signs that in the EU the social is being reunited with the economic in ways that relate to the realities of the global economy. It is also beginning to be recognised that social issues are a key factor in establishing the legitimacy of the EU's economic programmes. These are connections that this chapter seeks to unravel in the context of the gender policy.

2. Theoretical frameworks

Classical theories of European integration have not on the whole proved useful in gender analysis, since they tend to be focused on the nation state and the international arena while leaving a 'black box' where social issues are concerned (Kronsell 2005; Hoskyns 2008). However, recent theories are more open and two have proved useful in writing this chapter. The first is multilevel governance which helps to identify the different levels of analysis in EU decision making and the ways in which certain actors operate within and between levels (Hooghe and Marks 2001). Research from this perspective reveals how different combinations of actors, different constellations, operate in each area of decision-making and sometimes for each decision. It is difficult for women's networks and indeed social networks more generally to participate in this process. They are often unable to demonstrate the criteria of supposed neutrality and expertise which are considered necessary (Haas 1994).

The second useful tool is frame analysis (Schon and Rein 1994). This helps in policy analysis by examining how objectives are arrived at and the precise discourse used, and then asks the question: who does the framing of particular policies? This approach makes clear the extent to which policy is socially constructed: there are few absolutes and everything depends on how the issues are formulated (Mazey 1998). The idea of competing frames has been particularly useful in revealing the process by which gender policy is constructed. Very often the initial position or frame becomes subordinated to a second and dominant frame which finally transforms the outcomes. This ties in with mobilisation of bias theories which illustrate how certain ideas and positions are filtered out as the policy process develops (Stratigaki 2005).

Both of these approaches are used in an excellent and comprehensive study of the trajectory of gender policy in the EU: Anna van der Vleuten's *The Price of Gender Equality- Member States and Governance in the European Union* (2007). None of these approaches has yet been used to integrate unpaid work and social reproduction into the more general analysis. The new trends in theory, however, open up the space to do so.

In the light of these approaches, this chapter goes on to examine three key moments in the history of the EC/EU when economic and social interests interact in particular ways. These are seen through the prism of the gender equality policy. The three moments are:

1957 which saw the adoption of Article 119 (now Article 141EC) on equal pay. This was at the height of the application of embedded liberalism.

1992 before and after the Maastricht Treaty which saw the clear need for a strengthened social dimension at EU level coming up against entrenched positions in the member states. The gender policy both benefitted and suffered from this situation.

The present when social and economic issues are becoming more closely intertwined and it is becoming apparent that a new model of embeddedness is required. The gender policy itself has now been broadened into a new equality framework. There are indications that for the first time this may enable issues of care to be raised at European level.

3. 1957 Article 119

The adoption of Article 119 on equal pay, as part of the Treaty of Rome, the founding document of the EC, is now a well known story (Hoskyns 1996, Van Der Vleuten 2007). However, it is worth recapping in this context. The basic aim of the Treaty of Rome was to establish a general common market between six member states, based on the four freedoms already discussed. This core activity was implemented by binding legal requirements enforced by the European Court of Justice (ECJ). At the same time, in the aftermath of war there were strong social concerns in the member states, concerns which led to the formation of the welfare state in the UK and to provisions in continental Europe which now define the European social model. As a result, there was considerable debate about what kind of social harmonisation might be required at European level. The answer at the time was 'not much'. Social welfare, it was thought, could best be assured at national level - with distortions ironed out by the free play of the market. Only in the area of free movement of labour between the member states were strong and binding provisions thought necessary as the negotiations continued (Collins 1975). However, this was not the end of the story and as another 'frame' came into play concessions on social policy became necessary to ensure that France remained central to the new European market. One of these measures was Article 119 which committed the EC to the principle of equal pay for women. The measure concerned only women workers and pay, and pay related benefits. There was no concern at the time expressed about the overall situation of women or with unpaid work in the home, but there was a concern about the labour shortages which women workers might fill. Because the measure concerned the labour market its provisions were formulated as binding economic law.

These provisions were enforced and expanded by activist women and by a campaigning Court throughout the seventies and eighties. At a time when the legitimacy of the EC was in question, new strong Directives were adopted which expanded the remit for women workers from pay to a much broader concept of employment equality. In 1976 in an important ruling in the ECJ (the second Defrenne case) the Court confirmed that the EC had social as well as economic objectives.[1]

These provisions provided, albeit in a narrow field, a strong social restraint on the right to compete. In other words, companies could not gain comparative advantage by paying their women workers less. Such protections have become an important element in European labour regulation and provide an example of how the social can come into the economic at EU level even while the paradigm of embedded liberalism remains strong. However, it is important to note that Article 119 embodies social regulation which is also in the long term interests of the market, in the sense that it helps to free up a new labour force. Economic objectives

---

[1] Three cases were brought in the ECJ around the situation of Gabrielle Defrenne, a Belgian air hostess who suffered a number of different forms of gender discrimination. These cases established the direct effect of European law in this context as well as the social role of the EC. ECJ cases: C-80/70, *Defrenne v Sabena (No 1)*, ECR, 1971, p. 445; C-43/75, *Defrenne v Sabena (No 2)*, ibid., 1976, p. 455; C-149/77, *Defrenne v Sabena (No 3)*, ibid., 1978, p. 1365.

normally take precedence over the purely social but when, as in this case, they are combined the case for action becomes compelling.

4. 1992 the Maastricht Treaty

The next key moment involves a jump to the early nineties. This is the period before and after the 1992 Maastricht Treaty, a time when the EC experienced one of its most serious political and economic crises. The sense of crisis began in the eighties with economic stagnation and rising unemployment. New member states were joining from the south and from Scandinavia: the fall of the Berlin wall in 1989 suggested possibilities for expansion to the east. How could the EC revitalise itself and incorporate this new and expanded membership?

The challenge was met by a dramatic increase in economic integration with the move to the Single Market, involving new levels of coordination, and then the adoption of economic and monetary union and the common currency. All of this was rolled up in the Treaty, adopted in 1992, together with the new name of European Union.[2] The Treaty introduced the concepts of citizenship and human rights into the ethos and management of the Union, thus expanding its competence with regard to people beyond the category of worker. At the same time qualified majority voting (QMV) was introduced in the Council of Ministers to speed up decision making.

All of this represented a significant increase in economic integration, moving further into the interstices of the member states and influencing in a much deeper and more all embracing fashion, the delivery of social policy. What kind of a social policy might be needed in these circumstances at European level? In recognition of this new situation a Social Protocol was signed by eleven member states in 1992 amid worries that unless firm standards were set, the new members, particularly Spain, Portugal and Greece, might be able to undercut wages and conditions in the former member states. The Social Protocol, although rejected by the UK, acted largely to reproduce aspects of the European Social Model at the level of the EU. It was clear that there was both a need for greater coordination in the social field and also great reluctance to concede new powers to the European Commission or adopt policy in this field by the old and binding 'community method'.

On the gender side this new concern with social policy unblocked the log jam of policy initiatives which had built up in the late eighties and

---

[2] Treaty of European Union (Maastricht Treaty) 1992.

allowed further Directives to be adopted. New ideas which came in here embodied gender mainstreaming (the introduction of gender into all aspects of policy) and the reconciliation of work and family life which gave partial recognition to the unpaid work and family responsibilities restricting the employment opportunities of many women. The adoption of the reconciliation policy provides a classic example of the competing frames dilemma. An initiative which started out with the purpose of benefitting women became increasingly used to support casual and temporary work (Stratigaki 2004).

As a result of these developments, we can see the scope of social and gender policy becoming broader and the contact with economic policy clearer. This allowed more focus to be placed on the interface between employment and unpaid work. At the same time, member states were wary of ceding too much control in the social field. The result is more comprehensive policies but developed through consensual methods and with fewer legal requirements. An indication of this was the fact that the important European Employment Strategy (EES) was adopted and implemented though a process which came to be called the Open Method of Coordination (OMC). The EES involves a complex array of guidelines, benchmarks and reporting requirements, and relies on monitoring and peer pressure rather than legal enforcement (Porte and Pochet 2002) The involvement of social movements and the public in this new process is still minimal.

5. Interlude

Lying behind all this and crucial to any interpretation of economic and social interaction are the changing labour markets developing at the end of the twentieth century. In contrast to what had gone before, by the nineties the most advanced areas in the economy were dealing not with the production of goods but with information, services and complex relationships. Calling this 'immaterial labour', Hardt and Negri see it as the 'hegemonic form' that is the shape of things to come. This type of labour is linguistic and affective (relating to the emotions) and thus well suited to the general characteristics of women workers. However, it may well not benefit women in terms of status and income but does make them desirable as a subordinate labour force (Hardt and Negri 2004). This analysis is extended by Diane Perrons who writes about the 'weightless economy' resting on the one to one care economy. She also sees women as particularly suited to both these kinds of work but unlikely to benefit overall (Perrons 2003) As far as campaigning and activism is concerned, many women benefitted from the new openness and the reduction of traditional barriers, but in the process much of the earlier emphasis on class differences and poverty was lost (Fraser 2009).

6. The Present – 2002 onwards

The final key moment is located in the early years of the twenty-first century, from 2002 onwards. This is again a time of crisis and change. By this stage, enlargement to the east has almost been completed with the total number of member states reaching 27 in 2007. This creates a whole new situation for decision making and the shape of the institutions. As in the earlier period, radical change is envisaged to deal with this new situation. But this time it is at a political and constitutional level rather than in the sphere of economics. The idea of a constitution that would reshape and re-energise the EU was first mooted in 2002 and a European Convention set up to prepare a draft. The need for a new form of legitimacy was evident. However, the drafters underestimated the extent of popular disillusion, and when the constitution came up for approval in 2005 it was turned down by referenda in France and the Netherlands. The degree of common policies and politics envisaged at EU level went beyond what populations could support, especially as they had hardly been involved in the debate. This illustrates the flaws in the embedded liberalism model and the consequences of keeping the social/political and the economic separate. Since then a more limited Reform Treaty has been proposed which in most countries can be approved by Parliaments rather than by popular vote. It is striking that radical change in the nineties in the economic field to deal with a crisis was possible, whereas a similar move in the political field in the present decade has proved much more difficult.
As far as gender policy is concerned, the main change has come through Article 13 EC on non-discrimination which was adopted in 1997 and gradually implemented over the following decade. This extends the grounds for discrimination from gender alone to a range of other categories including race, disability and age. Though this appears to take the focus off gender it in fact allows for 'combinations of discriminations' including gender to be tackled in new ways. The different aspects of Article 13 have been implemented in a number of strong Directives which are gradually coming through to the ECJ for interpretation. In 2006 six of the existing gender equality Directives in the employment field were amalgamated into a single 'recast' Directive (2006/54/EC) which came

into force in 2009. Despite these new developments, the economic rationale remains dominant and market reasons are increasingly being seen as a justification for narrowing the application of gender policies.

The upshot of this is that the gender policy has a broader focus along with new political and social needs and the interface with the economy has become closer over a range of issues. However, the political forms which should go along with this, and particularly participatory democracy, are missing at the European level. Nevertheless, this situation is permitting new concerns to emerge including issues to do with domestic work and care. The arbitrary and erratic way in which this is happening is illustrated by a brief look at two aspects: new forms of gender research and the recent case law in the European Court.

7. Beyond the world of work

Traditionally research on gender at the level of the EU has been focussed very substantially on labour market policies and law, since this is where the emphasis and the progress have been. In addition, there has been analysis of the political dynamics of policy making in the gender field and the trajectory over time. More recently, however, there has been an attempt to move out of the straitjacket imposed by EU policy and take a broader and more comprehensive stance. Typical of this new trend have been two projects funded by the EU Framework Programmes which test out gender equality processes at both national and European level and take a broad sweep beyond employment. The aim is to produce comprehensive data and make it 'theoretically interesting'.

The first of these, entitled 'Policy Frames and Implementation Problems: the Case of Gender Mainstreaming' and given the acronym MAGEEQ, ran from 2003 to 2005. The researchers took a range of non standard topics such as family policy, prostitution and migration and examined them predominantly in the smaller EU member states. The emphasis was on different interpretations of gender equality, the relation of these to other forms of discrimination, and the importance of regional and sub-regional contexts. The results, now published, add a greater depth and complexity to the understanding of gender equality and the policy making process, and are particularly critical of the emphases on inclusion and homogeneity which too often appear to be the underlying assumptions (Verloo ed. 2007).

The second project is Quality in Gender Policy (QUING) which runs from 2006-09. This has a more extensive reach and aims to collect data from all

27 member states. The topics covered include policy towards 'non-employment' and, unusually, the project looks centrally at social reproduction and the domestic context. The data produced should throw light on the complex relationship between paid and unpaid work and the implications of current policies.

8. Recent case law in the European Court of Justice

Examining cases before the ECJ is always instructive. Because the majority of cases are referred up from the national courts they illustrate the kinds of dilemmas and problems that ordinary people face. And yet the rulings and interpretations reflect a collective view which has to take account of different material interests and cultural contexts. Recently the Court has been faced with some difficult decisions in the social field which derive from the economic and social changes outlined above. In the two examples discussed here, the first (*Laval*) concerns a labour dispute involving competing member state interests and the second (*Coleman*) an individual case centring on disability discrimination by association and the interpretation of Article 13 EC.

In *Laval*[3] the issue concerned the right of Swedish trade unions to enforce a collective agreement on a company using lower paid Latvian workers to fulfil a service contract in Sweden. The trade unions blockaded the workplace and used secondary picketing against the company. The reference to the ECJ from the Swedish labour court posed the rights of establishment of the Latvian company against the right of the Swedish trade unions to take action to preserve living standards and working conditions. The ruling in December 2007 on the one hand recognized the right to strike and confirmed the social function of the EU but on the other affirmed the right of companies to offer services across the EU. The ruling stated, however, that trade union action 'must be proportionate'. This was particularly controversial since it seemed to bring the courts into industrial disputes in a way that is against Scandinavian traditions.

The ruling was an attempt to strike a compromise and maintain balance in a situation that pitted Swedish anti-dumping concerns against Latvian employment opportunities. It suggested, however, that the different traditions of social protection existing from the past would be hard to maintain in the current market system which now incorporates services and penetrates into every corner of society. In these circumstances, the

---

[3] Case C-341/05, *Laval un Partneri*, ECR, 2007, p. I-11767.

principles of non-discrimination and fair competition which were the cornerstones of the 1950s trade off, are in danger of being undermined. If this is the case, the consequences for low paid workers and for gender issues more broadly are considerable.

In contrast to the above, *Coleman*[4] dealt with the position of the individual in this new situation. It was one of the first tests of the scope of Article 13 EC and the Framework Directive (2000/78/EC) adopted to implement it. Sharon Coleman who brought the case saw herself as a worker and a carer and gave equal importance to both roles. While working as a legal secretary in a UK law firm, she gave birth in 2002 to a severely disabled child. Struggling as a single parent to care for her child, she claimed that she was discriminated against and treated unfairly by her employers because her child was disabled. Mothers with normal children received better treatment. She thus claimed disability discrimination by association, a claim not at that time recognised in UK law except in the case of race discrimination. The London South Employment Tribunal referred the case to the ECJ asking whether European law could supply an alternative reading in this case and whether disability discrimination by association could be seen as being covered by Article 13 and the Framework Directive. Using a variety of arguments, both humanistic and material, the Advocate-General and the full Court came out in Coleman's favour. Though the final judgement was quite narrow, relating only to parents of a disabled child, it has had the effect of broadening the scope of European law in this area and confirming its supranational effect. It also went some way towards reducing the hierarchy between productive and reproductive work and establishing the economic value of the latter (Hoskyns, Niccolai and Stewart, 2008).

9. The Future

The scenarios described above illustrate the extent of change over the last fifty years. The intensification of economic activity together with the importance now being given to immaterial labour, services and communication brings the economic into every aspect of social life. It is no longer possible, even rhetorically, as it was in the fifties, to talk about the separation of the social from the economic and the taming (or embedding) of economic liberalism at national level. The embedding of neo-liberalism, if it were to take place, would have to be at very different

---

[4] Case C-303/06, *Coleman,* ECR, 2008, p. I-5603.

level with social concerns being dealt with in parallel and on the same scale as the economic.

There are as we have seen some indications that this is beginning to happen. The acceptance of citizenship and human rights at the level of the EU moves concerns on from those just of the worker. And gender mainstreaming for all its limitations has expanded the scope of the equality policy into new areas as has the adoption of Article 13 and the Framework Directive. It is evident also that the new policies being adopted under the Lisbon agenda aim to link economic and social objectives more closely and to dovetail implementation and reporting. This is particularly true of the recent emphasis on 'flexicurity' – a term which is intended to bring together the economic need for flexible employment with the human need for social protection and security. Pioneered in Denmark and the Netherlands, policies based on this linkage are now being promulgated by the European institutions as the new form of the European Social Model (Rogowski 2008). Such policies are pursued through the consensual forms of policy making as developed in the OMC and work through guidelines, plans and monitoring rather than through hard law and enforcement. The obvious danger here is that the economic need for flexibility will receive greater priority than the accompanying human needs, unless hard law and public pressure are involved.

Gender equality remains one of the objectives of the flexicurity policies, if only because flexible work so clearly involves women and the ambitious employment targets set by the Council and Commission can only be met by moving more women into employment. Nevertheless, as *Coleman* suggests, these facts and concerns in themselves open the way for care issues to come to the fore. The bringing together of the social and the economic involves the linking of the productive and reproductive spheres, as the emphasis in new gender research suggests. However, this on its own is not enough to shake what Susan Okin has called 'the cycle of socially caused and distinctly asymmetric vulnerability by marriage' – that is the process by which labour markets exploit but do not recognise the power of women and continue to undervalue their roles in both the economy and the family[5]. Nancy Fraser (2009) urges feminists to think big and make campaigns around gender justice and the recognition of care and work the key issues for the next decade, The current uncertainty and vulnerability of the economic sphere provide a rare opportunity.

---

[5] Cited in Fraser 2009.

Changing Images of Normal and Worthy Life. The Constitutional Potential of Economic Sensitivity in EU Gender Policies

Silvia Niccolai

Synopsis. This chapter reads EU Gender Policies as the terrain of a constitutional dialectic between national constitutional traditions and the EU, where an idea of exchangeability of gender roles has been constructed. The exchangeability principle reflects the two cornerstones underlying the European integration process: on the one hand, the optimistic vision of the market's social inclusiveness (which marks the European approach to the economic and to the social); on the other hand, the increased proximity between production and reproduction (which has historically characterized the recent European social and economic history and which is largely due to the massive entry of women into the marketplace). Obviously functional to the EU's economic goals, this path nonetheless involves important transformations in the judicial uses of the Anti-discrimination principle as well as in the language adopted by soft law's instruments. Further, it has the potential to translate and express a new and no longer hierarchical balance between paid and unpaid work, and care activities in particular. In order to recognize and foster these implications of EU Gender policies it is important to abandon readings that connect these policies only to the interests, needs and history of European women and men, as well as readings that underestimate the original economic aim of EU Gender policies. As the increasing contribution that migrants' work is making in many EU countries to the performance of such traditional women's activities such as care and household labour demonstrates, gender roles' transformations have connections with a number of social, economic and political factors. Thus, a contemporary understanding of EU Gender policies' scope and potential requires to read them as the centre of multiple links between the European social model, EU employment policies and EU migration policies.
Keywords: Anti-Discrimination Principle, Gender Equality, Paid Work, Care Work.

1. Introductory remarks. Understanding EU gender policies beyond gender

1.1. EU GENDER POLICIES: THE CONSTRUCTION OF THE IDEA OF EXCHANGEABILITY OF GENDER ROLES, REFLECTING THE INCREASED PROXIMITY BETWEEN PRODUCTION AND REPRODUCTION

This chapter suggests that EU gender policies have developed a European image of normal and worthy life based on the principle of "exchangeability" of roles between the sexes. This principle rejects the idea that different social roles pertain to men and women, ordered along the divide between productive and reproductive work[1]. It is the result – and the expression – of an optimistic understanding of the relationship between the economic and the social, openly trusting in the market's capability to perform as a socially inclusive player. The principle of exchangeability thus summarizes the contemporary spirit of the European integration process in comparison with the constitutional inheritance of post-World War II national constitutions. Here, a pessimistic view of the market economy was reflected in the idea that stable gender roles had to exist, in order – at the same time – to protect society from the market and the market from society. The principle of "exchangeability of roles between the sexes" thus operates as a sign of notable, even if ambiguous and complex, changes in the answer to the purely constitutional question: what is the relationship between life and the market that is today deemed opportune and just?

This principle has been shaped by EU gender policies and particularly by the anti-discrimination principle. Both represent, thanks to the particular economic sensitivity which has for years characterized the European integration process, a privileged lens through which the EU has focussed on women's entry into the market place. With its gender policies, the EU has paid attention to one of the most influential among the multiple transformations of the relationships between the market and society in our times.

This explains the fundamental and specific constitutional relevance of these policies; their undeniable and often noted "special" value within the integration process (Van der Vleuten 2007; Bell 2002), and their mixed nature, as opportunities for new ways of living together and as control devices for the developments and itineraries of individuals and society. It is a process of re-definition that EU gender policies, the anti-

---

[1] For more on these ideas see C. Hoskyns and S. M. Ray 2007.

discrimination principle and their result, the principle of exchangeability, are constantly shaping, and its outcomes can be influenced virtuously only by open debate, a debate eventually aware, most of all, of the fact that what is at stake is much more than the interests of the "disadvantaged sex". Far more importantly, what is on the table is the opportunity to reconstruct the relationship between the economic and the social, particularly between production and reproduction, paid work and care, in terms no longer hierarchical, as was characteristic of the symbolic order that had prevailed during the era of industrial capitalism in Europe, but also able to express the value of reproductive activities, and that of care in particular.

The chapter ends by suggesting that, since the gender issue in Europe is the issue which translates the shifting boundaries between production and reproduction, an understanding of EU gender policies "beyond gender" is required, one able to recognize and to accept the multiple and intertwined transformations which are occurring all along these boundaries - up to and including the increasing commodification of care and its delegation to non EU citizens, which should encourage the reconsidering the links between the European social model, EU employment policies and EU migration policies.

1.2. STANDPOINTS

This chapter rests upon two main points.
The first is the idea which reformulates the largely used clause of "gender contract", that the way in which a given legal order represents men and women, their roles and the normality of their life, is the synthesis of how that order conceives of the relationship between the market economy and society. The latter (which can also be described as the relationship between productive and reproductive work, production and reproduction) has a fundamental constitutional meaning. It influences what it is that is considered a "normal and worthy life" and, in this way, it conditions the meaning assigned to the basic constitutional principle of dignity, and the judgment surrounding what is fair and reasonable[2].

---

[2] For the general assumption that the image of the human person promoted by a given order can be drawn from its constitutional dispositions see Baer 2008, Dorsen et al. 2003, although different notions of constitutional law and constitutional law's sources are adopted here (see further in the text).
The idea that gender anti-discrimination policies operate at the level of a redefinition of the concept of dignity has been explored in Italian literature, for example in Pollicino 2005,

Therefore, norms or principles referring to gender, to men and women, are not to be understood as merely concerning equality between the sexes, women's rights etc. As Theresa Wobbe's chapter in this book makes clear, they encapsulate a larger set of issues, which are fundamental to the establishment of a political experience; they pertain to the symbolic level of socialisation (such as the distinction between public and private or the notion of citizenship); they have consequences on many levels of a legal system (e.g.: the choice for or against a given welfare model, labour regulation and rights, family law).

The second basis of this work is the idea of constitutional law it adopts. This is based on a historic and evaluative conception of constitutional law (Cervati 2009a; Repetto 2009a; Bascherini 2009; Cerrone 2009), which has many points in common with the idea of law as rhetorical knowledge (Mootz 2006). This work is thus based on the idea that constitutional law is not only made up of rules, principles or norms flowing from normative texts called constitutions (or from the interpretations provided by specialized judicial institutions called "Constitutional Courts"), nor does it correspond merely to a map of rights and prerogatives that the tradition called "Constitutionalism" has already completely identified and listed. Instead, constitutional law is a comprehensive collection of the values of living together that are currently accepted and recognized. These values are developed and consolidated through constitutions as well as through statutory laws, regulations and case law, the activity of public service and all those contexts which articulate the ideas, interests and opinions held by a variety of players, including institutions, political parties, trade unions, public opinion and culture in the broader sense (Cervati 2009a).

To study the EU from the point of view of its constitutional values is therefore possible also without a formal European constitutional document, and requires taking into consideration a number of other sources, not necessarily binding or formally legal, among which the Treaties, the ECJ's and TFI's case law, hard and soft law, action programs, Green and White Books have to be included. In this work, we will examine in particular the outcomes of the ECJ's anti-discrimination case law and the EU's soft law in the field of social and employment policies, considered as together having produced the European constitutional gender discourse.

---

although framed differently from the concepts discussed here. The characterising role of gender policy within European constitutionalism has been pointed out by Shaw 2000 and 2002; Kronell 2005.

2. The conception of the relationship between the economic and the social. The constitutional dialectic between national constitutional traditions and the EU

2.1. THE NATIONAL LEVEL: FIXED AND STABLE GENDER ROLES, SEPARATION BETWEEN PRODUCTION AND REPRODUCTION. AN ENGENDERED VISION OF A WELL ORDERED LIVING TOGETHER REFLECTING A PESSIMISTIC VIEW OF THE MARKET'S SOCIAL INCLUSIVENESS

How to conceive the relationship between the market and society has long been the terrain of constitutional dialectic between national constitutional cultures and the EU, which has developed by discussing and reinventing gender roles[3].

European post-World War II national constitutions accepted the market economy. They were nevertheless rooted in the history which had followed the Industrial Revolution of the mid 1800's (the establishment of "Self Regulating" or "Second" Capitalism) and they had inherited a pessimistic vision of the market economy, seen as socially disruptive, as well as the conviction that to protect and maintain social cohesion was the duty and responsibility of public institutions, the state first and foremost, and a duty that involved correcting the market[4].

Testimony to this pessimistic view of the market economy is offered in the wording of the Italian Constitution (1948) when recognizing the freedom of private economic undertaking. "Private economic undertaking is free. It may not be carried out against the common good or in a way that may harm public security, liberty, or human dignity" (art. 41 It. Const.). Straightforward enough, this paragraph blames private undertaking for naturally tending toward harming such fundamental human rights as liberty, security and dignity.

Such a pessimistic view of the market economy has numerous implications. It underlies the conviction that the economic dimension alone does not offer room to nourish the links that preserve a society. If the market is not able, and must not be considered able, to produce social links, the protection of society (as the theories on social rights developed during the 1950's clearly demonstrate[5]) can be realized only using means

---

[3] On the extent to which the historic legacy of gender arrangements is being transcended through the EU integration process, and namely through the Community equality script, see Theresa Wobbe's chapter in this book.

[4] Here I follow the reading proposed by K. Polanyi 1944.

[5] Such as the celebrated thesis of Marshall 1950. For interesting insights see: Deaking and Browne 2003.

that compete with the market economy, that is, via values considered different and alternative to it (health, family life, education, morals). As mentioned earlier, this belief was not a revelation in the second half of 20th century. It had already meant, in some late 19th century national legislation, granting women (and children) a series of (limited) protections, the basic consequence of which was to make it more difficult for these subjects to enter the market place. Men thus became the model for the standard worker, as subjects specialized in the productive arena due to their freedom from care responsibilities. The male breadwinner model had begun emerging in societies where at the same time, as an effect of the uprooting (Weil 1949) of peasant people from the solidarity of traditional country life, the spheres of human life had started to pivot around work and family, cut from the larger relational texture of life and time to which these two spheres had been connected before the Industrial Revolution (Thompson 1967[6]).

Accordingly, the pessimistic view of the market economy of post-World War II constitutions corresponded to an image of men and women, where the former was framed in the market place, the latter in family life. Looking again at the Italian Constitution it is worth mentioning, on the one hand, the tenor of article 29, according to which: "Female workers are granted the same pay as male workers for work of equal value. Working conditions must allow women to perform their essential family function and grant the mother and the child special and fair protection". On the other hand, art. 20 states: "Each worker has the right to a salary granting him and his family a free and dignified life".

A gendered division of roles was thus positioned as the basis of a well ordered living together. Corresponding to this division were prohibitions for women to enter many "male" jobs and professions, and the prohibition of night work, both often inherited from previous centuries. Similar examples are provided by the German Basic Law prohibiting women from working in the Army (modified after *Tanja Kreil*[7]) and by the norms of the German Civil Code which subordinated the capability of women to undertake a job or profession to the condition that they were able to perform their family duties, and could be taken from the normative systems in force in other founding states at the time the European integration process started (Van der Vleuten 2007: 32 ff.).

Recognizing equality in basic rights for men and women while placing them in different spheres of living and assigning women to family and

---

[6] Quoted by Moffat 2007: 157.
[7] Case C-285/98, *Kreil v Bundesrepublik Deutschland*, ECR, 2000, p. 69.

reproductive work meant reaffirming that a divide between the economic and the social existed and had to be maintained (Crompton 2006: 35). One of the many results of this, as much feminist analysis has pointed out, was to perceive and represent sexual difference as a cost (at least because it is a cost to protect the spheres over which it presides, which is to say, the family), and as a disadvantage, in that it was female difference that was featured as a liability with respect to the male model of normality, competence and capability. Another consequence was that, once production had been separated from reproduction and paid work chosen as the only public sphere, the market was allowed to remain indifferent to the conditions in which the work force it needed was reproduced and maintained (Moffat 2007: 157). In protecting society from the market, the gendered divide between production and reproduction had consequently also meant that the market was protected from society.

2.2. THE EUROPEAN LEVEL: REFRAMING GENDER ROLES WITHIN AN OPTIMISTIC VISION OF THE MARKET'S SOCIAL INCLUSIVENESS. A PATH ECHOED BY THE DIFFERENT STAGES OF THE INTEGRATION PROCESS

From its very first steps as the European Economic Community, the EU has adopted a positive view of the market economy as a socially inclusive player, able to perform favourably toward society (think of the Spaak Report's leading idea, according to which social cohesion would derive from the common market's establishment and development). Women as subjects defending basic social linkages such as family against the market and for that reason not participating in the market place, or participating in it in a more restricted and limited way than men, were not part of the EU's initial imagery. Since the former Art. 119's original wording, the EU has considered women as subjects of the market place, and invested in the market economy in order to address problems of social cohesion and personal development[8]. Since the late 1960's, this normative imagery has faced huge societal and economic transformations, namely the "Second Wave" of feminism in Europe. Having received from the Treaty a mandate to concentrate on women's work, in terms of parity of pay and treatment between men and women as workers, the EU has found it possible and necessary (and easier than it was for Member States) to intercept and govern societal transformations, and particularly the emergence of female subjectivity, which views the freedom to enter the

---

[8] The dialectic between the national language of protection and the EU equality approach is described in depth by Wobbe's chapter in this book.

market place as a fundamental element of female independence and emancipation.

On these premises a dialectic has developed, where a European approach promoting the idea that gender roles are exchangeable contrasts with the approach of post-World War II national constitutions, which understood gender roles as being permanently separated along the divide between productive and reproductive work. This shift is probably due to the fact that the changes in the relationships between men and women that were emerging in this period appeared functional to the integration process's objectives and ends. Nonetheless, it was an important step, which has the potential to lead to a transformed understanding of the relationship between market and society.

Before describing the European idea of exchangeability of gender roles it is important to stop for a moment and to dissociate from mainstream opinion which tends to underestimate the equal pay principle's original "economic aim" (Barnard 2007) as a merely initial, partial and insufficient approach. According to many scholars, what is valuable in EU gender policies is the fact that, over the course of time, they have overcome the integration process's merely economic dimension, revealing and fostering the capability to participate in the human rights field as well. From Maastricht to the Social Policy Protocol, to Amsterdam, to the Charter and the process of accession to the ECHR, the EU has consolidated a proper "social dimension" developing along lines that correspond to national constitutional traditions (De Witte 2005), and, in particular, to the tradition which assigns to social policy a market correcting function (Barnard 2007b).

Indeed, the fact that the EU has increasingly and more consciously recognized its place in the European fundamental rights tradition has had, has, and may have in the future undeniable and very important consequences in the contents of European policy, on the ECJ's lines of argumentation, and on the tenor of soft law documents (some of which will also be considered in this work). It remains nonetheless important to reaffirm that in the European approach to gender there remains an unbroken connection with integration's economic ends - a connection that, of course, is differently established and re-established along the different stages of the European integration process[9].

---

[9] The picture drawn here of EU gender policies rests mostly on the ECJ's case law and on soft law materials. It can be completed by taking into consideration a number of other factors, namely: national implementation policies; intra-institutional dynamics at the EU level; the role of feminist cultures and lobbying. In all these directions important

In other words, EU gender polices have not developed within an integration process constantly tied to a fixed range of objectives and priorities; instead, they have been a kind of litmus paper, reflecting evolving and varying objectives.

The policies' first component (the equal pay principle) originated, as is well known, from the fear that female work could operate as a social dumping factor (Van der Vleuten 2007, Hoskyns 1996). Art. 119 did not aim to boost women's participation in the market place, nor did it want to alter the traditional division of gender roles. Besides, a similar intent would have meant intruding on the "social" dimension that the Community foundation pact, according to its ordo-liberal essence (Joerges 2004) had entrusted to the Member States (for more about this "false duality" see Hoskyns' chapter in this book). Art. 119's objective was a fair and competitive market. This objective, extremely prominent at the time of the common market's construction, was still of the utmost importance when EU gender policy actually started, with the Equality Directives of the mid 1970's. As is well known, and as the three Directives' legal basis make transparent, the launch of European policy in the field of gender was the answer to the possible repercussions of women's massive entry into the common market. The intent was, in other words, to govern a societal transformation that appeared capable of having consequences for the common market.

Of course, the possible outcomes, in terms of increased legitimacy for the EU that were made possible by the alliance between the rhetoric of women's rights and the EU's anti-discrimination policies, were immediately felt. In 1976 *Defrenne II* distinctly pronounced two celebrated statements. Art. 119 has a double aim, economic and social, on the one hand, and on the other, the anti-discrimination principle is part of the equality principle[10]. These were foundational pieces of the doctrine that the Court was constructing at that time, according to which the Community has its own patrimony over fundamental rights, which is analogous to, but autonomous from, that of Member States.

Very quickly however, EU gender polices made clear the objective to enhance women's working opportunities. In the early 1980's the series of action programmes aiming to give women parity of opportunity at work started surrounding the Equality Directives. The objective of enhancing women's work, which was initially an indirect consequence of the anti-

---

instruments are provided by Hoskyns 1996, Wobbe 2003, Van der Vleuten 2007, Verloo M. (ed.) 2007, Wobbe and Biermann 2009.
[10] Case C-43/75, *Defrenne v Sabena (No 2),* ECR, 1976, p. 455.

discrimination policy's logic (a logic made by equality in treatment plus, in the limits accepted by Community law, parity of opportunity), became prominent once the single market had been realised (1982), against a background of transforming capitalism shifting towards globalisation and flexibility, where "immaterial jobs" fitting female competences were flourishing (see again Hoskyns' chapter on this point). It is in this context that the EU launches its social model, set up on the particular idea of activating society as a resource for the market economy (Villa 2009, Crompton 2006:63-85). At this stage, which is the present one, the EU gender policy objective is no longer to protect the building of a common competitive market, but to enhance employability. And framed this way, gender policy seems to start losing its individuality (Rubery 2005), becoming part of the all-inclusive European social policy, which is, in essence, employment policy (Sciarra 2005).

Many scholars agree that European social (employment) policies have a function which is social and market building at the same time (Deakin and Browne 2003). This means that economic reasons are once again the factor mobilising the EU's interest in society. Social rights that originate from this (such as the right to reconciliation, which will be discussed here) thus have an economic rationale as much as the equal pay principle had[11]. This change is found in the change in the integration process' economic objectives, no longer restricted to the building of a common competitive market, but enlarged to safeguard the competitiveness of "System Europe".

The ECJ expressed this change very clearly. Declaring that the former Art. 119's "economic aim" is now considered "secondary" to the "social aim"[12], the Court has narrowed the concept of the "economic aim" to the elimination of distortions to competition, which was in fact the core of the Treaty of Rome, but today, after enlargement, is no longer the most urgent of the EU's economic worries and interests[13].

---

[11] "To increase the income of families with children; to reduce poverty risks; to control social expenditure": these are, according to Villa 2009: 167 the economic goals which the EU tries nowadays to achieve by means of gender policies. Villa argues that the male breadwinner model (according to which women should live at home at the expense of public welfare or of their husbands' salaries) is no longer economically sustainable.

[12] Joined Cases C-270/97 and C-271/97, *Sievers and Schrage*, ECR, 2000, p. I-929. For a different reading of this ruling see Barnard 2007: 138.

[13] Far differently from the early stages of the European integration process, the EU today seems largely to accept the possibility of considering different labour costs as an opportunity to enhance competitiveness. The way in which the ECJ affronted the issue of low cost workers, one of the most significant consequences of enlargement on the common

2.3. FROM NON-DISCRIMINATED AGAINST TO EXCHANGEABLE: THE ECJ'S
CONTRIBUTION TO THE CONSTITUTIONAL REDEFINITION OF GENDER ROLES

The ECJ's case law has made a very important contribution to giving
EU anti-discriminatory law certain contents, instead of others. In
determining the interpretative paths adopted by the Court a number of
factors have had an influence. *Firstly*, there is the inclination of the Court
to privilege the negative and comparative traits of the anti-discrimination
principle. *Secondly*, the Court's noticeable loyalty to its role as guardian
of the correct interpretation of Community Law, which binds the Court to
giving a distinctive weight, in the balance of the interests that it makes, to
the integration process's specific objectives. *Thirdly*, there is the type of
judicial questions that have concretely reached the Court and in relation to
which the Court has explored the scope of the prohibition of
discrimination. This last factor includes, among other things, the
dimension of time, that is to say the different temporal contexts to which
the various Court's rulings belong, and, through this, is in its turn
connected with the first and the second above mentioned factors. It is the
combination of these three factors that has encouraged the Court to
develop a view of gender roles that hinges on the idea of mutual
exchangeability, and that has been constructed along with the notion of
the market economy as a non-discriminatory and inclusive player. Below,
I will refer mostly to the influence of the first and the second factors,
whilst I will consider the third in the conclusive part of this work.
In shaping the idea of gender roles promoted by the Court the strictly
comparative way in which the Court understands and applies the anti-
discrimination principle has played a determining role. A purely
comparative logic (to treat the like alike and the different differently)
permeates the fundamental line of this case law. According to it, only
pregnancy, the delivery of a baby and breastfeeding, which for biological
reasons pertain to women and not to men, justify special treatment in
favour of women (*Dekker*[14]). Any other special treatment in favour of
women, and aiming to compensate (in terms for example of a better
retirement scheme or more flexible treatment at work) the disadvantages
women suffer at work as a consequence of their family responsibilities, is
discriminatory and illegitimate, because: "as parents, men and women are

---

market, reveals the openness to this. See Case C-341/05, *Laval un Partneri*, ECR, 2007, p.
I-11767.
[14] Case C-177/88, *Dekker v Stichting Vormigscentrum voor Jong Volwassenen Plus*, ECR,
1990, p. I-3941.

equal", as in *Commission vs France*[15], and: "neither men nor women have a special relationship with family (care) or work": *Griesmar* [16].

Statements like these bring directly into question the constitutional legacy of Member States. In their light, it is the traditional interpretation of equality between men and women adopted by many national legislations that appears discriminatory, notwithstanding how deeply it was rooted in their constitutional and cultural texture and accepted, even fostered, by their national constitutional courts[17]. This was the traditional interpretation according to which, given the different social role of men and women, it was reasonable for the law to differentiate between men and women in order to compensate for the disadvantages women undergo in their working life due to their family burdens. From this interpretation of what is discriminatory to the one promoted by the ECJ, the shift is in the judgment of what is considered reasonable, normal, acceptable, and desirable in the relationship between women (and men), their family life and their work - a shift well exemplified by the prohibition of women's night work. Up until the mid 1980's it was still widespread among many European legislations, and was considered a typical example, as noted by Italian Constitutional Law reference books for instance, of a "reasonable" (and for that reason not discriminatory) difference in treatment between men and women[18]. It was then dismantled throughout Europe, as a direct or indirect consequence of the various infringement procedures brought by the Commission after the deadline for the implementation of the equality directives had expired.

Of course, the Court has had to pose the question of how to establish in which cases a difference in treatment between men and women is reasonable, justified and not discriminatory. Here the role of the Court as guardian of the correct interpretation of Community law enters into play. Once men and women had been defined as "equal" in every aspect of their life except for pregnancy, delivery and breastfeeding, thereby eliminating the "female family role" from the list of the grounds justified in differentiating women's treatment at work from men's, the Court has had to select a different set of criteria. This is the "objective justification" criterion, with which the Court has solved a number of indirect

---

[15] Case C-212/86, *Commission v France,* ECR, 1988, p. 6315.

[16] Case C-366/99, *Griesmar v Ministre de l'Economie, des Finances et de l'Industrie,* ECR, 2001, p. I-9383.

[17] This can be seen emblematically in the case of the German Federal Constitutional Tribunal and its jurisprudence in matters of equality between men and women as studied by Sacksofsky and Rodriguez 2005.

[18] See, as an example among others: Pizzorusso 1982.

discrimination cases in which men and women claimed to have been discriminated against, in terms of pay or treatment. With this criterion the Court has stated that, although they have more negative effects on women than they have on men (given for example women's lesser availability to work overtime due to family responsibilities), no time schedule nor pay scheme can be considered discriminatory if it is based on economic reason, strategy undertaken or business needs (from *Jenkins*[19], to *Cadman*[20]) (Beck 2007). Within such reasoning, there is an unquestionable logic: whilst the "female family role" does not form part of the values recognized and protected by the community legal order, the economic development entrusted to undertakings and business do. It is in light of this latter value that the Court has carried out its mandate to provide the right interpretation of Community law.

When the European Employment Strategy (EES) was launched in late 1990's, scholars were stimulated to reflect on the EU's hugely controversial tendency to subordinate rights to the market. Long before this moment, the Court, in deepening the scope of the anti-discrimination principle, had taught that it is normal, reasonable and justifiable to balance a fundamental right such as gender equality (Tridimas 2006: 308) with a business undertaking's needs - a balance, where it is the latter to influence significantly the way in which the former is structured and conformed. And this is not the only element, among those that over the course of time have become salient within the "European Social Model", to have initially taken form in the Court's case law.

Whilst suggesting that, instead of the market economy, it is the protective national legislations handing down traditional visions of gender roles that threaten individuals' rights, the Court's case law has fostered a view according to which the anti-discrimination policies' essential aim is not to protect people from possible assaults on their rights coming from the market, but to allow a larger number of people to enter the market place. This is the moral of the famous "parity of opportunity" case law. In it, the Court has stated that it is illegitimate for a national legislation to guarantee women automatic priority (quotas) for appointment or promotion. Instead, measures guaranteeing women (or other disadvantaged categories) some priority in vocational training or educational guidance, which do not guarantee a job, but the opportunity to successfully apply for one, are deemed consistent with the non-discrimination principle. This point of

---

[19] Case C-96/80, *Jenkins v Kingsgate*, ECR, 1981, p. 911.
[20] Case C-17/05, *Cadman v Health and Safety Executive,* ECR, 2006, p. I-9583.

view, already demonstrated by *Kalanke*[21] in 1995, entails the same "procedural" understanding of social rights, which scholars have recognized as being present in European employment policies since 1997, the year of the first EES (Sciarra 2005).

Besides, the Court has held the view according to which being a worker is an essential pre-condition to a full entitlement to citizenship's rights. In the twin cases *Drake* and *Züchner*[22]), the Court defined the notion of an "active population" temporarily out of work, entitled by Directive 1979/7/E to equal access to social protection measures such as illness allowances. On these occasions, the Court stated very clearly that the Directive protects only those people who have had, even if for a short period, paid work (*Drake*), not those people who have always worked in the household, notwithstanding the fact that they perform duties that, given their complexity and difficulty, would otherwise be performed by a professional, for example a professional nurse (*Züchner*).

The idea according to which there is no social division of gender roles and that, instead, they have to be understood as exchangeable (biologically "special" situations like pregnancy, delivery and breastfeeding excepted), is thus framed in a case law which has always expressed the idea that rights, and fundamental rights such as non-discrimination above all, must be realized under the conditions made possible by the market economy. And here the abandonment of the gendered divide between production and reproduction has been joined to the idea that it is the participation in the market place that is the source of full social inclusion.

2.4. MAKING GENDER ROLES EXCHANGEABLE... IN ORDER TO KEEP THEIR VALUE UNCHANGED?

The reading according to which the ECJ has fostered the exchangeability of gender roles opposes a different interpretation, strongly upheld by a part of feminist opinion. According to this, the Court holds, on the contrary, a very traditional and conservative conception of gender roles, anchoring women to their maternal function (Montalti 2009; Masselot and Caracciolo di Torella 2001; McGlynn 2000)[23]. Evidence of this is typically drawn from the ECJ's case law on parental leave. Here the Court, on the one hand, appears reluctant to consider discriminatory

---

[21] C-450/93, *Kalanke v Freie Hansestadt Bremen*, ECR, 1995, p. I-3051.
[22] C-150/85, *Drake v Chief Adjudication Officier*, ECR, 1986, p. 1995; Case C-77/95, *Züchner v Handelskrankenkasse (Ersatzkasse) Bremen*, ECR, 1996, p. I-5689.
[23] See also on this point Ciervo's chapter in this book.

legislation granting this type of leave to women only. On the other hand, the Court includes in the term "maternity" not only the biological elements of pregnancy and delivery, but also the mother-child relationship following the delivery, a relationship which is not "biologically" but only "culturally" determined. *Lommers, Hofman, Aboulaje* and *Boyle*[24] are the rulings most often critically referred to.

As we will see, these opinions offer a precious opportunity to discuss ECJ case law more profoundly. But before this, let us focus a bit more closely on what these opinions mean and imply. Firstly, one must bear in mind that these critical opinions originate from one among the various possible conceptions about the right way to conceive of gender and to individuate women's needs. Precisely, these opinions are among those that define gender as an entirely cultural construct. Thus they believe that women's essential need is to be emancipated from traditional representations of the female role, considered by definition stereotyped. It is because they move from very precise and complete gender theories (which will not be discussed here) that these opinions do not often take into due consideration the margins of manoeuvre that a judge, such as in the case of the ECJ, concretely has. Whilst it is always possible, when reasoning on the basis of general theory on fundamental rights and gender, to draw purely logical and deductive conclusions, the same, generally, is neither possible nor opportune for a Court. Judges indeed have to take into account the concrete case, the limits of their own mandate, the extension of their jurisdiction and the predictable consequences of their decisions. All these elements assume different nuances depending on the time in which a decision is pronounced (Giuliani 1966). To put it differently, a theory of fundamental rights is a very important tool with which to criticize a Court in order to express opinions and points of view that could influence its future orientations. But it is not the ideal tool with which to investigate the interpretative dynamics that a Court adopts, as judges are called to evaluate concrete controversies, within a given timeframe.

Let us take the example of parental leave case law. Of course, extending the right to leave to fathers would have been logically coherent either under the premise that gender roles are exchangeable, or with the idea that gender is an entirely cultural construct. Nevertheless, in concrete cases, this would have meant for the Court to go far beyond the limits of Community Law. The Parental Leave Directive only *recommends*

---

[24] Case C-184/83, *Hofmann v Barmer Ersatzkasse*, ECR, 1984, p. 3047; Case C-218-98, *Abdoulaye and others*, ECR, 1999, p. I-5723; Case C-411/96, *Boyle and others*, ECR, 1998, p. I-6401; Case C-479/99, *Lommers*, ECR, 2002, p. I-2891.

Member States extend parental leave to fathers too; neither it is motivated by a desire to change gender roles and working parents' rights (Van der Vleuten 2007: 151). In this frame, extending parental leave to fathers appeared impossible. The logical alternative to the idea of exchangeability was that of condemning as discriminatory leave granted to women only. Needless to say, this would have been a highly counterproductive choice, resoundingly conflicting with a very long and valuable history of labour protection in Europe that the EU, with the Parental Leave Directive, had proved willing to safeguard.

Pure logic is not a good counsellor for Courts, and in this light we come to our second objection: where the question of the use of the term "maternity" in ECJ case law must be discussed. First of all, one should bear in mind that in many cases, the Court seems to use this term simply as a synthetic expression aiming to summarize "pregnancy, delivery, breastfeeding" while the exact boundaries of this notion remain obscure. But the point is that whilst obscurity is not a good quality in deductive logic, it has undeniable benefits in legal reasoning. Hinting at the "relationship between mother and child" that deserves to be protected after delivery, the Court avoids the risk of the very non-discriminatory solution of considering the granting of post-partum parental leave only to women who breast-feed, and denying it to those who bottle-feed (after all, men also can use the bottle) - a risk that a merely "biological" approach to maternity, along with anti-discrimination logic, would otherwise imply. Thanks to the imprecise notion of maternity it adopts, the Court avoids logical paradoxes (which could find the support of market forces), and realizes a very delicate and precious equilibrium: that of holding the general premise that "as parents, men and women are equal", without using it to the detriment of existing maternity protection laws.

Thirdly, a point that must be given its due weight is that protecting maternity has never meant, in the Court's words, protecting a female "family function". Let us reconsider for a moment the implications of a highly disputed case like *Lommers*. On this occasion, the Court stated that making subsidized nursery places only available to women employees is not discriminatory on the employer's part, because such a measure aims to eliminate the causes of women' reduced access to employment and thus improves their competitive position in the labour market (Tridimas 2006: 116-117). The Court carefully added, in a pure *Griesmar* logic, that male officials who brought up their children by themselves were to have access to the nursery scheme.

Of course *Lommers* expresses the difficulties the Court (and the entire EU) faces in imposing on Member States costly protections (Van der

Vleuten 2007). But what is far more important in this case is how explicitly it says that maternity is an obstacle to women's entry and permanence in the job market[25]. The coherence with *Commission v France* or *Griesmar* is then transparent. On those occasions, it was found to be discriminatory where protection consisted of compensating women for the periods they spent *away* from work and dedicated to family. In *Lommers*, considered lawful were those measures which protect women by helping them to come back to work after maternity. Clearly enough, a view emerges according to which the normal and worthy life of a woman, the one the law protects, upholds and considers valuable, is not to remain out of the job market in order to look after the children (and to be compensated at the expense of the public system for the economic or career losses connected to this), but to participate in the job market and be able to re-enter it after maternity.

What is true, on the other hand (and this is the important point that the opinions we are discussing help to discover) is that, in the above mentioned decisions, there is - and not because of what they decide, but because of the wording they adopt - a very problematic element. They describe maternity and child rearing as "obstacles" to returning to work. This language displays a negative characterization of care (painted as an undesirable and superfluous "obstacle" to the full realization of one's self, which consists of having a paid job). It demonstrates an order of values where care and unpaid family work are subordinated to paid work, which appears as the only value worth pursuing (overcoming the "obstacle" of children).

This is one of the most relevant traits of ECJ anti-discrimination case law. The Court has insisted on many occasions that women and men are equally entitled to care and reproductive work, but at the same time it has done very little, if not to say nothing, to signal a change in the traditional view according to which, between paid and unpaid work, it is the first that counts[26]. More generally, it is true that protecting non-discrimination between men and women has never meant, for the Court, promoting an understanding of work, of the conflicts that take place at work, renewed by a sensitivity to the different points of view, practices, experiences, exigencies and competencies that women bring with them to the job market. There are many examples of this, and one particularly significant

---

[25] Some praise this ruling for having recognized that maternity represents an obstacle to work different from that of paternity (Costello 2003: 125).

[26] This is the philosophy that also emerges from cases such as *Drake* and *Züchner.*

remains *Enderby c. Frenchay Health Authority*[27], on a case of indirect
discrimination. A speech and language therapist claimed to be
discriminated against because in the clinic where she worked,
psychologists and pharmacists (mostly men) were paid better than speech
therapists (mostly women) although they had the same qualifications. The
Court did not find a case of indirect discrimination, given that the higher
pay of psychologists and pharmacists was "objectively justified" by the
employer's need to attract that type of worker, less available on the job
market than speech therapists. In this case, as in many others, very well
known and statistically proven facts like women's inclination to
interpersonal work based on the use of language (from speech therapist to
teacher) have not lent any weight to their cases and the moral *Enderby*
communicates is that women can aspire to better pay by simply going
along with men's working choices and preferences. This is a message that
reaffirms that it is the market to establish the importance and value of
roles, activities and skills – a task that tradition, culture, habits cannot
instead legitimately perform.

Nevertheless, *Enderby* is not the expression of a hidden male chauvinism
within the Courts but more simply the consequence of the purely negative
and comparative use of the anti-discrimination principle, preferred by the
Court, and applied in a time where the workplace was still basically male
dominated. Under these conditions, it was almost inevitable that the
indirect-discrimination syndicate[28] would also lead to interpretations
suggesting that women can obtain protection and recognition by
conforming to male behaviour, leaving very little room for explicit
evaluative conflicts to emerge.

2.5. THE ENTRY OF NEW SOFTER MODES OF GOVERNANCE: DESCRIBING THE RELATIONSHIP BETWEEN PRODUCTION AND REPRODUCTION WITH NEW NUANCES, WHILE RE-TUNING GENDER DIFFERENCE WITH A POSITIVE NOTE

The anti-discrimination principle, especially when applied with
formalist severity, is not, in its comparative and negative dimensions, the
best instrument with which to lead to the recognition of new or newly
tuned values and rights (Repetto 2009b; Costello 2003).

---

[27] Case C-127/92, *Enderby v Frenchay Health Authority*, ECR, 1993, p. I-5535.
[28] Notwithstanding the fact that it appears closer, according at least to some scholars, to a
substantive review able to go beyond a formalistic assessment of identity and difference,
and to appreciate more concretely how given measures and situations impact on men and
women: Somek 1999, Schiek 2002.

At the EU level, the task of selecting and proclaiming new values, of pointing out the need to recognise new interests, or to signal objectives that the EU considers relevant is normally performed by the ICG's or ICJ and EC's final declarations, by the Council's and the Commission's declarations and recommendations, and, moreover, by the rich and articulated web of assessments, points of view, suggestions and evaluations which, especially within the European Occupation System, are the fabric of action programs and coordination methods. Here, political prescriptions are translated into soft law measures and implementative actions which involve social partners and national institutions.

According to many, from the first European Employment Strategy onwards, the EU has concentrated its attention on society, seen as a resource that needs to be activated in order to improve market performance. This has meant putting the objective of "employability" at the core of EU gender policy, developing new discourses and adopting new instruments. These changes have pushed in new directions that which European gender policy and the ECJ's case law had already consolidated.

There is, however, a large area in which traditional ECJ assumptions about gender relationships ("as parents, men and women are equal") and the contents and objectives of equality action programs do simply overlap. This area is that of the fight against gender stereotyping, a cornerstone of action programs from the early battle against female "segregation" at work to the more recent battle against the gender pay gap (Florio 2009). Parallel to ECJ case law outcomes, more than twenty years of action programmes enhancing actions against gender stereotyping wind up a long narrative which blames past ways of life as unreasonable and discriminative (precisely those on which the image of men and women were based according to the national constitutions of the post-World War II period).

It was indeed with the launch of the EES and the Lisbon Strategy that the picture began to change and the representation of gender roles started assuming new and more articulated nuances. An example is the Council Declaration on Equal Participation of Men and Women in Private and Public Life[29], contemporary to the launch of the Lisbon Strategy. Here, the image of gender roles exchangeability, at that time largely settled in case law, is used in a very innovative way.

According to this declaration, up to now both men and women have been discriminated against: women, for having being too long excluded from public life; men, for having being too long excluded from family life. The

---

[29] OJ 2000/C 218/02.

21st Century – the age of a "new social pact between genders" – should be the time when men will learn how to enjoy family life more, and women public life more.

The declaration is an emblematic expression of the EU's growing awareness that society holds a lot of weight in conditioning the success of a given economic model (Villa 2009). It is society indeed that the declaration refers to when evoking men's and women's behaviour and preferences, and pointing out the weight that cultural and symbolic pre-conditions have in orientating one or the other to different life-choices and careers. Up to this point, there had been nothing other than the old fight-against-stereotyping rhetoric. What is more interesting, and new, is that, besides this, the declaration communicates the feeling that some of the traditional disadvantages of female life – such as being trained to find occupation, self-realization and meaning in the private, family sphere, in care activities or child rearing – are now regarded as advantages in a world where labour structures and forms have deeply changed. In times of the global economy and flexible work, the European economic system urges men and women to be available to enter, to leave and to re-enter the job market many times over. The old female specialisation in the household and family becomes in this frame a psychological asset which men have to learn if they want to become able to overcome the challenges of a job market which exposes them to frequent periods of unemployment. In this, a shift occurs in the representation of gender roles, which goes further than case law's achievements, and implies abandoning an important corollary of the traditional reading of gender roles, those assigned to the female sphere, to domestic care activities, which traditionally pertain to women, the only sign of disadvantage. It is a shift which Ilenia Ruggiu's chapter in this book perceives as spreading across the entire European approach to diversity, which seems at times to lead to an approach to diversity as a public good.

A new tune in the attributions which are normally joined to the female sex and the care activities in which women have traditionally specialized is also presented by the themes which are actually placed at the core of European employment policies, namely gender mainstreaming and reconciliation. In particular, the entry of reconciliation means the entire perspective of family life, and thereby of care, has been discovered as a relevant field, which conditions women's and men's concrete chances of successfully participating in the market place.

As for the sincerity and effectiveness of the new European approach to care and reconciliation there is a huge discussion, and a high degree of distrust (Rossilli 2009). Scholars fear that the reconciliation idea was a token of feminist experience and reflection solely for the good and interests of market forces (Stratigaky 2004). Others argue that reconciliation policy means nothing other than keeping traditional gender roles unmodified (McGlynn 2001).

These critical remarks do point out limits and problems which are actually important. Nevertheless, to concentrate only or mainly on these components of EU reconciliation policies risks loosing sight of some others, which instead deserve being considered.

A reasonable starting point in addressing the complicated issue of reconciliation policies is that one can not definitely ascertain if these policies are good or bad, in that they express some degree of encouragement or acceptance of the fact that people, mostly women, are significantly involved, during the course of their lives, in care activities. As has been opportunely noted (Crompton 2006:51), we do not know why women tend to develop professional careers different from men's (more fragmented, for example, because of interruption of pregnancy). Maybe it is because they are unjustly burdened with care responsibilities. Maybe it is because they choose care positively, thereby preferring work or professional activities which allow them to carry out the family activities that they value. Maybe they are performing to stereotypes, or maybe they are just freely composing their own life path. Probably many different reasons are mixed and intertwined and differently weighted depending on the different circumstances of an individual's life (Barbera 2003b: 150, 160)[30]. What one can say is that our times seem in fact to signal an increasing heterogeneity in aptitudes displayed by women (and by men, too) towards the burdens and benefits of paid work and care (Moffat 2007: 155). It has been rightly noted that what counts is not that women and men make the same working or professional choices, but that the same importance and value is given to different choices, life conditions and behaviour. In other words, what is important to verify in European reconciliation policies is *what* they are able to modify within the relationship, traditionally hierarchical, between production and reproduction (Moffat 2007: 157).

The results of such an inquiry are conditioned by the type and intensity of expectations one has of the law and its institutions, their scope and their

---

[30] One of the most intuitive interpretations of the breakthrough connected to the contemporary relationship between women and care is probably that put forward by a reading of the "double yes" adopted by Italian feminist thought (Cigarini 2008), that notes how women today seem reluctant to establish any kind of hierarchy between their employment and care activities.

capability to condition and modify society. But it is difficult to deny that, whatever the concrete results of reconciliation policies are for the moment, these policies do put care and the dignity of time dedicated to it into the forefront. They cooperate in giving increasing recognition to the collective and public relevance of care, up to now totally relinquished to the private dimension. This does not mean, of course, that reconciliation policies in fact effectively overcome the traditional priority of paid work over unpaid work. The fact itself that reproductive work is not calculated in the Gross National Product has surely, among others, the important symbolic implication that the dominant vision of economy, development and production is up to now unwilling to recognize the contribution of unpaid reproductive work (Hoskyns and Ray 2007; Moffat 2007)[31]. Nevertheless, the fact that, within the reconciliation theme, a public discourse now exists which stresses that the world of work and the world of life must find ways to mutually adapt to each other is relevant, as Hoskyns suggests in her chapter. Indeed, it is a first step toward a possible, double transformation.

On the one hand, in that it recognizes that women (and men) are not able, neither do they want, to leave or to delegate completely their care responsibilities, the public discourse on care that reconciliation policies encourage is a contribution to a new shared awareness of the importance these responsibilities hold for individuals, for society, and for the productive world. For this reason, on the other hand, these policies can be used as a vehicle for the recognition that the productive world has responsibility toward the conditions in which the work force is reproduced, that is, towards society (Moffat 2007: 158). In other words, reconciliation policies (together with all the critical accounts that surround them) are a step towards putting into discussion the market economy's indifference and irresponsibility towards society, that traditional gender divisions had up to now cemented.

It is at this point that another much criticized aspect of reconciliation policies can be examined. These are based on the idea that the more flexible organisation of time-schedules, which are what most reconciliation policy consists of, correspond to a "coincidence of interests" between employer and employee. To many, this idea appears

---

[31] Recently, the perception that GDP is no longer a sufficient measure of a country's well-being tends to be more widespread. A good example is the report presented by 25 economists to the French President Sarkozy on the 14th of September 2009. The report adopts the view that in the evaluation of a country's economic situation, factors such as unpaid work available for homecare and child raising, and the balance between work and leisure time in general, need to be taken into consideration.

deceptive (Villa 2009: 175; Moffat 2007: 142; Crompton 2006: 111), and no doubt it can be seen as a trap. Nevertheless, with the image of the "coincidence of interests" rising, another one is slowly disappearing: the one according to which the woman is a flawed worker in which the market is not very interested, because women are costly workers and naturally cut out for other work (care and family). On the contrary, reconciliation policies reveal the job market's interest in female work.

This leads us to consider another frequent charge of European employment policy, and of gender mainstreaming most of all. As we have already mentioned, some of these policies are considered nothing but rhetoric which instead of improving the female condition have had the effect of weakening concrete and effective guarantees and eroding parity (Rossilli 2009: 15). These serious concerns must not mean losing sight of the fact that the EES period is, and thanks precisely to the type of discourse the EES adopts and develops (less focused on women's protection and special rights) - the age which has seen the overcoming of "women's disadvantage" rhetoric. Bearing witness to the focus shifting from the theme of protection for women (understood as a special category of workers) to research about what is needed in order to make the contemporary working world (now irrevocably composed of men and women) function well. This is a change in point of view which implies recognition of the social strength, public visibility, widespread and fully legitimised presence of women in society, and, in this way, of the fact that a definitive transformation in the relationship between men and women has taken place.

Rooted in the idea of the exchangeability of gender roles set up by the ECJ's anti-discrimination case law, European social policies are enriching the image of normal and worthy life by introducing new points of view, new discourses, figures and themes. According to the nature of "soft law" instruments, these approaches are considered remarkable persuasive paths. Neither univocal or all-inclusive, they imply an overcoming of the view of difference as a cost and disadvantage, in favour of the perspective of developing a sensitivity towards the importance of care, as a sphere no longer separated from productive work.

3. Conclusions. Towards a new order of values between production and reproduction

3.1. SPLENDID INSULATION OR MERE SELF-REFERENCE? HOW TO BRING EU GENDER DISCOURSE (AND ITS CRITICS) BEYOND THE BORDER: A) PUTTING THE OTHER INTO THE PICTURE

There are surely different permutations of gender representation that EU gender policy discourse (as constructed both by the ECJ's anti-discrimination case law and by gender policy in the social and employment field) has developed. As those feminist analyses convinced that there actually is a female difference to be protected and valued firmly denounce (Rossilli 2009), what we have called here "the exchangeability of gender roles" entails some degree of "neutralisation" of gender difference, and, framed by the ambiguities of the European Social Model, risks incorporating a view of normality of human life entirely constructed around the idea of a performing person merely functional to the logic of the market (Villa 2009).

Criticism of neutralisation has a point, which deserves nevertheless to be clarified. Otherwise, in its turn, it risks excessively downplaying the important transformations that, for the image of gender relationships, the EU integration process has actually involved. Secondly, it condemns as entirely negative and dangerous the EU's economic sensitivity, minimizing the fact that it was this sensitivity which allowed the EU to give attention to changes linked to women's entry into the marketplace; and thirdly, and most importantly, this criticism remains largely indistinct, being incapable of answering, in terms able to find a widespread consensus, the question of *what*, instead of the "neutralized-exchangeable" person, would be better placed at the core of the EU (or other) discourse on gender.

Which differences, if any, are the valuable features pertaining to one or the other sex is the matter of a huge and completely open debate. The great transformations following the end of patriarchy have not yet produced – nor (luckily indeed) they are likely ever to produce – a stable, homogeneous, permanent and shared "symbolic order" governing the relationships between men and women as effectively as patriarchy did. The huge variety of visions about female interests and women's worth – examples of which we have rapidly mentioned in the former pages – only demonstrate this unsettled state. For some, EU gender policy is unable to emancipate women from stereotypes, and, among these, from women's supposed natural inclination towards care; for others, it is incapable of protecting women's valuable social-building care roles against the market's utilitarian logics. Of course, this polyphonic discourse represents an important contribution to the collective elaboration of how to imagine a fair and reasonable relationship between human life and the market economy. On the other hand, it is difficult to deny that framing the debate in "women's interests" ends up weakening its critical grip and imaginative capacity.

In other terms, the criticism that perceives, within the EU representation of gender roles, a dehumanizing note, one which refuses to acknowledge men and women's real experience, could achieve greater depth by re-addressing the research that details these disowned experiences, facts, and values.

In 1996 Hoskyns pointed out a very problematic aspect of EU gender policies in the fact that they were all perceived and developed around the "European White Woman Model" (Hoskyns 1996: 199). Since then, the EU gender policy discourse's "self-referential" character, which, in the words used by Gianluca Bascherini in his chapter, could be called "provincial", has only increased. This is to some extent perceived and denounced by those who critically note the "Splendid Insulation" of EU gender policies (Van der Vleuten 2007), which communicate very little of their privileged status, huge "acquis" and intensive institutional creativity to other anti-discrimination and human rights policies (Bell 2002: 211).

Following the development and the tenor of EU gender discourse it is easy to think, on the one hand, that all the ingredients of emancipation is made up of (fostering women's access to productive activities; reconciling work and family; gender role's exchangeability) do echo and institutionalize all the classical items of the feminist revolution of the 1970's, unifying them with the slogan "go to work and be independent". From this point of view, the EU gender discourse is a great narrative, a magical mirror reflecting self-legitimacy and sense of identity, which reassure us EU citizens that great progress has been made, where the conflicts or injustices which had torn us apart have been repaired.

Strangely enough, this discourse is defined as if the actors on the stage were only European women and men, supported by their own goodness and civilized willingness to exchange their public and private roles and by a (recommended) policy of cheap public child care (plus some help for elderly people). Insisting that things will never change for women if men don't decide to take on more family responsibilities, feminist criticism contributes to this narrative. At the very core of it, there is nothing but a stereotyped vision of care and family responsibilities, regarded and evoked as a static series of activities, unchanged and unchangeable, focussing on child rearing and clearly separated from the workplace, which women have repeated the same way for years and men could easily perform, once adequately trained. This simplified narrative, firstly, does not take into account that women's (or men's) inclination to care comes from education, from inherited models of behaviour, from the types of structured life-expectations and desires which women today receive even less of, and men, in this context, are unlikely to receive significantly. Secondly, this narrative downplays the fact that what constitutes care and reproductive activity goes well beyond looking after children. Care is made up of an extremely long list of diverse activities ranging from cooking and shopping, to cultivating friendships and to caring for a disabled or ill family member. Towards this range of activities, each individual probably has a different attitude, which varies over the course of their lives, being conditioned by a number of factors, such as, to mention one, the present state of their own career. Lastly, the European static and simplified narrative, which reduces care to the art of juggling children between the age of 0-6 with work, fails to recall that men and women are increasingly attracted to the productive sphere and less trained to the mentality, behaviour and competencies that care requires, and are increasingly unlikely to be so heroic as to take on care in its entirety. Instead, they delegate it; but even when delegated, care remains care[32].

EU gender discourse neglects the key fact that enables most women and many men to remain in the marketplace. This is that, in many EU Countries, housework, care of children and the elderly, house-cleaning and home-services are provided by people being paid for this, very often non-EU citizens, and most of them women. Whilst providing a comfortable escape from the challenging remark according to which "Equal gender relations in western couples may rely on the employment of a third person" (Agustín 2007: 76), this narrative neglects to consider that the "third person's work", which sometimes substitutes, but in the majority of cases integrates and supports, the care work of EU parents or of adult children, changes substantially what reproductive and productive activities are. If the focus today is on care becoming "paid" work and thus being commercial (Le Baron: 2007), the fact cannot be denied that, as it is performed by a plurality of subjects within and outside the "family", care

---

[32] Indeed, as Lutz 2008b rightly observes domestic work "is insufficiently theorized if one reduces it to the issue of replacement of substitution. In care work emotional barriers play a specific role because, for example, mothers do not want to be entirely 'replaced' by a childminder, and housewives do not leave household tasks to another woman without making sure that their status and responsibilities are not in doubt".

activities are increasingly shaped by a relational network. This network is made up of the relationship between the cared for and the carer of course; but also by the relationship between the family (most often the mother) who hires the care-worker and is in contact with her; and is conditioned, among other things, by regulations governing domestic work. Care has become a word that indicates an ever growing multiplicity of connected subjects, challenges the labels of production and reproduction, and demonstrates a plausible sexed (or gendered) orientation[33], given that those who buy care are mostly EU women and those who sell it are mostly non-EU women, thus establishing a bridge[34]. This, far from entailing a merely monetary exchange, is for both also an opportunity for citizenship, self-realization and a dignified life: for the EU woman, who is enabled to accomplish her work (arguably: a consumer-oriented life); and for the non-EU woman, who from a healthy work relationship improves her stay and finds opportunities to answer needs, or desires, which moved her from home in the first place.

All this means, firstly, that the work of non-EU nationals is very important both for the European social and economic model and for the quality of life of individuals. Secondly, that a very strong connection exists, between the European system's development potentialities and the prospective for social inclusion of the so called "migrants". Thirdly, that a link exists between European employment policy and European migration policy. As a matter of fact, this link is very rarely considered. This lack of attention demonstrates how abstract and unrealistic (denying experience) the European mainstream reading is of the market economy, people's needs, and the relationship between production and reproduction.

This brings us back to Gianluca Bascherini's point that European migration policies differ from gender policies in that the former do not show much readiness to invest in the market's social inclusion aptitudes, which is a fitting way to reflect on the "splendid insulation" of European gender policies in a new way. It is actually true that the EU does not link its migration policies either to equality in treatment, or to fairness and competitiveness among market forces, nor does it demonstrate the intention to govern a process of entitlement to rights, as it did in the case

---

[33] This implies that "domestic work is not just another labour market, but that it is marked by the following aspects: the intimate character of the social sphere where the work is performed; the social construction of this work as a female gendered area; the special relationship between employer and employee which is highly emotional, personalized and characterized by mutual dependency; and the logic of care-work which is clearly different from that of other employment areas" (Lutz 2008b: 1).

[34] See on this: Bascherini 2007: 294, Lutz 2008b: 3.

of women. Nor does the EU seem to perceive "Migrants" and their rights
as a source of legitimacy, as fostering women rights was, when they came
together in women's entry into the market. All this demonstrates that
what gives EU gender policy its privilege and special nature, is its
constitutive link with the economic vehicle of integration[35].
Bascherini opportunely notes that the existing strong division between the
rights of EU citizens and non-EU citizens runs on the freedom to enter
and circulate within the European marketplace being considered
fundamental only for the former. It is a divide destined to deepen until the
silence, denial and stereotyping which hide the links which connects
Migrants' work to EU nationals' work are overcome.
As for the reasons why this theme is so difficult to explore, the existing
taboo surrounding it, especially for European women, deserves special
mention. The care-commodification theme comes across as traumatic for
European – and, in general, for Western – women, who seem embarrassed
about owing a large part of their independence to the poverty or less
fortunate circumstances that have forced other women to leave home[36].
From this – which could partly entail an attempt to escape from the need
to reconfigure the terms of sexual conflict in Europe - a process of
repression arises, which denies the conflicting and contradictory
components of the process of gender role transformation in Europe,
contributing to the risk that the European image of men and women comes
out as blurred, ineffective and therefore "neutral", that is to say:
misleading and as such strongly disciplinating.
    To start restructuring the space and values of production and
reproduction does imply a close and attentive view of the transformations
that care and the subjects involved in it are experiencing in Europe. It is
particularly vital to avoid the hasty equation according to which care

---

[35] Under this point of view the findings of Schwenken 2005 are revealing, which when
analyzing EU policies concerning migrant domestic workers note that "The EU is
relatively open to gender specific demands of undocumented migrants. Thus migrant
women's organizations and advocacy networks have an advantage compared to male
dominated or gender mixed organizations. But this more open opportunity structure for
female migrants is for the same reasons ambivalent, as the specific problems arising from
the lack of citizenship rights and restrictive immigration rules cannot be addressed
adequately". This suggests that, when detached from their link with the fundamental
economic freedoms of the European integration process (sources in their turn of full
citizenship rights), the mere fundamental rights dimension to gender issues is weak, if not
ineffective.
[36] See Hochschild 2000, asking "Are first-world countries importing maternal love as they
have imported copper, zinc and gold from third-world countries in the past?" (quoted by
Agustín 2008: 57).

work, when paid, simply becomes part of "production". This equation rids care work of its specialness, which exceeds a merely economic dimension (Lutz 2008b), and also ignores that care consists not only of dependence, passivity and marginality, but – through the multiple parts that participate in it – also of power, agency and pleasure (Marinelli 2008). To keep care from remaining aphasic, deprived of socialisation and doomed not to produce symbolic change, a great awareness movement is needed, capable of perceiving the challenges that care work does imply *because* it floats in the space between production and reproduction. It should be able to put gratitude, recognition and interdependence and the mutual legitimacy of different life projects in the place of the sometimes opportunist senses of guilt, and to recognise the central role played by women in this momentous flux.

Today, criticizing the European gender discourse from a gendered point of view requires focusing on the dynamics that the move from reproduction to production has had for European women (transforming both production and reproduction) and testifying to the centrality of what the re-productive sphere means for European living together[37]. It is instead European men and women's unwillingness to recognize the possibilities that performing care in their own way (which include boarding paid support, multiplying relationships, building mutual exchange and opening opportunities)[38] do include, that risks creating a true "delegation effect" where many of the implications of the restructuring of gender relationships are mislaid or forgotten. Such a step requires renewing the gender agenda from those issue, which had been built around the great 1970's cornerstone (and all pivoting on work and emancipation for European women). It is reassuring that, starting from the inspiring image of the "world as a domestic environment" (Preaetorius 2008), reflections are starting to blossom in this direction.

3.2. B) PAYING DUE ATTENTION TO THE CHANGING DEMANDS OF JUSTICE

The various limits that affect the EU gender discourse should not be seen only in negative terms. Instead, they are quite obvious consequences of the state of flux of the presiding symbolic order of gender roles, such

---

[37] A first, even if very little, step in this direction is the European Parliament Report on Regulating Domestic Help in the Informal Sector (EP: 2000). Even more interesting are the activities of the European Network of Migrant Domestic Workers (RESPECT, www.solidar.org).

[38] Described by Andall 2000, as "post-feminist paradigm".

that the re-definition process entailed by EU law is one of the components
of a collective process, the results of which can not be taken for granted.
For this reason, critical opinions and the introduction of different points of
view are important. They contribute to keeping the process open and they
all have a potential weight, considering that a large part of the process is
entrusted to those new soft modes of governance which are sensitive to
interests and evaluations capable of finding support and mention among
the series of subjects (from academic experts to activist groups) that have
a voice in the process.

If an open, pluralistic and active debate can influence the outcomes of the
European gender discourse, another channel to which attention must be
paid is legal experience. It is from this field, that the demands of justice
flow, stimulating not only judges but the entire collectivity to reflect on
their own values and imagine the form of an ordered living together.

At the EU level, cases and controversies are very often the expression of
the strategic engagement of lobbies and interest groups promoting and
supporting various claims due to their general political relevance. But as
happens in every legal system, cases and controversies are also
conditioned by the legal material, interpretative traditions included, with
which claims can be constructed. Another conditioning element is the
time frame, which makes certain themes appear more urgent and
important, and causes certain forms of reasoning, instead of others, to be
perceived as fair and reasonable.

When investigating the limits of ECJ case law, which repeats that gender
roles are exchangeable but is largely incapable of giving value to those
activities and life choices which are beyond the productive side, the
weight that the legal context, interpretative traditions and shared points of
view have in painting such a picture must be considered. All these factors
have a strong influence on the Court's responses, because they determine
the content of the judicial questions. It is difficult, in other words, largely
improbable and possibly inopportune, that a Court pronounces something
different from what people ask it for.

A glance at the Court's record shows the powerful parity approach of the
original Equality Directives working jointly with the remainder of
feminism's call for the emancipation of women (a word that dictionaries
define as "women's struggle to be given the same rights, opportunities,
etc. as men"), which dominated during the 1970's and the 1980's,
triggering off a sort of pursuit by the one sex not to be discriminated
against by the other. In preliminary rulings, this collection of elements has
produced three fundamental series of cases: *a*) the first, flowing directly
from the Equality Directive's parity goal, which includes controversies

originating from women claiming the right to be treated the same as men at work, notwithstanding the diversity of their career choices, time schedules, and lesser availability for overtime possibly due to their care responsibilities (from *Jenkins* to *Enderby*); b) another, consisting of the controversies, brought by men who claimed the right to the same treatment as women, arguing that their care roles were identical to women's (from *Griesmar* to *Lommers* to *Abdoulaye*); c) the third, consisting of controversies in which it was explicitly asked that the same rights be given to carers and workers (*Drake* and *Zuechner*).

This picture, drawn from case law until the end of the 1990's, communicates the idea that the unit of measurement of the value of activities, competencies and behaviour is that established by the traditional capitalist order, which considered the work provided by men – that is by a subject imagined as without care responsibilities – the normality and the norm. On the whole, anti-discrimination demands for justice have contributed to stressing the material and symbolic subordination of care to paid work.

It is not surprising then, that from such demands for justice, responses have come which have limited themselves to acknowledging that women and men perform exchangeable social roles, equally subordinated to the logic according to which the recognition of their importance is expressed by their market value. Worth noting here is only the coincidence of views between common sense, at least that shared by the majority of public opinion, and the interpretative path adopted by the judge.

What then becomes interesting is seeing if whether are changes in the tenor of the demands for justice that reach the Court. And in fact the earlier case law does signal some interesting elements.

Let us consider, in particular, two cases from the last decade: *Carpenter* and *Coleman*[39]. In the first one, a Philippine woman married to a UK national opposed a deportation order by saying she was entitled to the right to stay in the UK directly from Community Law. She claimed that by looking after her husband's children, she empowered her husband, who sold advertising spaces and travelled around Europe, to enjoy one of the fundamental freedoms granted by the Treaty, the freedom of the circulation of services. In the second case, a legal secretary, single mother of a disabled child, sued her employer for discrimination by association. By refusing to give her time off from work and the flexibility she needed to care for her child, and by surrounding her with a "hostile" atmosphere,

---

[39] Case C-60/00, *Carpenter*, ECRS, 2002, p. I-6279; Case C-303/06, *Coleman*, ECR, 2008, p. I-5603.

the employer is claimed to have discriminated against her, as a person associated with a disabled person. In both cases, the Court upheld the claimant's view. In fact, in *Carpenter*, the Court skipped the point of the woman's caring activities supporting her husband's productive work, and preferred to concentrate on the right to family life.[40] In *Coleman*, the Court stated that the parent, who is the first carer of a disabled child, can be the victim of disability discrimination (by association)[41].

Carpenter and *Coleman* are both of the utmost importance, and not so much for what the Court stated, as for the reading they imply of the situations they refer to. *Carpenter* shows the importance that non-EU women's work has towards the functioning of the European social and economic model. *Coleman* shows a mother who attaches value to her care role, without equating it with paid work. Both are demands for recognition that demonstrate the new placement of work and care in Europe today, and signal a common sense in change in which care work can start to discover its own dignity, and thereby, while also claiming recognition for its importance for production also, can thus emancipate itself from a symbolic subordination to the latter[42]. Both *Carpenter* and *Coleman* indeed claimed rights and entitlement – in a word: dignity – rather than money (in terms of salary or wages). They affirmed that their care activities are important *for what they made possible* (a child's wellbeing; a man's job), not for what they produce, and that thereby they are different and distinct from economic logic.

Demands for justice of this kind actually make it possible to agree that "Now, gender equality is placed in the context of other issues of liberty, equality, and indeed, dignity" (Costello 2003); and without demands being so laden with implications and scope, justice in Luxembourg would never be able to evolve towards "an authentic capacity to articulate issues of value" (Costello 2003: 124).

Today many factors are on the table, which mobilize the picture offered by European anti-discrimination law. *Carpenter* and *Coleman* reveal how

---

[40] On this case see also Bascherini's considerations in his chapter.

[41] On this case see also Hoskyns's considerations in her chapter.

[42] A similar change in values is that proposed from the part of scholarship (Fredman 2008: 16) sensitive to the fact that caring should be valued "because it is in itself a necessary and important social activity". One form of recognition of the value of care work can be seen in the legislation for the regularisation of the informal work situation of immigrants without permits of stay, that allows the regularisation of home workers and family assistants, as is happening in Italy (Lutz 2008b), even if in the entire picture remains ambiguous and difficult to decipher when viewed within the restrictions of these disciplines.

deeply those factors are working. They are the new grounds for discrimination; the increased adherence of the Court to the ECHR's principles; the presence itself of the EU Charter of Fundamental Rights, offering claimants both legal material either richer or more nuanced with which to construct their demands, and the expectation that the Court will listen to them. It is, plausibly, most of all the changed value that men and women recognize in themselves and their own life-choices which is starting to find its way into these new legal materials.

Today, scholars insistently ask the Court to start exploring the possibilities of a richer and more openly evaluative syndicate (Barbera 2003b). They recall that an understanding of anti-discrimination as principle oriented toward the positive recognition of rights and values, would enable the Court to go through the issues of fairness and justice (Masselot and Caracciolo di Torella 2001) that anti-discrimination claims always entail and that a purely negative and comparative use of the anti-discrimination principle severely silences (Repetto 2009b). As the reasoning developed in this volume by Giorgio Repetto with reference to the theme of sexual orientation well demonstrates, the chance of seeing the Court actively go down this path (and accordingly re-tune its legal reasoning) is conditioned by the diffusion of an enlarged sentiment of dignity, open to different possibilities, and capable of learning from the variety of ways individuals live their lives. It is only this sentiment that can change for the better the fabric of the European image of a normal and worthy life.

The Metamorphosis of Gender in the European Community: Shifting Forms of Social Inclusion from the *Nation-Building* to the *Market-Building* Frame

Theresa Wobbe

Synopsis. This chapter examines how societal inclusion works in the context of the EU and how it touches on the idea of gender equality. Using historical-sociological analysis and theoretical concepts of inclusion as points of departure, the chapter relates European gender politics to deeper structures of belonging and solidarity. It puts the historical *nation-building* and the unfolding European *market-building* as two analytical frames in which equality ideas are explored.

The chapter illustrates this by raising the concepts of labor, work, and gender: To what extent have ideas about work and (in-)equality been infused by the vision of sexual difference and in how far are the Community anti-discrimination principles contributing to its transformation? The principles of free movement and equal pay are used as a measure to examine variations of 'gendered inclusion'. By placing gender in this context we are able to illuminate the profound shift to including individuals as 'gendered persons' and conferring them with rights in a more broadly European historical context.

Keywords: Inclusion, Gender Equality, Nation/Market-Building, European Union.

Introduction

Since the Foundation Treaties of the 1950s, the concept of anti-discrimination took its own path in the European integration process. Both the free movement and the equal pay principle have embodied the two prominent anti-discrimination measures of the European legal framework, which have linked and are still linking the social and the economic in a distinct vision of equality. Together they have been serving as a backbone for the Community idea of equality, which is dedicated to that of equal opportunities (Ellis 1998; Ellis 2005; Craig and de Búrca 2008; Meenan 2007; Schiek and Chege 2009).

In this chapter, I will discuss the Community anti-discrimination principles from a historical-sociological perspective. This will be done (1) with respect to the European legacy of former national concepts of gender equality, and (2) regarding the unfolding European Community meaning of equality. By situating the anti-discrimination principles in the broader context of European modernity I want to illuminate the extent to which the historic legacy of gender arrangements is being transcended through the Community equality script.

In order to do so, two frames will be used. In the first step I will shed light on the historical frame of *nation-building* with respect to equality and, subsequently, relate this idea to that of the European *market-building* in the second part of the 20th century.

With the help of the institutionalist approach[1] I ask, to which extent concepts about work and (in-)equality have been infused by the idea of sexual difference and in how far the Community anti-discrimination principle contributes to its transformation (Wobbe and Biermann 2009). Since the early 19th century (in the context of the nation-state), gender difference has served as a fundamental defense for the legitimacy of unequal treatment. Thus, an underlying question of this chapter addresses the extent to which the European Community's gender norms are altering this modern heritage. In this context, the Community vision of women's work is telling, as it pervades the primary and secondary Community law (Ellis 1998; Ellis 2005).

A close reading of both the historic discourses and those of the EC brings to the surface the different meanings of work and equality while making visible the distinct visions of what constitutes 'women' and 'men' at work. This reading, in addition, offers an insight into the distinct concepts of rights as they have been institutionalized in the national and in the Community's legal frameworks.

Since there exists a rich body of sophisticated interdisciplinary research related to various aspects of my contribution, it is important to be clear about its focus and scope. This chapter is driven by a sociological perspective that seeks to identify the social forms of belonging and inclusion that emerge in the social system of the European Union (EU) as distinguished from those in the historical case of the nation-state. For this purpose two analytical frames will be employed.

Solidarity within the *nation-building* process started from the idea of collectively shared equality of certain privileged groups, while discriminating non-nationals, women, and various minorities (Anderson 1983). National solidarity was generated by the boundary making of a cultural difference, distinguishing the internal privileged 'we' from the 'others' in and outside the nation. In this manner, a particular group of

---

[1] For a (historical) sociological view on the broad field of institutionalist literature see: Collier/Collier 1991; Jepperson 1991; Thelen 2002, 2003.

individuals was included as nationals and conferred with the rights of national citizens in the legal context.

Quite to the contrary, the boundary making of the European *market-building* has contributed to economic difference, while drawing a major distinction between the common market (that of the shared competition rules of the emerging community) and market systems elsewhere in the world. The corresponding code of solidarity is built on the idea of collectively shared equality of market-participants who are conferred with basic social and economic rights in the market irrespective to their nationality[2], their sex, and further categories of collective belonging. By stipulating equal opportunities for individuals in the single market irrespective to their cultural diversity this equality script is challenging the historical national paths of cultural homogeneity in Europe. Against this background it becomes clear that the configuration of the economic and the social is undergoing a shift. The single market can be observed as a 'socially inclusion player' (Niccolai 2008: 24).

In the following, European integration will be considered as a process of transforming deeper structures of solidarity and rights, resulting in the formation of distinct forms of 'European' sociation (*Vergesellschaftung*) (Münch 2008a, b; Wobbe 2009; Wobbe and Biermann 2009). In this process former national arrangements of equality have been and are being blurred. It will be argued that because of the twin processes of transforming and blurring gender, too, is undergoing a profound change.

The chapter is organized in three steps. The first section addresses the gendered concepts of rights and work as they have been institutionalized in the course of the 19th and 20th century *nation-building* with respect to visions of difference (1). Next, the nature of the EU is discussed, while sketching the differences between *nation-building* and *market-building*: The principles of free movement and equal pay will be introduced as measures, contributing to include 'workers' as the key category to be addressed in the common/single market on the ground of equal treatment (2). Against this background I will discuss the prominent case law *Kreil/Bundesrepublik Deutschland* which has raised questions in the field of protection and equal treatment. (3). In my summary, I will ask, which meaning of the 'individual' and the *Menschenbild* is occurring and to which extent it is deeply interwoven with the alteration of gender.

---

[2] In the course of the history of the common market *nationality* signified the nationality of another EC/EU member state, while the status of third-country-citizens or stateless individuals has become a contested field (see: Craig/de Búrca 2008: 743; Shaw/Hunt/Wallace 2007: 281).

1. Constituting women as a non-standard employment group: protective labor legislation during the 19th and early 20th century

For the most part, social science literature emphasizes the modernity of the concept of the nation (Hobsbawm 1990; Anderson 1983). Basic rights have become institutionalized only in the context of the national citizenship model. The architecture of rights and identity, which emerged in the institutional context of the nation during the 19th and 20th century is deeply encoded through the idea of cultural homogeneity of every single nation's people. This presumed idea has historically been invested and reproduced by the concept of sexual difference. As a matter of fact, citizenship rights were first limited to men of property and then extended to the male citizens of the middle and the working classes. Against this background Benedict Anderson (1983) put the *nation-building* in the context of *horizontal comradeship,* which would herald the various routes to citizenship. In a more conceptual sense, Anderson considers the creation of the nation a new historical type of imagined community (i.e. solidarity) with respect to both the idea of equality between comrades and its programmatic horizontal sounding in contrast to former vertical models of communities.

Accordingly, the rise of the modern nation including its model of belonging was not a gender-neutral process. While modern social theory provided the concept of the abstract individual, which was disentangled from any corporal, cultural, and local context, in fact, European privileged men served as the prototype for this concept. At the same time the spirit of national solidarity, polity, and law was encoded with visions of masculine sovereignty (see: Scott 1996). Feminist critic of national citizenship therefore is not only dedicated to the exclusion of women as a social group, but it also focuses on the gendered nature of (adult) personhood and its underlying notion of sexual difference by which women have been included into the nation.

The meaning of work and equality provides a significant case to unpack these notions. Not only women's political participation was constituted as problematic and incomparable to that of men, but also their economic activities were designed as incomparable and nonstandard (see: Berkovitch 1999). The woman worker, who came into 'extraordinary prominence' during the 19th century, became 'a troubling and visible figure' in the eyes of governments, social reformers, women's and labor movements. Women's paid work attracted the attention of what became the *social question discourse,* which reflected efforts at coming to terms with the complex transformations to modern industrial society.

The 'problem' of the woman worker involved the compatibility between womanhood and wage-earning evoking an opposition between home and work, maternity and wage earning, femininity and productivity (Scott 1993: 399). The discourses on the national regulation of women's industrial work offer a nice example to reveal these visions on women workers who 'would always be second-class employees whose bodies, productive capacities, and social responsibilities made them incapable of the kind of labor that would win economic and social recognition of them as full-fledged workers' (Scott 1993: 425). During the 19th with industrialisation and women's move into the paid work labor market female night work figured as a symbol for protective labor legislation.

First efforts and protecting steps were taken in order to constrain women's work in underground mines. Britain, in 1842 prohibited women from underground work. Various national labour laws interdicted women's night work including Switzerland in 1877, Britain and Germany in 1878, France in 1892, Sweden in 1909, Spain in 1912, Russia in 1905, the Soviet Union in 1918, and Portugal in 1927. State regulated restriction of women's working hours started in Britain in 1844 (12 h.) and in 1847 (10 h.), in Germany in 1891 (11 h.), in France in 1892 (11 h.), in Italy in 1902 (12 h.) (see: Bock 2000: 218; Kessler-Harris, Lewis and Wikander 1995: 6f.; Lewis andRose 1995)[3].

By the late 19th century, women's factory labor became a focal point for intervening into gender relations. After 1890, in the course of international congresses and national investigations of women's working conditions, 'women's roles as workers became the principal subject for debate. Female factory and sweatshop workers found themselves in the centre of a controversy about the social value of restricting their wage work' (Kessler-Harris, Lewis and Wikander 1995: 7). The factors that pushed this debate were complex. The legislation was connected to the late 19th century revaluation of free market liberalism and the establishing of international competition standards. It was a response to women's increasing economic opportunities and the attempt to re-configure women's family work as a priority in the welfare state at the same time.

Seen from today's perspective, the discourses about protective labor legislation offered a field to create labor relations as a gendered realm according to the separation of place, type, and value of work.

---

[3] Various countries including Zurich in 1815, Britain in 1833, Prussia in 1839, France in 1841, Sweden in 1852, Austria in 1859 restricted the working hours of children at the same time. By the 1870s the laws interdicting children's work were common in Europe (Kessler-Harris/Lewis/Wikander 1995: 6).

What was the meaning of 'protection' and what did 'women' mean? What was the underlying vision of equality within these discourses? First, the language of protection touched on *hygienic* and *moral* dangers to which women would be exposed during their paid work to an exceptional degree (compared to men). Since the mid 19th century promoting health became a significant feature in order to identify social problems of modern societies. While observing phenomena such as emerging urban structures and life worlds, industrial work and urban prostitution, the discourse of hygiene signified both a technology for social control and a myth of (controlling) modernity. It produced a vision of health, which invoked discipline, civility, progress, and normalcy. In contrast, disease signified disorder, dependence, and backwardness (see: Frevert 1985).

Why, then, protecting women as a particular group? During the second part of the 19th century, political and scientific experts discussed the impact of wage-earning labor on the woman's body, on her ability to achieve maternal and familial roles including her moral capacities as mother and housewife (see: Lewis and Rose 1995: 102). In this context, the notion of hygiene, served as a medical and moral programme governing the reproductive resources of modern societies (see: Wikander, Kessler-Harris and Lewis 1995). By presenting high infant mortality and low birth rates national statistics contributed at the same time to the emerging evidence of the need to protect women.

In the 1890s, it appeared that the concern for two fields was at stake: While the men-women-relationship in the work place attracted the public eye, women's family duties were related 'to the need of the state and the future of the 'race'' (Wikander 1995: 30; see: Lewis and Rose 1995: 98). The issue of motherhood was interconnected to these fields. It figured as a common thread across the international debates on protecting women's labor, spanning different political fields from the Second International to national governments and the international women's movements (see: Wikander 1995).

The discourses preparing protective legislation contributed to generate ideas about men and women at work as on the working floor as well: 'They advanced and strengthened the idea that the 'working woman' and later the 'working mother' were contradictory terms' (Lewis and Rose 1995. 90). These discourses around legislation resulted in 'a widespread acceptance of social conventions that assigned different jobs to men and women' (Wikander 1995: 54). The clustering of women's work in certain low-paying, unskilled jobs reflected the priority of women's maternal und familial duties as distinguished from those of the skilled male worker with a life-long occupational commitment: 'The "problem" of the woman worker, then, was that she was an anomaly in a world where wage labor and family responsibilities had each become full-time and spatially distinct jobs' (Scott 1993: 400). It is against this background that, with respect to employment, women became a special case, a non-standard.

In other words all women, by not distinguishing between age, marital status, race, social position, were converted into a species that was in need of protection (*Schutzbedürftigkeit der Frau*). Restrictions in working hour and site as well as in occupational tasks constituted the core of protective labor legislation in Europe (see Wikander, Kessler-Harris and Lewis 1995). Simultaneously the issue of night work became a myth in the self-description of modern societies: The state, with the help of administrative and scientific experts, carried the banner of protecting the *mothers of the nation*, and so did the mainstream labor and women's movement and social reform. Legislators and social reformers maintained that these measures were in the interest of the nation. While the distinct focus of the concern could shift from sexuality to the relevance of domesticity 'legislators portrayed the control of women, as workers, as fundamental to social order and the health of the body politic' (Lewis and Rose 1995: 94). Around 1900, this meaning was institutionalized in the national labor legislation across Europe. It took place in the context of the welfare-state formation, which was interconnected with national health insurance, social security measures, population and family policy (see: Bock and Thane 1992; Wikander, Kessler-Harris and Lewis 1995). In the aftermath of the Second World War these measures have been extended to various national welfare regimes (see: Lewis 1993). It was only in the 1970s that Western European countries transformed their labor and family law by addressing women as persons participating in economic activities as 'individuals' and comparable to men. The next section will show to what extent this legacy has been challenged by the Community legal framework.

2. From protecting the 'woman worker' to promoting women as equals in the labor market

When in 1991 the European Court of Justice decided in Stoeckel/Tribunal de police d'Illkirch[4] that national provisions forbidding women's night work were inconsistent with the principles of the Equal Treatment Directive (76/207/EEC), the French and Italian governments

---

[4] Case 345/89, *Stoeckel/Tribunal de police d'Illkirch*, ECR, 1991, p. 4047.

argued that the prohibition would protect women. The ECJ, however, considered women's exclusion from this work as a source of discrimination[5].

As becomes clear, both claims provide different views on equality in employment. The French government argued in the frame of women's anomaly status in the market. It claimed that night work exposed women to risks of violence, and, in addition, their family responsibilities resulted in more and extra work. The Court, on the other hand, underlined its understanding of equal treatment. This would mean 'with regard to working conditions (…) that men and women are to be offered the same conditions without discrimination of sex' (Art. 5 ETD 76/207). With respect to sexual assaults and women's family work, the ECJ argued against the general protection of women. In case the risks for women exceeded those for men, employers had to take measures. As far as family responsibilities were concerned, the Court refused strictly any intervening[6].

Contrary to the language of *protecting women* the ECJ invoked the principle of equal treatment that should work irrespective to the notion of difference including women's family work. These different perspectives demonstrate the contested visions about gender and work. The dispute illuminates the ongoing dynamics between the European legacy of gender difference and shifting gender arrangements, which are grounded in the Community idea of equal treatment of the sexes irrespective to their family status. Why, however, does the EU promote this meaning that alters the former concept and in which broader frames is it embedded?

During the second half of the 20th century, the idea of gender equality increasingly spread across the globe (Berkovitch 1999; Heintz and Schnabel 2006; Wobbe 2003). For the purpose of this essay, the most important factors are the codification of human rights as an organising principle worldwide, the new face of labor migration, and the emergence of multi-level polities, most prominently on the European stage. Mainly in the discourse on human rights and social progress, gender codes underwent a shift from difference to equality. During the 1950s and 1960s, with the help of international organisations, the primacy of women's family roles became less tenable and acceptable.

Simultaneously, individual rights of women were institutionalized as international standards as the International Labour Organization (ILO) convention 100 (1951) that was dedicated to equal pay of men and women

---

[5] Ibid., at pa. 19.
[6] Ibid., at pa. 17.

(Lubin and Winslow 1990). While establishing the historically new common market, the European Economic Community (EEC) contributed to this reconfiguration of rights by stipulating anti-discrimination norms in its legal framework (see: Ellis 1998).

The EEC Treaty (EECT 1957) provided two anti-discrimination principles dismantling the barriers as been anchored in the *nation-building* frame during the 19th century. Both the principle of free movement and that of equal pay have since embodied the two distinct anti-discrimination measures in Community law, which served and still serve as the backbone for equal treatment.

Each of them is deeply entangled with international labor standards as entitled in the ILO conventions. As a consequence of the extent of international migration, free movement gained increasing relevance following 1945. The ILO Migration for Employment Convention (No. 97) of 1949 prohibited discrimination on several grounds, including nationality and sex:

> 'Each Member (…) undertakes to apply, without discrimination in respect of nationality, race, religion or sex, to immigrants lawfully within its territory, treatment no less favourable than that which it applies to its own nationals (…).' (ILO, 97, Art. 6.1).

This principle, which prohibits discrimination against persons on various grounds, in the EEC was referred only to with respect to the nationality of one of the Member States: 'Freedom of movement for workers shall be secured within the Community by the end of the transitional period at the latest. 1. Such freedom of movement shall entail the abolition of any discrimination based on nationality between workers of the Member States as regards employment, remuneration and other conditions of work and employment. 2. It shall entail the right, subject to limitations justified on grounds of public policy, public security or public health (…)' (Art. 48, EECT). Historically, the right of free movement constituted one of the basic rights established in Europe during the 19th century in the context of the nation-state and bound to national territory. In the EEC, the national boundaries of this right have been transcended and extended to those of the common market. Complementary, a shift has taken place from 'citizens' to 'workers': Persons are being addressed and entitled as workers, i.e. as participants of the market, but not as (national) citizens.

The meaning of this core term 'worker' was, however, not defined in the Treaties. It has been shaped by the case law of the ECJ and is to be considered a distinct Community law term, an *'autonomer Begriff des Gemeinschaftsrechts'* (Haratsch et al. 2004: 316), i.e. a Community concept in its own. From the beginning the Court has insisted, that this definition was a matter of the Community law, not of the national (Craig and de Búrca 2008: 747). In the case *Hoekstra/Bestuur der Bedrijfsvereiniging* the Court declared:

> 'If the definition of this term were a matter for the competence of national law, it would therefore be possible to each Member State to modify the meaning of the concept 'migrant worker' and to eliminate at will the protection afforded by the Treaty to certain categories of person (...) Articles 48 to 51 (now 39-42) would be therefore deprived of all effect and the above-mentioned objectives of the Treaty would be frustrated of the meaning of such a term could be unilaterally fixed and modified by national law'[7].

Contrary, this notion should attain a single meaning in every Member State. The Court was claiming 'ultimate authority to define its meaning and scope'. As Federico Mancini put it, the Court conferred on itself a 'hermeneutic monopoly' (Craig and de Búrca 2008: 747). The free movement measure in the sense of equal treatment of workers was and still is the key principle for inclusion, as workers are the most privileged category of people under Community law. The term has been interpreted widely in order to grasp the plurality of the common/single market participants (Shaw/Hunt/Wallace 2007: 281 ff.).

While the political and legal processes of *nation-building* contributed to the emerging category of the citizen, *the common-market-building* gave birth to the key component of the worker. With respect to these latter processes, the notion of the worker serves as a medium for inclusion, because it reduces the barriers between the Member States in order to create free movement within the evolving market area. This measure as stipulated in Art. 48 EEC was the starting point for the mutual opening of national markets to a transnational level in the Western-European region.

The Treaties of Rome also provided a second anti-discrimination principle, which altered the core term 'worker'. The free movement principle established the worker as the key subject to be included into the common market. By prohibiting unequal pay on the grounds of sex, Art. 119 (now 141) was dedicated to fair renumeration of women's and men's work.

As Hoskyns (1996) has pointed out, the equal pay provision also owes its existence and particular form to the debate that took place in international organisations. The Equal Remuneration Convention (No. 100), which was

---

[7] Case 75/63 *Hoekstra/Bestuur der Bedrijfsvereiniging voor Detailhandel en Ambachten*, ECR, 1964, pp. 177, 184.

drafted and adopted in 1951, is the second international measure in the context of the *market-building*. Ultimately, however it may have been modified, the principle of equal pay enshrined in Art. 119 is in accordance with the equal pay principle of ILO Convention No. 100 (Hoskyns 1996; Wobbe and Biermann 2007; Wobbe and Biermann 2009)[8].

While the EEC aimed at creating a common economic area with shared rules on competition, a shift in perspective took place: Formerly distinct economic units became individual parts of an emerging supra-national system in which previous differences now appeared as internal differentiations of the same system.

Negotiating the Treaties of Rome, the creation of a common competition scheme for the coming market challenged the six member states due to their different economic and social policy models (see: Hoskyns 1996: 47; Vleuten 2007: 35). The different constitutional principles regarding men's and women's work became among others a point of debate. In particular, France was concerned that it would be placed at a competitive disadvantage in prescribing equal pay more thoroughly than other Member States.

They set up a section on social standards in which they included the equal pay provision for men and women:

> 'Each member state shall during the first stage ensure and subsequently maintain the application of the principle that men and women should receive equal pay for equal work. (...). Equal pay without discrimination based on sex means a) that pay for the same work at piece rates shall be calculated on the basis of the same unit of measurement, b) that pay for work at time rates shall be the same for the same job' (Art. 119, EEC Treaty).

This article prescribes sex as an irrelevant ground of evaluating the outcome of work. Instead of this it stipulates that it would be the outcome which serves as the definitive criteria in contrast to that of the sex of the worker. Given the historical meaning of the 'woman worker' this phrasing of the treaty appears to be a *caesura* as it reverses the meaning of work from incompatibility to comparability.

As Silvia Niccolai put it, Art. 119 represents the first European constitutional document that addressed women '*only* as subject of the

---

[8] Moreover, international expectations in the field of economic harmonization are essential for market building. Due to both the liberalization code of the Organisation for European Economic Cooperation (OEEC) and the rules on competition laid down in the GATT agreement, the chosen common market model must adhere to international standards.

market, as factors of production or 'human resources' (Niccolai 2008: 31).
I suggest underscoring this historical perspective by illuminating that Art.
119 is also the first European document requiring comparability of work
irrespective to sex.

While reforming the trade code of the Kaiserreich, to raise the German
case, in 1891 free movement explicitly was restricted to male worker.
Women were considered to require protection from the state due to their
weakness (Schmitt 1995). As further European countries demonstrate,
women and children were portrayed as victims of the factory system,
while the state as well as husbands were called on to advocate on behalf of
them. Through the lens of legal reformers women were no free agents,
rather the national law included women and children as needing its
protection (see: Lewis and Rose 1995: 95ff., 101). In the context of this
broader frame, both female domesticity and male breadwinning were
identified 'as the test of a civilized society' (ibid. 99). The equal pay anti-
discrimination measure dismantles the barriers of these former notions of
national legal regulation.

In the light of institutionalization, equality norms are understood as shared
meanings and taken-for-granted scripts (Jepperson 1991).[9] Accordingly,
change will occur when a prevailing script is replaced by another. In this
view, evolving Community gender equality norms reflect a celebration of
the 'woman worker' as a market participant comparable to the 'man
worker'. In the process the notion of women as a non-standard worker has
being replaced by the idea that they are full fledged workers.

Starting with the equal pay principle, the European Community gradually
established a distinct structure for gender equality that challenges national
conceptions. In particular, notions of equal treatment are now
transcending national borders in the drive to establish free movement and
competition in the new common market area (Ellis 1998 and 2005).
Against this background, in the following I will illuminate the entwined
institutional history of Community anti-discrimination principles and
gender equality with respect to a prominent legal case.

3. Evolving anti-discrimination principles and gender equality

The sex equality principle was originally divided into three
dimensions: equal pay for work of equal worth, equal treatment in access

---

[9] Accordingly, institutionalization is defined as 'the construction over time of a social
definition of reality such that certain ways of action are taken for granted as the 'right' if
not the only way to do things' (Scott and Meyer 1994: 234).

to and conditions of employment, and social security as enshrined in the Directives of the 1970s, which have been consolidated in the Directive 2006/54 (see: Craig and de Búrca 2008). In addition, there has evolved a rich amount of soft law such as action programs, road maps, etc. (see: European Commission 2006).

It was the ECJ ruling in the *Defrenne* cases[10] that was a landmark, as it stated that formerly Art. 119 had direct effect in Member States. In other words, women could rely on this article in national court irrespective of domestic law; from then on this article was fully enforceable in national courts and conferred subjective rights to individuals.[11] Since then the equal pay principle has been expanded and extended. In the context of the second *Defrenne* decision the Court stated that the economic aim pursued by Art. 119 is secondary to the social aim pursued by the same provision, which has the status of a principle Community right.[12] According to the third *Defrenne* ECJ ruling in 1978, the sex anti-discrimination principle gained the status of a fundamental human right.[13]

It becomes clear, already from these rulings, that the sex equality principle spread across the Community legal framework gaining increasingly more authority while being widened to additional social fields. Until 2008, Art. 119/141 as well as the three Directives from the 1970s have become the backbone of Community litigation as they cover around 80 % of the references of the cases (Wobbe and Biermann 2009: 100, graph 1).

Against this background, the case *Kreil/Bundesrepublik Deutschland* serves as an instructive example to illuminate the scope of the Community equal treatment principle. At the same time, it offers a nice case for a contrast between the *nation-* and *market-building* frame.

In 1996 Tanja Kreil sued the German armed forces, claiming in particular that the rejection of her application on grounds based solely on her sex was contrary to Community law. She stated that the application of Article 12a of the Basic Law for the Federal Republic of Germany amounted to direct discrimination[14] in violation of the Equal Treatment Council Directive (ETD 1976)[15]. The core of Kreil's argument was that

---

[10] Case C - 43/75, *Defrenne v. Sabena (No. 2)*, ECR, 1976, p. 455.

[11] Cichowski 2001: 120.

[12] Case C- 43/75, *Defrenne v. Sabena (No. 2)*, at pa. 8, 11, 12.

[13] Case C- 149/77, *Defrenne v. Sabena (No. 3)*, ECR, 1978, p. 1365, at pa. 26, 27.

[14] Case C-285/98, *Kreil v. Bundesrepublik Deutschland*, ECR, 2000, p. 69, at pa. 11.

[15] Article 12a of the German Basic law then stated: '(1) Men who have attained the age of eighteen years may be required to serve in the Armed Forces, in the Federal Border Guard, or in a Civil Defence organisation.' Women, however, were not allowed access: 'They may on no account render service involving the use of arms' (*ibid.*: Article 12a

Community law may not prohibit a woman from access to the occupation she wishes to pursue[16]. Thus, she referred to Article 2 (1) ETD, which sets out that 'the principle of equal treatment shall mean that there shall be no discrimination whatsoever on grounds of sex either directly or indirectly by reference in particular to marital or family status'[17].

The German government refuted Kreil's view, arguing that 'Community law does not in principle govern matters of defence, which form part of the field of common foreign and security policy and which remain within the Member States' sphere of sovereignty'[18]. Even if the Directive could be said to apply in these circumstances, the German constitutional provisions could be justified under Articles 2 (2) and 2 (3). Article 2 (2) of the ETD allows for exceptions, or, 'the right of Member States to exclude from its field of application those occupational activities and, where appropriate, the training leading thereto, for which, by reason of their nature or the context in which they are carried out, the sex of the worker constitutes a determining factor.' Article 2 (3) states that the directive 'shall be without prejudice to provisions concerning the protection of women, particularly as regards pregnancy and maternity'[19].

The main points of the Court's judgement concerned, on the one hand, the military as an employer in the public service, and thus as a part of the labor force. As a consequence, access to the military had to come under the authority of the ETD. On the other hand, by underlining the equal treatment principle as a fundamental right, the Court emphasised the principle status of gender equality norms. In doing so, the Court of Justice rejected the central points made by the German government.

First, on the argument of sovereignty, the Court of Justice stated that the area of security and defense was indeed under the authority of the Nation State. That did not mean, however, that decisions in the area of internal and external public security would fall entirely outside the scope of Community law. By referring to its judgment in the *Sirdar* case, the Court

---

(4)).The access for women to military posts in the Bundeswehr was governed by Article 1(2) of the Law on Soldiers ('the SG') and by Article 3a of the Regulation on Soldiers' Careers ('the SLV'), according to which women were allowed to enlist only as volunteers and only in the medical and military-music services.

[16] *Kreil*, at pa. 11.

[17] OJ 1976 L39/40.

[18] *Kreil*, at pa. 12.

[19] OJ 1976 L39/40.

of Justice continued to expand its jurisdiction in the area of public security from internal to external aspects[20].

Second, the Court of Justice did not accept the exceptions based on distinct historical reasons, which the German government sought to emphasize. Germany argued for the historical specificity of the German case in relation to National Socialism and, following from that, for Germany's distinct moral obligation to protect women. In 1955 the German Parliament had decreed the exclusion of women from the military service in order to distinguish women, as a group within the civilian population, from combatants, and in order to protect them in accordance with the Geneva Convention of 1949. Hence, the protection of women could only be realized through their complete exclusion from the status of combatants. The exclusion was thus justified through the notion of protecting women.

Against the background, the argument of the German government for protecting women for historical reasons could not override the authority of equal opportunity law[21]. In consideration of the equality norm, General Advocate La Pergola argued that it was beyond the principle of proportionality to exclude women from access to almost 330,000 posts within a work organization, which were, in particular, posts with a high degree of stability[22]. Hence, the Court stated that the Community equality principles cover all occupation areas and do not allow exceptions due to distinct historical narratives or particular sectors.

In addition, the ECJ stressed the function of Art. 2 (3) of the ETD that was related to special conditions, but argued that it could not 'justify greater protection for women against risks to which men and women are equally exposed'[23]. Rather, the Court pointed to Art. 9 (2) of the Directive, which states that 'Member States shall periodically assess the occupational

---

[20] Case C-273/97, *Sirdar v. The Army Board, Secretary of State for Defence*, ECR, 1999, p. 7403, at pa. 9, footnote 19. The first time the ECJ applied questions of public, internal security to the ETD was in Case C-222/84, *Johnston v. Chief Constable of the Royal Ulster Constabulary*, ECR, 1986, p. 1651.

[21] With respect to these dimensions see my discussion in Wobbe 2003:100 ff.

[22] Closing Opinion, October 26, 1999, Case C-285/98, *Kreil v. Bundesrepublik Deutschland*, at pa. 35; Williams (1989: 9) points to this economic dimension of sex segregated occupations, i.e. it 'works out to the benefits of men'. Kilpatrick (2001: 100) underscores the diverse dimensions in the meaning of proportionality. According to her the decisions in *Sirdar* and *Kreil* show 'that, while the ETD may be effective in preventing a blanket ban of women from positions involving the use of arms, more specific exclusions will readily be excused following *Johnston*, under Article 2 (2) ETD, provided that the national court finds the exclusion in question proportionate'.

[23] *Kreil*, at pa. 14.

activities referred to in Art. 2 (2) in order to decide, in the light of social developments, whether there is justification for maintaining the exclusions concerned. They shall notify the Commission of the results on assessment'.[24] In this way the ECJ underscored the historical and cultural meaning of occupations with respect to special treatment and protection.

The key idea of the equal treatment principle as a fundamental right takes us back to the transformation of Art. 119. Until the late 1960s member states had not implemented the equal pay provision in their legal system. The involvement of women initiated change in this respect. Belgian advocate and academic lawyer Eliane Vogel-Polsky, arguing for a strong definition of Art. 119, 'attempted to test out her contentions in the court' (Hoskyns 1996: 60). This first test was to take ten years and would involve the three Defrenne cases[25].

According to the judgment in *Defrenne (No. 3)*, Art. 119 was an enforceable right with the status of a fundamental Community right: 'In view of this it seems to me that the prohibition of all discrimination based on sex (particularly on the subject of pay) protects a right which must be regarded as fundamental in the Community legal order as it is elsewhere'[26].

Kreil could exploit not only these dimensions of the equality provision. In addition, the Treaty of Amsterdam enforced the status of gender equality as a 'fundamental principle' of Community policies. By including equal opportunity and a new non-discrimination clause into its new provisions on fundamental rights, the Community obliged itself to the promotion of gender equality.

Against the historical background, the Kreil case demonstrates the complex shift from *protecting women* to promoting their equality as comparable participants equal within the single market. As the ECJ decision reveals national particularities to protect women in the name of the nation are being layered by Community principles of non-discrimination.

---

[24] *Kreil*, at pa. 4.
[25] Ibid., at pa. 60-77.
[26] Case C-149/77, *Defrenne v. Sabena (No. 3)*, at pa. 26, 27; consider, the Court referred to both the European Social Charter (1961) and to the ILO Convention 111 (1958) concerning discrimination in respect of employment and occupation (ibid., 28).

Concluding remarks

The purpose of this chapter was to bring new insight in the dynamics of the historical legacy of gender arrangements and its current reconfiguration in the Community context. To this end it investigated the transformation from equality concepts within the frame of the *nation-building* to those in the *market-building* frame. In the first one, women were addressed as a particular group, demanding state protection as workers and mothers. In the second one, women were addressed as individual workers and as such entitled to participate in the labor market. Whereas in the 19th and most part of the 20th century the category of the 'standard worker' was restricted to skilled male full-fledged workers, the European Community altered this meaning while opening it up to both sexes. In the first equality concept women are considered incompatible with men, the latter demands their comparability and considers inequality a problem that requires intervention.

Two frames, that of *nation-building* and *market-building* have been employed in order to identify the extent to which the historic legacy of gender arrangements is being transformed through the European Community equality script. As the first and second section reveal, the meaningful construction of work and gender in the national and the supra-national context differ considerably.

In the course of the *nation-building* solidarity was built on the idea of collectively shared equality between comrades, while discriminating women. Whereas the category of the 'individual' represented the disembodied male privileged person, female persons were invested with the difference of their sex, from which followed distinct problems that required particular control and restriction. All women were converted into a species that needed of protection (*Schutzbedürftigkeit der Frau*) due to its assumed weakness. This arrangement was institutionalized through protective labor legislation around 1900 and in the long run it was extended to national welfare-regimes.

During the second half of the 20th century in the context of the European *market-building* the idea of equality has been built on the collectively shared equality of market-participants who are invested with basic social and economic rights. Solidarity is not built on the national 'we', rather it is dedicated to the shared fairness of free movement and same living conditions. To this end, men and women should be observed as compatible and equals in the market context. Due to this mission and as a result of highly contingent institutional constellations, women are considered individual workers and as such addressed to equal treatment and equality of opportunity, which became the core component of the Community equality model. This transition does not mean, that inequality has vanished, rather it means that the reproduction of gender arrangements is shifting due to changed social forms of inclusion.

Against this background, in the third section, the Kreil case was discussed as a highly symbolic legal controversy about special treatment as anchored in the national constitution or equal treatment in the single market. The dispute about the meaning of protection and the close reading of the ETD reveal the ongoing dynamics between the two frames.

The entire anti-discrimination frame of post-Amsterdam is contributing to a further altering of former national scripts. While deepening the provisions for gender equality, the anti-discrimination Directives are extending the equal treatment principle to further grounds of discrimination such as race, ethnic origin, religion, age, handicapped, sexual preference (see: Fredman 2001; Fredman 2006). Given the historical weight of cultural homogeneity in the *nation-building* frame, the recent generation of anti-discrimination Directives illuminates the blurring of this legacy.

As the post-Amsterdam Lisbon processes are bringing to the surface the antidiscrimination scheme is closely coupled with the politics of competitiveness and growth, i.e. to bring as much as possible persons into employment and to include as many 'human resources' as possible into the single market: given the fact of the plurality and diversity of workers, an equal treatment frame appears to be adequate. Through this lens equal treatment has become the key mechanism for inclusion as the market itself is changing it's face. Since economic life becomes 'the notion of normal and worthy life, of dignity' (Niccolai 2008: 39), the configuration of market and society is undergoing a shift.

The main sociological belief behind the chapter is that European anti-discrimination offers a legal provision for new modes of solidarity and social inclusion in Europe. These new modes have been explored in the frame of the new structure of the single market and Community law. The transformation of deep social structures that is taking place in Europe can only be understood in connection with the *market-building* and the Community legal system.

Embedded as it is in the supranational notion of equality, the case of gender equality offers intriguing insights into these dimensions of anti-discrimination, including its transformation over 50 years of European integration. Whereas the historical equality concept restricted solidarity to the privileged (male) members of the national community, the Community script has opened it up to a diversity of workers.

The effort of this contribution was to identify the ways of inclusion in different frames. It has become clear that the EU cannot be adequately captured by national notions of belonging, membership and inclusion. In more methodological terms, the essay does not assign the nation-state a privileged status as the exclusive unit of analysis, rather national standards of inclusion served as the point of reference for a comparative perspective. Put simply, instruments of national inclusion such as citizenship or welfare rights are considered historically contingent 'cases' that are open to change. It is therefore important to note that the chapter is much more about the 'how' of various modes of social inclusion than about their 'rightness' or 'wrongness'. It was, rather, an attempt to situate the Community anti-discrimination idea in a broader frame of European modernity in order to identify shifting ideas of equality. In this framework we can grasp a deeper understanding of the transition, which is taking place in the European region.

PART II

SHAPING THE VALUES OF A POST-PATRIARCHAL
SOCIETY: ANTI-DISCRIMINATION DISCOURSE
IN LEGAL REASONING
AND NATIONAL IMPLEMENTATION

Towards a "Equal Dignity": the Spanish Organic Act 3/2007, of March 22nd, on the Effective Equality Between Women and Men

Yolanda Gómez Sánchez

Synopsis. The convenience of the elaboration and adoption of a law on equality between women and men has been a subject of discussion in Spain since the adoption of the Constitution in 1978. Some sectors of the legal doctrine have been in favor and others have refused this initiative. The opponents of such a proposal argue that the equality principle must be strictly observed by the authorities, but cannot be developed by a law because this would be a simple reiteration of the Constitution, which already establishes and guarantees equality. Thirty years after the entry into force of the Spanish Constitution, the accumulated experience clearly shows that a further development of equality and of other constitutional rights is necessary. Organic Act 3/2007 of March 22nd, on the effective equality between women and men implements into the Spanish legal system two Directives on equal treatment and other relevant principles on effective equality. This Act also establishes the necessary legal changes in other laws.
Keywords: Gender Equality, Spanish Act on Equality, Effective Equality.

1. Constitutional and European background

Equality is a demand in many different countries and national legal systems to try to eradicate all forms of discrimination. The fight for equality is different in each country and each adopts different legal forms. However, there is a relevant relationship between the protection against discrimination in nation States and at the international level, especially in the Council of Europe and in the European Union.

The Spanish Constitution guarantees different forms of equality:

a) as a superior value of the legal system in Article 1.1;
b) as *material equality* or *effective equality* in Article 9.2;
c) as *formal equality*, referring to the traditional principle of equality *before and in the law* in Article 14; and
d) lastly, alongside the text of the Constitution one can find concrete examples of equality deriving from Article 14 (for example, equality of children, and equality of mothers, in Article 39).

With regard to guarantees, all these Articles are protected by appeal to unconstitutionality if their legal development does not respect their constitutional contents. However, only Article 14 is protected by judicial guarantees at the highest level, since Article 14 is subjected to preferential and summary proceedings and is also guaranteed by an individual constitutional appeal for protection (*amparo*).

The right to equality, on the other hand, is directly in force from the very moment of the Constitution enters force, as the Constitutional Court has often pointed out.[1]

It has been discussed whether the equality of Article 14 is a *principle* or a *right*; the references in the decisions of the Constitutional Court are not useful in this sense, since the Court uses both the concept "right" and "principle". In recent years, the opinion in favour of considering it as a *right* has prevailed (Freixes, Sanjuán 1999, 186; González Rivas 2003). I share this view, since equality has, in my opinion, the structure of a right and a scope that public powers must respect.

The Spanish Constitutional Court has confirmed that the right to equality in Article 14 includes both a) *equality in the application of the law* (which compels a uniform application and interpretation of the law regardless of the subject concerned); and b) *equality in the law* (equality in the contents of the norms, equal treatment in the norms).

In spite of the broad reception of equality in the Spanish Constitution cited above, until 2007 the Spanish Parliament had not passed a Law on Equality.

The convenience of the elaboration and adoption of a law on the equality between women and men has been a subject of discussion in Spain since the adoption of the Constitution in 1978.

Some sectors of legal doctrine have been in favor and others have refused this initiative. The opponents of such a proposal argue that the equality principle must be strictly observed by the authorities, but cannot be developed by a law because this would be a simple reiteration of the Constitution, which already establishes equality. In 2008 Spain celebrated three decades since the coming into force of the Spanish Constitution and the experience accumulated during this period clearly shows that a further development of Equality and the other constitutional rights is necessary.

What is the normative context of this Act?

First of all, the already cited article 14 of the Spanish Constitution stipulates the right of equality and of non-discrimination on the grounds of

---

[1] See among others Judgment 7/1983 of 14 February by the Spanish Constitutional Court (*Telefonica Case*).

sex. This article led to abundant jurisprudence in the Spanish Constitutional Court on the range of the article and the reasons for the prohibition of discrimination included in it.

Article 9.2, in turn, ratifies public authorities' obligation to further conditions that will ensure that individuals, and the groups of which they form a part, enjoy real and effective equality. This article contains the so called "principle of true equality" or "political principle of equality", taking into consideration that the mandate to the legislator is rather to enact the necessary measures to ensure that equality becomes not just a "formal right", but a reality. Full recognition of formal equality before the law, while undisputably constituting a decisive element of the rule-of-law states, has proved to be insufficient. The principle of "true equality" has made it possible to complete the range of the right to equality and to implement equality activities that benefit the people in a direct way.

Equality between women and men is a universal legal principle acknowledged in a number of international texts on human rights, most prominently the Convention on the Elimination of all Forms of Discrimination against Women adopted by the United Nations General Assembly in December 1979 and ratified by Spain in 1983. Regarding this matter, significant advances have been introduced by dedicated world conferences, such as that in Nairobi in 1985 and Beijing in 1995.

Likewise, equality is a fundamental principle in the European Union. Since the entry into force of the Treaty of Amsterdam on May 1st 1999, equality between women and men and the elimination of the inequalities between them constitute an objective that must be integrated into all policies and actions undertaken by the Union and its members.

Under the provisions of former Article 111 of the Treaty of Rome, the Community has developed an *acquis* on equality between the sexes of great depth, whose rightful transposition is largely the aim of the present Spanish Act.

In particular, this Act introduces into the Spanish legal system two Directives on equal treatment, namely 2002/73/EC amending Directive 76/207/EEC on the implementation of the principle of equal treatment for men and women regarding access to employment, vocational training and promotion, and working conditions; Directive 2004/113/EC implementing the principle of equality of treatment between men and women in access to and supply of goods and services, and Directive 97/80/CE on the burden of proof in cases of discrimination on grounds of sex which has been reflected in the Act on Civil Procedure and in the Act on Contentious-Administrative Jurisdiction.

Gender violence, wage discrimination or the problems reconciling working and family life stand as evidence that the attainment of full, effective equality between women and men remains an unfinished task, whose completion demands further legal instruments. It is absolutely necessary to continuously enact legal norms to combat all subsisting *direct* or *indirect* expressions of discrimination on grounds of sex and to promote true equality between women and men, removing obstacles and social stereotypes that hinder its attainment.

2. Principles of the Spanish Act on Equality between women and men

The Spanish Act on Equality is based on a set of principles:

1) Principle of prevention of discriminatory behaviour.
2) Principle of the establishment of active policies to make equality effective within the different legal domains and within the social, cultural and economic domains, where inequality may be generated or perpetuated.
3) From the previous principle derives the principle of *gender mainstreaming*. In this context, article 4 of the Act on Equality provides that "Equal treatment and opportunities for women and men is a basic precept of the legal system and, as such, will be integrated and observed in the interpretation and enforcement of legislation".
4) According to the territorial principle, the Act refers to all public policy in Spain (at the central, regional and local levels). The Act has been adopted under the competence of the central government "to regulate the basic conditions that guarantee the equality of all Spaniards in the exercise of their constitutional rights". The Act contains more detailed regulation in domains where the central government has basic or full legislative competence.
5) The principle of application of the Act both in the public and the private sector (art. 1).
6) Principle of "positive action". The Act provides for a general framework for the adoption of such so-called positive action. In this regard, it mandates all public authorities to reverse verifiable de facto situations of inequality that cannot be remedied by the mere formulation of the principle of legal or formal equality. And where such action may involve the formulation of an unequal

right in women's favor, precautionary and conditioning requisites are established to ensure its constitutional legitimacy.

7)   Principle of distinguishing between *direct* and *indirect* discrimination (art. 6).

8)   Principle of "reversal of the burden of proof". According to the provisions of the law of the European Union, the Spanish Act also includes the principle of reversal of the burden of proof. In proceedings in which the plaintiff alleges discriminatory conduct on the grounds of sex, it will be incumbent upon the defendant to prove the absence of discrimination in the measures adopted (art. 13). This principle will not be applicable to penal proceedings.

3. The content of the Act on Equality

3.1. THE PURPOSE AND SCOPE OF THE ACT

According to article 1 of the Act, the purpose of this Act is to ensure equal treatment and opportunities for women and men, in particular the elimination of discrimination against women of whatever circumstances or background and especially in the political, civil, occupational, economic, social and cultural domains.

To this end, the Act establishes the principles governing the action of public authorities, regulates natural and legal persons' public and private rights and duties; and lays down measures designed to eliminate and correct all forms of discrimination on the grounds of sex in the public and private sectors.

The Act prohibits all direct or indirect discrimination on the grounds of sex, in particular as regards maternity, the assumption of family obligations or marital status (art. 3).

Regarding its scope, the Act establishes that all persons possess the rights deriving from the principle of equal treatment and the prohibition of discrimination on the grounds of sex. The Act is to be applied to all natural and legal persons present or acting on Spanish soil, regardless of their nationality, registered address or residence.

3.2. EQUAL TREATMENT FOR MEN AND WOMEN REGARDING ACCESS TO EMPLOYMENT, VOCATIONAL TRAINING AND PROMOTION, AND WORKING CONDITIONS

In its article 5, the Act establishes that equal treatment and opportunities for women and men, applicable in the domain of private and public employment, will be guaranteed as provided in the applicable legislation in:

a) access to employment;
b) vocational training;
c) vocational promotion;
d) working conditions including remuneration and dismissal; and
e) affiliation in trade union and employers' organizations.

The Act on Equality allows the establishment of positive action measures to favour women's access to employment and the effective implementation of the principle of equal treatment for women and men and nondiscriminatory working conditions (art. 43).
Nevertheless, the same article provides that "difference of treatment based on a sex-related characteristic will not constitute discrimination in access to employment, including the necessary training, where, in light of the nature of the particular tasks concerned or the context in which they are performed, such a characteristic constitutes a genuine and determining occupational requirement, provided that the objective is legitimate and the requirement is proportionate". These are the criteria already established by the jurisprudence of the Constitutional Court to judge on the existence of a discrimination situation.

3.3. SEXUAL HARASSMENT AND HARASSMENT ON THE GROUNDS OF SEX

The Act on Equality establishes that sexual harassment and harassment on the grounds of sex will be considered to constitute discrimination under any and all circumstances. The conditioning of a right or expectation of a right to the acceptance of a situation constituting sexual harassment or harassment on the grounds of sex will likewise be regarded to be discrimination on the grounds of sex.
The Act stipulates its own definition of "sexual harassment", which is "any form of verbal or physical conduct of a sexual nature with the purpose or effect of violating the dignity of a person, in particular when creating an intimidating, degrading, or offensive environment" (art. 7).

On the other hand, the Act also defines "harassment on the grounds of sex" as "any behaviour prompted by a person's sex with the purpose or effect of violating his or her dignity, creating an intimidating, degrading or offensive environment" (art. 7).

3.4. PROHIBITION OF DISCRIMINATION ON THE GROUNDS OF PREGNANCY OR MATERNITY AND MEASURES FOR THE CONCILIATION OF FAMILY AND WORKING LIFE

The Act establishes that any less favourable treatment of women relating to pregnancy or maternity constitutes direct discrimination on the grounds of sex. The dismissal of a woman, a domestic employee, for being pregnant has been declared null and void by a recent judgment of a labour court.

At the same time, the Act also provides measures to foster the integration of men in the family responsibilities and in the raising of the children, permitting women to reconcile family and working life (art. 44).

3.5. POSITIVE ACTION

As noted above, the Act on Equality introduces the possibility to adopt "positive action" measures favouring women when other measures cannot correct situations of inequality in a concrete case. The Spanish Act refers to women and not to the "less represented gender" as the provision of the law of the European Union does.

Article 11 of the Act establishes that in order to ensure the effectiveness of the constitutional right to equality, public authorities will adopt specific measures favouring women to correct situations of obvious de facto inequality with respect to men. Such measures, which will be applicable while the situation subsists, must be reasonable and proportional to the objective pursued in each case.

Natural and private legal persons may also adopt such "positive action" measures.

3.6. DESIGNATIONS MADE BY PUBLIC AUTHORITIES AND BALANCED PRESENCE IN THE PUBLIC SECTOR

Another very important element of the Spanish Act on Equality is the equality between women and men in the so-called "public sector".

In this context, article 16 of the Act establishes that public authorities will attempt to abide by the principle of a balanced presence of women and men in their appointments and designations for positions of responsibility. Balanced membership will be understood to mean the presence of women and men in a manner such that neither sex accounts for more than sixty nor less than forty percent of the total (Additional provision one). This balanced presence regards the management bodies of the Public Administration, selection bodies and evaluation committees etc. (art. 52 and ff.).

An example of this in Spain is President Rodríguez Zapatero's government appointing more women than men (9 women and 8 men) and the country's first woman Minister of Defense. Also for the first time, a Ministry for Equality has been created.

Furthermore, the Additional provision two has added a new article 44 bis into the Organic Act on the General Electoral System stipulating that the Spanish electoral lists must have a balanced presence of women and men, with each of the sexes accounting for at least forty per cent of the total number of candidates on the list. When the number of positions to be filled is under five, the number of women and men will be as close as possible to this balanced presence of 60% - 40%.

In the elections for the Parliaments of the different regions (Autonomous Communities) in Spain, the respective laws on the different electoral regimes can introduce measures that favour a greater presence of women in the election lists.

3.7. EQUALITY IN EDUCATION

Another very important measure provided by the Spanish Act on Equality is a set of measures for the integration of equality at all levels of education. These measures have an important significance since they promote habits of behaviour of the population.

The Act on Equality establishes that education authorities have to give special attention to the curriculum of women and men in all stages of education and to further the equality and the integration of women in school management and supervisory bodies.

The Act also pays attention to equality in the domain of artistic and intellectual creation and production, where women have often been discriminated against. The Act establishes that the public authorities may adopt "positive action" measures in this area.

3.8. INTEGRATION OF THE PRINCIPLE OF EQUALITY IN HEALTH POLICY

One of the domains most "forgotten" by the public authorities regarding the right of equality is health. The biological differences between women and men are often not taken into consideration in the frame of health policy or of biomedical investigation. Therefore, the regulation of this area by the Spanish Act on Equality is of significant relevance.

First of all, the Act establishes that health policies and programs will integrate women's and men's differing needs and the measures required to suitably meet them (art. 27). Secondly, the public authorities will guarantee equal rights to health for women and men, preventing the generation of inequalities between women and men due to biological differences or the associated social stereotypes.

Finally, the most important provision of the Act concerning health is the one establishing that scientific research must take into account the differences between women and men in terms of both clinical tests and care.

3.9. EQUALITY AND THE INFORMATION SOCIETY

Another aspect of particular interest covered by the Act on Equality is related to the information society. According to the Act, the Government will further women's full mainstreaming in the information society with specific programs. Furthermore, public authorities must ensure the absence of any sexist language (or language that violates the dignity of women) or content in information and communication technology projects wholly or partially financed with public funds.

In the same context, the Act considers illegal any advertising that involves discriminatory conduct pursuant to the Act (art. 41).

3.10. EQUALITY IN THE ARMY AND IN THE POLICE FORCE

Regarding the Army and the police force, the Act establishes that the provisions of the Act on their personnel will secure the effectiveness of the principle of equality between women and men, in particular with respect to access, training, promotion, stationing and administrative status (art. 65, 66 and 67).

3.11. LEGAL PROTECTION

The Act expressly establishes that any person may call upon the courts to protect the right to equality between women and men, in a summary and preferential process. Subsequently, the constitutional complaint to the Constitutional Court can be lodged, pursuant to the terms of Article 53.2 of the Spanish Constitution, which stipulates the judicial guarantees of the fundamental rights and of the right of equality, which obtains the same guarantees.

In cases of sexual harassment or harassment on the ground of sex, only the person subject to such harassment has the legal capacity to institute the respective legal action. This is an adequate measure to avoid interference and pressure on the victim.

3.12. LEGISLATIVE MODIFICATION

The most significant achievement of the Act on Equality is that it contains not only general principles and measures, but a multitude of concrete legislative modifications. The Organic Act on the Electoral System, the Organic Act of the Judicial Power, the Act on the Ministry of Prosecution, the Act on Contentious-Administrative Jurisdiction, the General Act on Health, the employment laws, etc., have been amended by the Act on Equality.

In conclusion it also has to be pointed out that the Spanish Act on Equality has introduced into the internal legal system not only the provisions of the EU Directive, but other, new aspects as well. The Act represents a very important advance in combating discrimination in Spain.

4. Main lines of the doctrine on equality in the Spanish Constitutional Court

The Spanish Constitutional Court has developed an important doctrine concerning equality. Among the decisions of the Court, we can point out two especially important decisions from 2008: Decision 12/2008 of 29 January and Decision 59/2008 of 14 May.

Decision 12/2008 of 29 January decided upon the constitutional review brought by the Contentious-Administrative Court number 1 of Santa Cruz de Tenerife and the appeal for constitutional review filed by over fifty members of parliament of the Popular Parliamentary Group in relation to article 44B of the Organic Law 5/1985 of 19 June, on the General

Electoral Regime, introduced by the second additional provision of Organic Law 3/2007 of 22 March, on the Effective Equality between Women and Men. The appellants considered that the cited Article breached Article 23, in connection with Articles 6 and 14 of the Constitution. Article 44B introduces parity measures in the electoral lists, thus reducing the freedom of political parties to organize their lists.

The Constitutional Court, after analyzing the international criteria (specifically those deriving from the Rome Convention and these emerging from European Union Law), concluded that all of them refer to the aim of both formal and material equality between women and men, which is a pillar of international human rights law and EU law.

On the other hand, the Constitutional Court stresses that the freedom of political parties to form their electoral lists is an activity which is also subjected to the Constitution and to the law, as Article 6 of the Constitution points out, so that the freedom of political parties in this sense is not and cannot be an absolute freedom. The legislator, considering other constitutional values and goods, has limited this freedom by imposing on political parties certain conditions for the elaboration of electoral lists (for example, conditions on the candidates to be elected, their place of residence, or referring to closed and blocked lists). Thus, the new restriction based on the gender of the candidates, regulated by the amendment of the Electoral Organic Law, is neither the only one, nor does it lack constitutional basis, in the view of the Constitutional Court.

The Constitutional Court also states that the parties' freedom to select candidates is clearly limited by all of these parity requirements introduced by the Organic Law. However, that restriction on the parties' freedom is perfectly constitutional and lawful, as it is reasonably instrumented and does not infringe fundamental rights. The parties' freedom to select candidates is not even a fundamental right, but rather implicitly conferred in the Constitution (Article 6 of the Spanish Constitution), which is granted by the legislator (expressly authorised by that article to do so) - a legislator who enjoys a broad freedom of configuration, which, although of course not absolute, does allow him to include parity in the general electoral regime. The constitutional validity of these measures is clear in view of the consideration that their aim is to achieve effective equality in the field of political participation (Articles 9.2, 14 and 23 of the Spanish Constitution).

For all these reasons, the Constitutional Court considered that the electoral reform was in accordance with the Spanish Constitution.

The second very relevant decision on equality by the Constitutional Court was Decision 59/2008 of 14 May, which decided upon the constitutional review brought by the Criminal Court number 4 of Murcia, regarding Article 153.1 of the Criminal Code. In this reform of the Criminal Code, the description of the crime was amended by including new aggravating circumstances when the victim of the crime is a certain group of persons: "In case of physiological damage or in case of violence against the wife or ex-wife or woman with a similar relationship with a man, with or without living together, or any other specially vulnerable person". The gender factor is fundamental in this new subtype of crimes. There is a distinction between the subject and the victim of this type of crime depending on their gender, which was the object of the constitutional control by the Constitutional Court.

First of all, the Constitutional Court refers to its doctrine on Article 14 of the Constitution, which distinguishes two concepts of equality: a) the principle of equality; and b) the prohibitions of discrimination.

The first paragraph of Article 14 includes the general clause of equality between all Spanish citizens. This general principle has been regarded by the Constitutional Court's doctrine as an individual right of citizens to be treated equally, so that public powers shall respect this right. Equal circumstances have equal legal consequences. "The introduction of differences shall be justified on reasonable arguments, according to generally accepted criteria that consequences shall not be disproportionate" (Decision 200/2001 of the Constitutional Court, argument number 4). After Decision 222/1992 of 11 of December, "the conditions and limits imposed on the legislator, deriving from the principle of equality, require three different demands: a clear and legitimate aim, a logical form of pursuing such aim, without imposing disproportionate measures on the rights and duties of groups and individuals (argument 6; also Decision 155/1998 of 13 July, argument 3; Decision 180/2001 of 17 September, argument 3).

In addition to the general clause of equality, Article 14 refers to the prohibition of discrimination on grounds of a series of concrete features. "This expressed reference to a number of grounds of discrimination does not imply a closed number of reasons of discrimination" (Decision 75/1983 of 3 August, argument number 6), but does point out an expressed prohibition of discrimination on a number of historical grounds which have not only meant for certain groups of citizens unfavourable situations, but are also contrary to the dignity of the individual, as guaranteed by Article 10.1 of the Constitution (Decision 128/1987 of 16

July, argument 5; 166/1988 of 26 September, argument 2; 145/1991, of 1 July, argument 2).

The Constitutional Court, either in its general regard for all grounds cited in Article 14, or regarding one of these grounds specifically, has always declared "the unconstitutionality of the different legal treatments based only on one of the grounds of discrimination prohibited by Article 14" (Decision 200/2001, argument 4). However, as the cited Decision states, "this Court has also accepted that the grounds for discrimination prohibited by the constitutional Article can also be exceptionally argued for justifying a different legal treatment (regarding gender, among others, Decisions 103/1983 of 22 of November, argument 6; 128/1987 of 26 July, argument 7; 229/1992 of 14 December, argument 2; 126/1997 of 3 July, argument 8, etc.), although in these cases the control of the constitutional character of the legal differences shall be more strict when analyzing the legitimacy of the different treatment and more rigorous its justification" (argument 4).

The Constitutional Court remarks that the object of the constitutional review is the legislator's option to consider a certain conduct as a crime, which is the exclusive option of the legislator. The legislator can decide what constitutes a crime "with a broad margin of freedom if the Constitution is respected. The legislator's freedom is based on his constitutional position and on his specifically democratic legitimacy" (Decisions of the Constitutional Court 55/1996 of 28 March, argument number 6; 161/1997 of 2 October, argument number 9; Resolutions of the Constitutional Court 233/2004 of 7 June, argument number 3; 332/2005 of 13 September, argument 4). After the Court, the legislator shall decide "which goods are protected by criminal law, which conduct shall be punished, how this conduct shall be punished, and which proportion there shall be between the conduct to be avoided and the foreseen punishments" (Decisions of the Constitutional Court 55/1996, argument 6; 161/1997, argument 9; 136/1999 of 20 July, argument 23).

The legislator shall establish the criminal policy (Decision of the Constitutional Court 129/1996 of 9 July, argument 4), shall determine the conduct to be punished, and shall distinguish which conduct deserves greater penalties to prevent it. All these activities respond to "a complex analysis of legal, social and political opportunity which is much more that a simple or mechanical application of the Constitution". Thus, the task of the Constitutional Court is "restricted to the constitutional suitability of the norm, and shall not consider its opportunity, effects or quality". Therefore, the analysis of Article 153.1 of the Criminal Code is restricted to examination of respect of the limits of the principle of equality imposed by the Constitution on the legislator.

The different consideration of men and women for the purpose of this article of the Criminal Code is based on the legislator's decision to punish with greater sanctions some aggression that he considers more serious and socially reprehensible, since this conduct "reflects the discrimination of women in sentimental relationships, a discrimination which has very serious consequences on individuals with a subordinate position, that shall not be accepted from a constitutional point of view".

The Organic Law on Protection Measures to Fight Gender-based Violence, which has been the legal basis for the amendment of the Criminal Code, pursues the prevention of aggression in sentimental relationships as a form of control of men over women in such a context. Its purpose is to protect women in a context where the legislator appreciates that women's basic goods (life, physical integrity, health) and their freedom and dignity are not well enough protected. Another aim of the Law is to combat a type of violence that arises in a context of inequality. All these considerations were made by the Constitutional Court's decision.

Effective equality is "the defining element of the concept of citizenship" (Decision of the Constitutional Court 12/2008 of 29 January, argument 5). Gender-based violence in which a man attacks a woman who is or was his sentimental partner directly violates effective equality. The Constitutional Court considers especially serious and reprehensible violence that seeks to limit the freedom of the partner in the most private sphere and to deny the victim's equal dignity.

For all of these reasons, the Constitutional Court rejected the constitutional review and declared Article 153.1 of the Criminal Code constitutional.

EU Gender Policies beyond the Marketplace: the Good and Services Directive and its National Implementation

Anna Lorenzetti

Synopsis. In December 2004, the Council of the European Union adopted Directive 2004/113: the purpose was to implement the principle of equal treatment between men and women in the access and supply of goods and services. The Goods and Services Directive seems to mark the beginning of an ambitious period for Anti-discrimination Law as it passes from the labour market, the traditional sphere of gender equality, to the market of goods and services. Directive 2004/113 closes an important gap and strengthens the principle of gender equality under EU law. In this light, there is a question that needs to be taken into consideration: where does the Goods and Services Directive stand within the overall framework of EU equality law? A further issue is whether Directive 113 improves the coherence and uniformity of European Anti-discrimination Law.
Keywords: Gender Equality, Goods and Services, Anti-Discrimination Law.

1. Preliminary remarks

Directive 2004/113 which implements the principle of equal treatment between men and women in the access and supply of goods and services was adopted in December 2004, in the middle of the 'new golden age' of Anti-discrimination Law (Barbera 2003a: 399), as part of the new package of anti-discrimination directives which have been adopted since 2000.
These represented and still do represent an unprecedented round of anti-discrimination law reform across the Member States, expanding significantly the grounds under EU protection.
Firstly, the Racial Equality Directive (2000/43/EC), which implements the principle of equal treatment between persons irrespective of racial or ethnic origin.
Secondly, the Framework Directive (2000/78/EC), whose purpose is to fight discrimination on the grounds of religion or belief, disability, age or sexual orientation in employment and occupation.
Lastly, the Equal Treatment Directive (2002/73/EC), which amends Council Directive 76/207/EEC on the implementation of the principle of equal treatment for men and women, as regards access to employment,

vocational training and promotion, and working conditions; this was included in Directive 2006/54/EC, on the implementation of the principle of equal opportunities and equal treatment of men and women in matters of employment and occupation. The so-called 'Recast Directive' consolidates the 7 existing Directives dealing with equality between men and women in employment and interpretative case law[1].

2. Background

Given that real equality, irrespective of gender, depends on actions in a number of areas, of which the world of work is only one, the Commission proposed a new directive to implement the principle of equal treatment between both sexes in the access and supply of goods and services. In setting out a Community framework strategy on gender equality, the Commission undertook to present a proposal for a Directive based on Article 13 of the EC Treaty, implementing the principle of equal treatment between men and women in matters other than employment and occupation[2].

Subsequently, in December 2000, the European Council called on the Commission to reinforce equality-related rights by adopting a proposal for a directive on promoting gender equality in areas other than employment and professional life[3].

On 5 November 2003, the Commission adopted the proposal, rejecting the idea of extending it to education, taxation and media portrayal of the sexes on the ground that the most effective way of tackling discrimination in these areas was still being debated[4]. There were several criticisms of this proposal: in the opinion on the draft of the Directive, the Committee of Regions stressed that the principle of equal treatment in the access to and supply of goods and services might be applied more widely[5]. It

---

[1] i.e. Dir. 75/117/EEC, the 'Equal Pay Directive'; Dir. 76/207/EEC, the 'Equal Treatment Directive', as amended by Dir. 2002/73/EC; Dir. 86/378/EEC, the 'Occupational social security Directive', as amended by Dir. 96/97/EC; Dir. 97/80/EC on the reversal of the burden of proof in cases of discrimination based on sex, as amended by Dir. 98/52/EC.

[2] See COM(2000)335. In the Social Policy Agenda published in June 2000, the Commission announced its intention to present a proposal for a directive to prohibit sex discrimination outside of the labour market. COM(2000)379.

[3] The preamble refers to the Council Decision 2001/51/EC, which established a Programme relating to the Community framework strategy on gender equality (2001-2005).

[4] See COM(2003)657.

[5] See the opinion delivered on 22 April by the CoR.

emphasised that, in addition to legislative instruments, it was important to achieve equality between men and women in all areas of life, and particularly in the political and professional spheres. To this end, the Committee called for the adoption of measures to change attitudes and promote a better understanding of gender issues.

The European Economic and Social Committee has also urged the Commission to ensure that equality of access to educational opportunities for both boys and girls is available[6].

Despite this advice, at a Council meeting of the 4 October 2004, the political agreement on the final text of this instrument was reached. This was restricted to the area of access and supply of goods and services.

The result is the so-called 'Goods and Services Directive', based on Article 13 of the European Community Treaty and adopted in December 2004 by the Council of the European Union[7].

Article 1, titled 'Purpose', manifests the law's objective, which is 'to lay down a framework for combating discrimination based on sex in access to and supply of goods and services, with a view to putting into effect in the Member States the principle of equal treatment between men and women'.

3. Structure and contents of Directive 2004/113

As regards its contents and structure, Directive 113 is set out in four chapters: General Provisions (Chapter I), Remedies and Enforcement (Chapter II), Bodies for the Promotion of Equal Treatment (Chapter III) and Final Provisions (Chapter IV).

In line with other Anti-discrimination Directives, it defines the concept of discrimination, covering direct and indirect discrimination, harassment, sexual harassment and instruction to discriminate.

Direct discrimination occurs where one person is treated less favourably, on grounds of sex, than another is, has been or would be treated in a comparable situation (article 2). This provision also defines indirect discrimination as where an apparently neutral provision, criterion or practice would put persons of one sex at a particular disadvantage compared with persons of the other sex, unless that provision, criterion or practice is objectively justified by a legitimate aim and the means of

---

[6] See the opinion delivered on 3 June by the EESC.
[7] The Community enjoys competence in this area as a result of its powers in relation to freedom to provide services and consumer protection.

achieving that aim are appropriate and necessary[8]. In the cases of both direct and indirect discrimination, no motive or intention is required on the part of the discriminator. The test causation is an objective one.

Article 2 also defines harassment and sexual harassment. Harassment as 'where an unwanted conduct related to the sex of a person occurs with the purpose or effect of violating the dignity of a person and of creating an intimidating, hostile, degrading, humiliating or offensive environment'; sexual harassment as 'where any form of unwanted physical, verbal, non-verbal or physical conduct of a sexual nature occurs, with the purpose or effect of violating the dignity of a person, in particular when creating an intimidating, hostile, degrading, humiliating or offensive environment'.

Article 4(1) provides that less favourable treatment on grounds of pregnancy or maternity in goods and services is direct sex discrimination. Articles 4(3) states that such harassment and sexual harassment are to be deemed to be discrimination on the grounds of sex. It adds that a person's rejection of or submission to such conduct may not be used as a basis for a decision affecting that person. As in the case of the other Anti-discrimination Directives, Directive 113's Article 4(4) prohibits giving instruction to discriminate, but does not give any definition of what is meant by this term.

Article 3 states that the prohibition of discrimination should apply to persons providing goods and services, which are available to the public and which are offered outside the area of private and family life, and to the transactions carried out in this context[9]. On the concept of goods and services, recital 11 of the preamble states that 'goods should be taken to be those within the meaning of the provisions of the Treaty establishing the European Community relating to the free movement of goods. Services should be taken to be those within the meaning of Article 50 of that Treaty'.

The Directive stresses that it does not cover the content of media and advertisements, employment, education and tax.

Paragraph 2 of Article 3 does not prejudice the individual's freedom to choose a contractual partner as long as an individual's choice of contractual partner is not based on that person's sex.

The key provision of the Directive is Article 5 (Actuarial factors), which aims to tackle the issues of premiums and benefits in the insurance sector.

---

[8] Article 4(5) justifies the differences in treatment between men and women if the provision of goods and services, exclusively or primarily, to members of one sex are made with a legitimate aim and the means of achieving that aim are appropriate and necessary.
[9] See also recital 13.

It is in fact common practice to offer insurance products on different terms to men and women: this is an exception to the general absence of differential rules based on sex. In the majority of cases, women either pay higher premiums for pension and annuities or else the plan pays out less per year. This is justified by the industry on the grounds that women live longer.

Actually, actuarial factors are broken down by sex in order to evaluate the risk of insuring men and women separately in various parts of the insurance market, but especially in life, health and car insurance and in the calculation of annuities. The factors taken into consideration include variations in average life expectancy, but also different patterns of behaviour (particularly in car insurance) and consumption (in health insurance).

However, there are a number of factors, that are not linked to sex, which are equally important in establishing life expectancy, such as socio-economic or marital status, the region a person lives in or levels of smoking. Sex is at the very best a proxy for other indicators of life expectancy[10].

Against this background, Article 5(1) of the Goods and Services Directive states that Member States shall ensure that in all new contracts the use of sex as a factor in the calculation of premiums and benefits, for the purpose of insurance and related financial services, shall not result in differences in individuals' premiums and benefits.

Article 5(2) allows Member States to defer the implementation of this article for a transitional period: it provides that insurance companies are allowed to continue taking into consideration actuarial factors based on sex for a transitional period of eight years, in order to make the necessary adjustments to their practices[11]. Member States that decide to make use of this transitional period should notify the Commission and must compile, publish and update detailed life expectancy tables for men and women, so that the market is sufficiently transparent for the consumer[12]. In point of fact, Member States have the right to derogate from the principle of equality and may 'permit proportionate differences in individuals' premiums and benefits where the use of sex is a determining factor in the assessment of risk based on relevant and accurate actuarial and statistical data'.

---

[10] COM(2003)657.

[11] See COM(2003)657.

[12] The Directive refers to 'accurate data relevant to the use of sex as a determining actuarial factor'.

Article 5(3) requires that any costs relating to pregnancy and maternity should not result in differences in individuals' premiums and benefits.

In article 6, the Directive indicates the possibility of positive actions.

Member States remain free to introduce legislation that is more favourable to the protection of the principle of equality in the access and supply of goods and services (art. 7, par. 1). The provisions that the Member States adopt for enforcement of the Directive must not be regressive, which means that the level of protection afforded against discrimination must not be reduced (art. 7, par. 2)[13].

Chapter II (Remedies and Enforcement) is made up of four articles, the first of which (article 8) requires Member States to ensure that judicial and/or administrative procedures (including conciliation procedures) for the enforcement of the obligations are available to all persons who consider themselves wronged by failure to apply to them the principle of equal treatment to them, even after the relationship in which the discrimination is alleged to have occurred has ended (par. 1). Furthermore, Member States shall introduce into their national legal systems such measures as are necessary to ensure real and effective compensation or reparation, as the Member States so determine, for the loss and damage sustained by a person injured as a result of discrimination, in a way which is dissuasive and proportionate to the damage suffered. The Directive does not fix a prior upper limit for compensation or reparation.

Article 8(3), which provides for enforcement by organisations acting on behalf of individuals, has considerable importance in the practical efficacy of the principle of equality. It states that 'Member States shall ensure that associations, organisations or other legal entities, which have, in accordance with the criteria laid down by their national law, a legitimate interest in ensuring that the provisions of this Directive are complied with, may engage, on behalf or in support of the complainant, with his or her approval, in any judicial and/or administrative procedure provided for the enforcement of obligations under this Directive'. On the same provision, in the other Anti-discrimination Directives Ellis (2005: 267) stresses that 'In a system which relies heavily on individuals' complaints, it is necessary to support such complaints both financially and morally, since

---

[13] By laying down minimum requirements, the Directive leaves the Member States a wide margin of manoeuvre for the purposes of attaining its goal and in particular allows those with a higher or broader level of protection for citizens to maintain those levels. A Directive leaves the Member States sufficient flexibility as to how to provide this protection in practice.

individual litigants will inevitably lack the money and the psychological strength to pursue all their lawful rights. In addition, a claim on behalf of a number of complainants is more likely to produce results since it operates as a greater threat to the respondent. A body with representative enforcement powers is also able to take a more strategic view of the overall direction and development of the law that an individual can do it'.

Given that a complainant in any discrimination claim normally faces considerable difficulty in proving the case, the Goods and Services Directive, as with all other European Directives on matters of equal treatment[14], provides the reversal of the burden of proof. Article 9 requires that where a complaint of discrimination in relation to goods or services is brought, if the aggrieved person can provide evidence that discrimination has occurred, then it is for the goods or services provider to prove that there has been no breach of the principle of equal treatment. This approach is aimed at improving the effectiveness of access to justice for those who consider they have been subjected to sex discrimination. However, this article does not prevent Member States from introducing rules of evidence that are more favourable to plaintiffs (art. 9, par. 2); but it does not apply to criminal proceedings and need not be applied to inquisitorial proceedings.

Article 10 is concerned with the victimisation of those who allege a breach of the principle of equality in the access and supply of goods and services. The Directive sets out a broad rule in this respect[15].

In accordance with article 11, Member States shall encourage dialogue with relevant stakeholders who have a legitimate interest in contributing to the fight against discrimination on grounds of sex in the area of access and supply of goods and services.

Article 13 requires the Member States to take the necessary measures to ensure that the principle of equal treatment is respected in relation to the access and supply of goods and services within the scope of the Directive. This article is a classic provision, contained in all previous Community instruments on discrimination, which concerns compliance with the Directive by the Member States. Equal treatment involves the elimination of discrimination arising from any laws, regulations or administrative

---

[14] See Dir. 97/80; art. 10, Dir. 2000/78; art. 8, Dir. 2002/73; art. 19, par. 1, Dir. 2006/54.
[15] 'Member States shall introduce into their national legal systems such measures as are necessary to protect persons from any adverse treatment or adverse consequence as a reaction to a complaint or to legal proceedings aimed at enforcing compliance with the principle of equal treatment'.

provisions. The Directive therefore requires the Member States to abolish any such provisions.

As with earlier legislation, the Directive also requires that any contractual provisions, internal rules of undertakings and rules governing profit-making or non-profit-making associations contrary to the principle of equal treatment are, or may be, declared null and void or are amended.

Finally, the Directive requires that sanctions, which may comprise the payment of compensation to the victim, shall be effective, proportionate and dissuasive (art. 14). It also requires Member States to set up national equality bodies to promote equality in the access and supply of goods and services (art. 12).

The Directive obliges the Member States to send the Community all necessary information in order to enable it to draw up a report on the application of the Directive for the submission to the European Council and Parliament (art. 16).

4. Implementation process

Given that the Directive represents an effort to harmonize the laws of the Member States in relation to the principle of gender equality in the access and supply of goods and services, the way in which the Member States are implementing the Directive represents an important issue for the future (and possible) evolution of EC Anti-discrimination Law.

An overview of the measures that the EU Member States have taken in order to transpose into national law the provisions of the Directive shows that the majority of the Member States did not respect the deadline[16] (S. Burri, A. McColgan 2009).

In some countries the existing legislation already contained the prohibition of sex discrimination in the area of goods and services and only slightly adaptation was needed[17].

While these countries had already prohibited gender discrimination in access and supply of goods and services in broadly similar terms to the Goods and Services Directive, in most of the Member States this matter

---

[16] In fact the transposition was still ongoing after the deadline (21 December 2007); for instance in Austria, Belgium, Cyprus, Finland, France, Ireland, Malta, Portugal, Romania, Ireland, UK. At the time of this writing, the implementation is still to be implemented in the Czech Republic, Poland, Estonia. For an overview of the transposition measures see the report edited by S. Burri, A. McColgan, 2009.

[17] Denmark, Hungary, the Netherlands, Sweden, the UK.

has been explicitly regulated only with the transposition of Directive 2004/113.

In Belgium, Cyprus, France, Germany, Luxembourg, Malta, Portugal, Romania, *ad hoc* laws have been introduced specifically to implement it, sometimes the provisions of the Directive being reproduced *verbatim*[18].

In most countries the existing legislation was amended[19]. In Italy, although the existing Code of Equal Opportunities between men and women was amended[20], the implementation was purely *pro forma*, in the sense that it was a 'cut and paste' operation, without any reference to the former national framework[21].

In some Member States the transposition was combined with the implementation of the other Equality Directives and regulated discrimination on multiple grounds; for instance in Germany this Directive has been implemented together with other Anti-discrimination Directives in the so-called AGG, *Allgemeines Gleichbehandlungsgesetz*, the Act on Equal Treatment[22]. Belgium also adopted a Gender Act, implementing all the relevant EC Directives on Gender Equality[23]. France approved the *Loi* n° 2007-1774, transposing many European Directives in the insurance sector and the *Loi* n° 2008-496 to complete the implementation of all the relevant EC Anti-discrimination Directives; Luxembourg transposed Directive 113, also amending the penal code and the law on the insurance contract[24] and Spain approved the *Ley Orgánica 3/2007, de 22 de marzo, para la igualdad efectiva de mujeres y hombres*, which also implements the Directive 2002/73.

Despite the fact that the majority of Member States have provided protection against gender discrimination in the access and supply of goods

---

[18] Belgium, France, Luxembourg, Malta, Romania.

[19] Austria, Bulgaria, Denmark, Finland, Hungary, Ireland, Latvia, Lithuania, the Netherlands, Slovakia, Slovenia, Sweden, the UK.

[20] Italy amended with the Decree (*D. Lgs.*) 196/2007 the D.Lgs. 198/2006.

[21] This deals with the direct effect of the Directive and with the possibility to invoke it, irrespective of the national implementation.

[22] Germany transposed the four directives 2000/43/CE, 2000/78/CE, 2002/73/CE, 2004/113/CE into the *Gesetz zur Umsetzung Europäischer Richtlinien zur Verwirklichung des Grundsatzes der Gleichbehandlung*, German law for transposition of European Directives to achieve equality principle.

[23] *Loi 10 mai 2007 tendant à lutter contre la discrimination entre les femmes et les hommes*). The Act was amended on 21 December 2007.

[24] *Loi du 21 décembre 2007, égalité de traitement entre les femmes et les hommes dans l'accès à des biens et services et la fourniture de biens et services.* See also Act nr. 5739/2007.

and services, some of them have not completely fulfilled their obligations[25].

The Commission had already executed infringement proceedings against twelve Member States for non-communication of national transposing measures, six of which were still open at the end of 2008[26].

In January 2009, in accordance with the procedure under Article 226 of the EC Treaty the Commission sent a referral to the Court against Greece and the Czech Republic for failing to notify measures to transpose Directive 2004/113. On 14 May 2009 the Commission referred Poland to the European Court of Justice for non-transposition of 2004/113, despite a "Reasoned Opinion" (second stage warning) sent by the Commission in June 2008.

Given that the transposition measures reflect the variety of legal framework which exists in this field (i.e. the absence or the pre-existence of anti-discrimination legislation) it is interesting to analyse the contents of the transposition of this Directive and its impact on the current domestic body[27]. Thus the Directive provides an opportunity to study the relationship between national and EU Anti-discrimination Law.

As the Goods and Services Directive was passed fairly recently, neither the National Courts[28] nor the European Court of Justice have, as yet, rendered any judgment on it[29], so it might be interesting to analyse the

---

[25] For instance, some countries didn't transpose the requirements of establishing a gender equality body and the reversal of the burden of proof.

[26] This is the case of the Czech Republic, Estonia, Greece, Latvia, Poland and the United Kingdom (but the UK had an existing legislation partially covering gender discrimination in the access and supply of goods and services that only needed to be amended).

[27] A further issue is whether the implementation into the domestic legislation reflects the "gender regime" in the Member States, i.e. the configuration of gender relations within a particular setting, such as the gender presence in national and the international institutional context.

[28] Malta was in delay with the transposition process: the National Commission for the Promotion of Equality (NCPE), the Maltese equality body, reported that it had received a number of complaints in relation to access and supply of goods and services. In the light of the possible direct effect of this directive, it will be interesting to see if the directive will be invoked.

The Administrative Court of the Republic of Slovenia rejected a claim concerning the leasing of a non-profit apartment. The plaintiff claimed indirect gender discrimination as a result of the use of unisex criteria that must be fulfilled by a young family in order to be placed on a priority list for the allocation of a leased non-profit apartment (judgment No U947/2007-12 of 20 March 2008).

[29] On the use of actuarial factors based on sex see the judgment of the Court of First Instance of the European Communities of 18 March 2004 in Case T-204/01, *Lindorfer v Council* to the extent that it dismissed Ms Lindorfer's action on the ground that there was no discrimination based on sex and the appeal Case C-227/04 P ('The use of factors which

way in which the Courts use the discretion entrusted to them in this instrument.

5. Final remarks: the dual reading of Directive 2004/113

Commentators have offered a dual reading of Directive 2004/113. On the one hand, it has been understood as a form of self restraint of the Community Institutions, on the other the Goods and Services Directive seems to be the beginning of an ambitious period for Anti-discrimination Law as it moves from the labour market to the market of goods and services[30]. This is in line with the general trend of applying the anti-discrimination principle to fields outside the workplace, the traditional sphere of gender equality, being still only in an embryonic and experimental form (Guariello 2007: 471)[31].

The 2004/113 is not the first Directive aimed at tackling discrimination outside the workplace. As is well known, in 2000 the Council adopted the 'Racial Equality Directive' which outlaws discrimination on the grounds of race or ethnic origin within the workplace and outside: this was earliest than the Article 13 Directives and provided the most extensive protection till then, extending protection beyond employment, occupation and training to social protection, social advantage, education, access and supply of goods and services. Directive 2000/43 is an example of the way in which the opening up new areas of protection has also led to positive results with regard to gender discrimination (Guaglione 2007: 287).

Directive 2004/113 has been understood as a form of self restraint of the Community Institutions, which have preferred not to touch on tricky areas such as political representation but limit the scope of the Directive to the implementation of the principle of equality between men and women only to the consumer market sector, among those outside the labour market (La Rocca 2007: 316). The author has put forward the idea that there could be a strategic decision behind this Directive to give pre-eminence to the sphere of civil law protection of individual rights (La Rocca 2007: 293). Moreover, there has been a series of critical comments on the wording and

---

vary according to sex ... constitutes sex discrimination which is not justified by the need to ensure sound management of the Community pension scheme').

[30] In practice the scope deals with sex segregated services such as housing, transport services, financial and insurance services, healthcare and social services, leisure services (hairdresser, nightclubs, etc.).

[31] See, however, the proposal for a Directive on implementing the principle of equal treatment between persons irrespective of religion or belief, disability, age or sexual orientation, COM(2008)0426.

definitions used in it: La Rocca points out that the language used to define the type of contracts affected by the Directive appears to be lacking in the terminological precision which typified private law; she also stress that an effort at greater accuracy could have been made (La Rocca 2007: 328).

As is partially evident from the outline given above, what should be underlined is the way in which, although some provisions in the Directive appear to be of great importance, this importance could be merely hypothetical.

This factor has been and is reflected in the implementation acts as well as in the overall judgement of the value of this Directive.

Even if it is true that with this Directive the European Union has closed a gap and strengthened the principle of gender equality, it is also true that the impact and potential of the Directive have been conditioned by some compromises. For example, the explicit recognition of the need to safeguard contractual freedom (art. 3, par. 2) that was not envisaged in Directive 2000/43 (race and ethnic origin) but was stated in Directive 113, is one such compromise (La Rocca 2007: 309[32], Centini 2007: 2405-2449[33]). If on the one hand, this rhetorical provision seems to take a firm stand, on not permitting alterations in the equilibrium of commercial brokerage, on the other, it also seems to admit the risk that full contractual autonomy might be subject to some limitations (La Rocca 2007: 289).

Article 5, whose introduction was the result of animated discussions, may also be considered as a compromise between the position of the European Commission and that of the insurance industry (Caracciolo di Torella 2005)[34].

---

[32] The author mentions an *excusatio non petita* which demonstrates the fear that this prohibition of discrimination might alter the logic of commercial brokerage.

[33] The author points out the different positions on non-discrimination in private law transactions.

[34] The European Commission stressed that differences in treatment based on actuarial factors directly related to sex are not compatible with the principle of equal treatment and should be abolished. This position is in line with the ruling of the European Court of Justice in *Coloroll* (Case C-200/91), to the effect that different contributions for men and women to an occupational pension scheme are discriminatory. The other European Institutions supported the thesis that differences in premiums or benefits derived from insurance products should not be based on gender. The Commission stresses that studies show that sex is not the main determining factor for life expectancy. Other factors have been shown to be more relevant, such as marital status, socio-economic factors, employment/unemployment, regional area, smoking and nutrition habits. Lifestyle can be seen as a multidimensional factor, which has a significantly higher impact on an individual's life expectancy than sex. The inference that can be drawn from studies is that the practice of insurers to use sex as a determining factor in the evaluation of risk is based on ease of use rather than real value as a guide to life expectancy. Commentators have

The result of the different positions was article 5, which introduces the dangerous precedent of justifying direct discrimination and suggests that in the area of goods and services there is more room for manoeuvre in the expansion of measures and behaviour. In fact this provision could well lead to a diminished protection in this area.

Despite the fact that gender equality is a fundamental principle that should always prevail, as the Commission acknowledged, due to the complexity inherent in the issues involved in the access and supply of goods and services, gender might be considered a factor justifying discrimination in certain cases. That said, if the insurance industry is to be given the opportunity to derogate from the gender equality principle, this must be based on clear and specific principles and subject to strict interpretation (Caracciolo di Torella 2005).

Directive 2004/113 closes an important gap and strengthens the principle of gender equality under European law. In this light, there is a question that needs to be taken into consideration: where does the Goods and Services Directive stand within the overall framework of EU equality law? A further issue is whether Directive 113 improves the coherence and uniformity of European Anti-discrimination Law.

Some authors stress that there are reasons to be sceptical (Caracciolo di Torella 2005).

Firstly, although Directive 113 has a number of features in common with the Article 13 Directives, it is not consistent with them. Despite these Directives having established a basic common core of legal concepts and provisions for the covered grounds apart from nationality, the Racial

---

noted that insurers are more likely to pool together the healthy and the unhealthy than men and women. Different pricing should instead be linked to individual behaviour and choices such as eating habits, smoking or the use of alcohol.

The insurance industry stressed the fact that a total ban on using gender when calculating insurance premiums would have a considerably detrimental effect on companies' competitiveness and ultimately on consumers who would be forced to pay higher premiums.

The Commission recognised that the current widespread use of such factors cannot be changed overnight without causing disruption and turbulence in the market and accepted, therefore, that it may be necessary for insurance companies to continue to take account of actuarial factors based on sex in certain cases during a transitional period.

Furthermore, it was emphasized that because at present only a relatively limited number of women have annuities in their own right, any change towards a unisex criterion would only affect small numbers. Additionally, the industry argued that since women more usually depend on the annuity of a male relative for their retirement income, they could potentially lose out under a unisex system. A further point it made was that close attention should be paid to the costs passed on to consumers as a result of bringing uniformity to premiums and benefits. See COM(2003)657.

Equality Directive, for instance, appears more extensive covering matters of social protection, social advantages and education.

Secondly, there is a lack of coordination with the other gender equality Directives, for example with Directive 86/613 (equal treatment for self-employed[35]) which doesn't contain a provision on positive action and doesn't provide sanctions. This lack of coordination fails to take account of the impact of women's unequal position inside the workplace or their financial circumstances outside it.

In Directive 2004/113 the principle of non-discrimination is spelled out in similar but not wholly identical terms to those in the Recast Directive. As in the Framework Directive (2000/78), Directive 2006/54 is confined to its application to the workplace, whilst the Racial Equality Directive (2000/43) and Goods and Services Directive are not so restricted.

However, the fact that Directives 2000/43 and 2004/113 provide protection against discrimination outside the field of employment is not enough to ensure that all persons are adequately protected.

The traditional idea of a hierarchy regarding different grounds, with race enjoying the greatest protection followed by sex leaving the other grounds the least protected, was reinforced by the Goods and Services Directive.

Nevertheless, despite an initially low profile at the EU level, the access and supply of goods and services is going to be covered for grounds other than sex. As soon as the new proposal (2008/0426) is approved, the protection against discrimination in relation to social protection, social advantages, education, access and supply of goods will be extended to discrimination on the grounds of religion, belief, disability, age and sexual orientation[36].

From this perspective it must be considered that there will be a disparity among the grounds, with race and other grounds attracting the most protection.

While this outline could dismiss the idea of a clear hierarchy of protection regarding sex and race, gender can not be considered as another ground of discrimination, its promotion being a 'positive obligation'[37].

---

[35] On October 2008, the Commission published a proposal for a new directive, COM(2008)636.

[36] COM(2008)0426.

[37] Preamble to Dir. 2006/54, recital 2 (and preamble to Dir. 2002/73, recital 4) 'Equality between men and women is a fundamental principle of Community law (…). Those Treaty provisions proclaim equality between men and women as a 'task' and an 'aim' of the Community and impose a positive obligation to promote it in all its activities'.

In fact despite the wider scope of application of the racial anti-discrimination Directive, some provisions suggest a pre-eminence for gender.

Firstly, the legal basis reflects the strong will of the EU legislator to stress a difference between gender and the other grounds. In fact, only for gender discrimination the legal basis (Art. 141 TEC) states a prohibition, while Art. 13 TEC only enables the Council to take appropriate actions to fight discrimination on all grounds.

Secondly, a further point to be noted is the creation of a specific European Body, which does not exist for the other grounds: the reference is to the so called European Institute for Gender Equality (art. 20, Recast Directive).

Finally, as Gender Equality is a 'task' and an 'aim' of the European Community the Principle of Gender Mainstreaming becomes a central provision in the Recast Directive (Article 29)[38]. In the other Anti-discrimination Directives it requires Member States to provide an assessment of the impact of the measures taken on women and men[39].

In that way the European legislator seems to highlight that gender has a transversal value and a central position in the European Anti-discrimination framework, which is not the case for the other grounds.

The interaction of gender and its negative impact in the combination or intersection with other grounds seem to lead to the introduction of a further ground of discrimination, i.e. multiple discrimination: this seems to lead to the charge of a new centrality of gender.

In conclusion, despite the criticism stressed above, it is important to recognize that even the introduction of this limited instrument must be considered a very important step in the creation of more coherent National and European Anti-Discrimination Law.

---

[38] 'Member States shall actively take into account the objective of equality between men and women when formulating and implementing laws, regulations, administrative provisions, policies and activities in the areas referred to in this Directive'.

[39] See Dir. 2000/43, art. 17, par. 2; Dir. 2000/78, art. 19, par. 2; COM(2008)0426, art. 16, par. 2, all titled 'Report'.

The Rhetorical Strength of the Anti-Discrimination Principle: Insights on the Case of Sabine Mayr vs Flöckner OHG

Antonello Ciervo

Synopsis. The case of Sabine Mayr vs Flöckner OHG (ECJ, C-506/06, 26.02.2008) demonstrates how the rhetoric of equal opportunities and non-discrimination between the sexes, within the European Community labour market, is extremely efficient because it is able to neutralize feminist criticisms against the European regulatory system.

With an "hermeneutic slip", the Court of Justice identifies, in Directive 1976/207 concerning equal treatment of the sexes at work, rather than Directive 1992/85 regarding *tout court* dismissals, a higher degree of security in favour of Ms Mayr, who was dismissed while undergoing IVF treatment.

Thus, the Court of Justice uses Directive 1976/207 rhetorically, as if it were a kind of "Grundnorm" able to keep the entire anti-discriminatory framework of EU law working.

Keywords: Principle of Equality, Anti-Discrimination Law, Feminism and the Law, Pregnancy, Medically Assisted Procreation, IVF Treatment.

1. The Law between the principle of equality and philosophy of "difference"

Feminist literature discussed, at length, the importance of the law and its use within a logic of emancipation: in fact, women stand within, but also outside the law, since the male-female relationship is already given in judicial regulations, but in such a way as to restrain female requirements (Cigarini 1995).

In analyzing Italian feminist thought, particularly the trend of gender literature defined "of difference" or "Thinking about Difference" (Negri 2005; Muraro 1991: 13), the problem of the relationship between women and the law is proposed radically.

In fact, women are inserted into the legal system "in pieces": it means that they can only be protected by law to the extent in which female interests coincide with male interests. But as soon as there is a male-female conflict (as much inside the home as at work), the regulatory system is no longer able to guarantee effective legal protection to women, because, in the science of law, the conflicts between sexes have always been neutralized by the formal principle of formal equality (Cigarini 1995: 110; Libreria delle donne di Milano 1987: 70).

In practice, political institutions and regulatory law ignore the sense and value of the difference between the sexes; they are presented as if they were neutral and forcefully confirm their claim of neutrality, especially at times when they effectively endorse the male sex.

It was not by chance that, for a long time, feminist literature confronted the problem of the "concrete" changing of the law, in order to have sexual differences come to light and be recognized. In proceedings before a third, impartial judge, a mere voice of the law, this trend of studies identified a preferential place, where the gender-sensitive and, thus, discriminatory character of the law can be made clear (Libreria delle donne di Milano 1987: 77).

Actually, analyzed from this point of view, the proceedings can be considered a "practice" that allows to unmask the false pretence of the law to set itself up as the sole instrument for mediating social relations between men and women within society.

In this way, feminist thought laid down the construction of a "different" view, regarding as much social relations as the legal process itself, a view that was able to neutralize the "double blind" that binds the universality of the law to the claim of universality by males (Cigarini 1995: 119).

This female practice, implemented within the proceedings, attempts to bring to light a fundamental fact that is completely neglected by the judicial science of a regulatory matrix, i.e. women who work in the field of law (attorneys, judges, and scholars) may build up, among themselves, a network of significant relationships that removes them from the judicial homologation effected by the male legislative model (Libreria delle donne di Milano 1987: 76).

Thanks to this new vision, as much of the regulatory system in its entirety, as the legal process, feminist literature began to work up a series of juridical principles able to affect the regulatory system, in order to characterize it within a "sexed" or gender logic.

These new principles are as follows:

a) female freedom, understood as a special form of freedom that is construed differently from the male form; it results in a breach as to the classical conception of *habeas corpus*;

b) the inviolability of the female body that must be understood as a protection from any form of patriarchal control, as much by individuals as by disciplinary institutions, for example prison (Davis 2003);

c) the creation of new political forms (according to the famous slogan: "the personal is political") capable of defining an idea of "common good", produced starting from personal experiences that converge into public space, but can no longer be classified within classical political concepts, like the majority principle or the system of liberal-democratic representation (Cavarero 1987; Cigarini 1995; Olivito 2002).

Like work-ups from feminist jurists and philosophers, these principles tend to put even the *fulcra* of constitutional law into a critical position, a law that has shown itself to be incapable of breaking out of its considerably rigid dialectics that constantly oscillate between the principle of equality (formally recognised from a regulatory point of view) and the impossibility of conceiving the gender differences between men and women within the society (differences ignored by law as being mere situations of fact, "natural" and non produced by any cultural-type matrix).

However, the European Community juridical horizon is also subjected to severe criticism by feminist thought.

In fact, the same European "gender mainstreaming" tends to neutralize the sexual differences between men and women, owing also to the pervasiveness of the economic aspect, which actually establishes a streamlining of fundamental rights as a function of market logics.

Nonetheless, one must acknowledge, as was correctly noted by the some scholars (Niccolai 2006: 609), that the construction of European policies in general has always been driven by a multitude of legal instruments (from directives, often interpreted by the Court of Justice, to practices, up to concrete economic interventions).

These instruments have built up a much more articulated representation of the relationship between the sexes as the one supplied by post-war constitutionalism.

In any case, this "invasive" European economy-based vision has established a kind of fungibility for parties within the labour market that did not actually bring about a substantial change in quality of the formulation of the male-female relationship, embodied in national constitutions written at the end of the second world war.

Of course, the Treatises that set up the European Community do not formally state that the essential function of women is that of mother and wife, "angel of hearth and home", whose main task is to raise and educate children. However, treatises remain strongly linked to a vision of relations between the sexes in terms of identity and equality. In this vision, the principle of non-discrimination steadily upholds its cultural hegemony.

Female labour, for example, is boosted and guaranteed on the same conditions as male labour: one need only think of night work, regulated by

Directive 1992/85 (although the directive literally regards the "non-obligation" to carry out night work, more than prohibiting it).

This directive was adopted into the Italian legal system through Legislative Decree 645/1996. In the decree, in order to avoid pre-establishing a general layout of the regulation on night work, starting with the more protected female workers, preference was made to refrain from specifying the "non-obligation" provided in the directive.

Therefore, in accordance with article 6 of the aforesaid legislative decree, law-makers limited themselves to referring to the regulatory and contractual provisions in force and already provided for in Italian laws. In its decision dated 4 December 1997 (case C-207/96), the Court of Justice reproved Italy, since it did not correctly implement the Community regulation, but introduced an unjustified limit on women's access to night work. This limitation opposed the principle of equality of the sexes, a principle that can only be deviated from, if the woman herself states she is pregnant.

In fact, only in this case, due to rational reasons of protecting the health of both the future mother and the foetus, may this type of work be prohibited. However, the prohibition only lasts until the child is one year old, just sufficient time for the woman to return to work normally.

In practice, in the Community, women's access to the labour world consists of a simple extension of the male labour model to females, an extension that can be deviated from if the woman cannot carry out the same tasks of a man, due to physical traits typical of women, such as, obviously, pregnancy (Craig, de Búrca 1998: 810).

Hence, the integration of female work into the formal principle of legal equality tends to cancel out the concrete, real differences (biological, symbolic) between men and women, relegating the "natural" differences of gender to a regulatory exception.

Therefore, women could also reach a higher level of social emancipation, by accessing the labour market under the same conditions and benefit from the same guarantees and career prospects as men, as long as they deny their sexual difference and uncritically accept the imposition of a single, male-style model (white male worker, who produces wealth, hereby guaranteeing himself economic autonomy and independence).

This conception of relationships between the sexes, which typifies the economic and social aspect of the European Community, produces, in practice, a series of aporias that may be evaluated in their intrinsic inconsistency, particularly through the analysis of concrete legal cases (Tega 2008).

2. The Case of Sabine Mayr: the "hermeneutic slip" of the Court of Justice

In light of the observations made in the preceding paragraph, I would like to carry on my analysis by dwelling on a recent judgement by the Court of Justice of Luxembourg, dated 26 February 2008: the case of *Sabine Mayr v. Flöckner OHG* (Grand Chamber, C-506/06).
This decision appears interesting to me because it demonstrates how the rhetoric of equal opportunity and non-discrimination between the sexes, within the Community labour market, is quite effective, not only from a legal point of view, but also from a "symbolic" point of view. It manages to neutralise gender and feminist criticisms against the European regulatory system.
The possibility of being able to recognise a diversified plurality of guarantees and legal protection at work, as far as the difference in sex of men and women is concerned, only seems to surface when the regulation clashes with the female body and the woman's wish to have a child.
The leading figure in our case, Ms. Sabine Mayr, was working as a waitress for Flöckner OHG and, during attempts at in-vitro fertilisation, following on extensive hormone treatment, a follicular specimen was taken on 8 March 2005. To that end, her physician prescribed a week's leave of absence from March 8th to March 13th. Two days later, on March 10th, Flöckner informed Ms. Mayr by telephone of her dismissal with immediate effect. On the same day, the woman's physician informed her that, as a result of the follicular specimen, the transfer of the fertilised ova into the uterus, would occur on March 13th.
The problem in the purpose of the lawsuit concerned Austrian law on maternity protection (*Mutterschutzgesetz*, MSchG). Article 10 of this law provides that female employees may not be dismissed during the period of pregnancy or during the four months subsequent to birth, as long as they have informed their employers of their expecting a child.
Ms Mayr found that the aforesaid article 10 had to be applied in her case, whereas Flöckner found that, at the moment the woman was notified of her dismissal, she was not yet pregnant and, thus, no state of pregnancy existed.
At the *Landesgericht* of Salzburg, the Austrian judge of the first instance received the petition from the woman, deeming that the application of article 10 of the MSchG must begin with the fertilisation of the ovum, since only from that time one can speak of the onset of pregnancy from a legal point of view.

However, the *Oberlandesgericht* (i.e. Court of Appeal) of Linz overturned the decision of the first instance, deeming that it was impossible to imagine a pregnancy separate from the body of the woman. Hence, in the case of in vitro fertilisation, the beginning of the pregnancy must be considered the moment in which the fertilised ovum is transferred into the body of the woman.

The appeal decision was contested before the *Oberster Gerichtshof* for a *Revision*: the Austrian Supreme Court was called upon, for the first time, to pronounce judgement on a very particular question, that is, according to Article 10 of the MSchG, started from what moment may a pregnant woman benefit from protection against dismissal in case of in vitro fertilisation.

The Oberster Gerichtshof immediately suspended judgement and submitted the following preliminary question to the Court of Luxembourg: "Is a worker, who undergoes in vitro fertilisation, a "pregnant worker" within the meaning of the first part of Article 2(a) of [Directive 92/85] if, at the time in which she was given notice of dismissal, the woman's ova had already been fertilised with the sperm cells of her partner and "in vitro" embryos thus existed, but had not yet been implanted within her?"

Through this request, the Austrian judge asked if Directive 92/85, concerning dismissals and equal treatment of men and women at work, could also be applied to the concrete case in point and if the petitioner could be considered an expectant mother.

Having formulated the preliminary question before Community judges, the Attorney General of the Court of Luxembourg immediately showed great sensitivity to the problems raised by the case. In fact, he confirmed that medical science and common sense usually define "pregnancy" as the process comprised between conception and delivery, whereas the term "gestation" tends to identify the development of a new being in the maternal womb (point 38, conclusions of the Attorney General).

Having made this brief linguistic premise, the Attorney General proposed three categories of argument, based on which he sustained that the legal protection of the expectant mother must be considered as beginning with the implantation of the fertilised ova into the woman's uterus (Trucco 2008).

The first argument begins with analysing what occurs in medical science and specialist literature: in this regard, the Attorney General cited the works from the Committee for the ethical aspects of human reproduction from the International Federation of Gynaecology and Obstetrics (IFGO) and, in particular, the declaration made in Cairo in March 1998 (see http://www.figo.org/about_guidelines.asp).

On the other hand, the second argument tends to assess the actual meaning of the term "pregnancy", commonly identified as the development of a new being in the maternal womb.

Finally, the third argument is based on the consideration of non-applicability to a pregnancy that occurs through in vitro fertilisation, i.e. that of Ms. Mayr, within the rationale of Directive 1992/85, a directive that is limited to promoting an improvement in the safety and health of expectant female workers, but only with regard to the physical conditions of said workers.

In addition, in the last argument, the Attorney General noted a possible protraction of the protection against dismissal *sine die,* in cases in which the transfer of the embryos into the woman's uterus does not occur immediately, but may even take place after several years. Some national laws also recognise this possibility to women who accede to medically assisted procreation techniques (for an analysis on the comparative point of view, Bagni 2008: 637).

Moreover, one must emphasise how, regarding the last argument, which had the most affect on the final decision, the Court of Justice gave less importance to the point concerning the "defence" and "protection of procreation", but made Ms. Mayr secure from a dismissal that appeared, to all intents and purposes, discriminatory.

According to the Attorney General, in the hypothesis of in vitro fertilisation, since the woman may withdraw her consent to undergo the medical intervention until the moment of transfer of the fertilised ovum, one must calmly deem that there is no life within the maternal womb until the embryo is implanted there.

In their judgment, the judges in Luxembourg immediately declared that "… *the Court is not called upon, by the present order of reference, to broach questions of a medical or ethical nature* but must restrict itself to a legal interpretation of the relevant provisions of Directive 92/85, taking into account the wording, broad logic and objectives of that directive" (point 38 of the judgement).

Upon advice from the judges of the Grand Chamber, Directive 1992/85 could not be applied to Ms. Mayr's case, but this did not exclude the fact that the national judge might refer to other regulations in Community law, although they had not been taken into consideration when the preliminary question was formulated.

Thus, also taking into consideration the observations presented by the Commission and Greek and Italian governments, the Court of

Luxembourg deemed that the question could be resolved by using Directive 1976/207 against discriminations based on gender.

However, this directive establishes minimum protection against unjustified dismissals of women due to maternity leave or for reasons linked to their state of pregnancy, or for a reason based on a substantially similar situation.

This kind of dismissal can most certainly only concern women and not men.

Upon advice by the Court, this directive may be applied for the protection of Ms. Mayr, because Flöckner OHG's reasons for dismissing her were not clear from the formulation of the preliminary deferment by the Austrian judge. In any case, the judges in Luxembourg found it clear that the dismissal occurred when the woman was on sick leave, in order to undergo a treatment of in vitro fertilisation.

Workers, whether male or female, may quite probably find themselves in special situations, which hinder them from carrying out their ordinary duties.

However, in the case of Ms. Mayr: "… the treatment in question in the main proceedings – namely a follicular puncture and the transfer to the woman's uterus of the ova removed by way of that follicular puncture immediately after their fertilisation – directly affects only women. It follows that the dismissal of a female worker essentially because she is undergoing that important stage of in vitro fertilisation treatment constitutes direct discrimination on grounds of sex." (point 50 of the judgement).

The Court of Justice concluded by confirming that Council Directive 1992/85/EEC of 19 October 1992 on the introduction of measures to encourage improvements in the on-the-job safety and health of pregnant workers and workers who have recently given birth or are breastfeeding (tenth individual Directive within the meaning of Article 16(1) of Directive 1989/391/EEC); in particular, the prohibition of dismissal of pregnant workers provided for in Article 10(1) of that directive must be interpreted as not extending to a female worker who is undergoing *in vitro* fertilisation treatment when, on the date she is given notice of her dismissal, her ova have already been fertilised by her partner's sperm cells, so that *in vitro* fertilised ova exist, but they have not yet been transferred into her uterus.

Article 2(1) and 5(1) of Council Directive 1976/207/EEC of 9 February 1976 on the implementation of the principle of equal treatment for men and women as regards access to employment, vocational training and promotion, and working conditions, preclude the dismissal of a female worker who, in circumstances such as those in the main proceedings, is at an advanced stage of *in vitro* fertilisation treatment, that is, between the follicular puncture and the immediate transfer of the *in vitro* fertilised ova into her uterus, inasmuch as it is established that the dismissal is essentially based on the fact that the woman has undergone such treatment.

Despite the Community regulatory approach to sexual discrimination at work is criticised rather often by the most solicitous, sensitive policy on such subjects, it seems to us that, in this case, the Court of Justice most effectively guaranteed the right of the female worker to accede to medically assisted procreation techniques, equating the conditions of Ms. Mayr with those of "normal" expectant workers.

Moreover, the argumentative route taken by the judges indicates in-depth reflection by the Court on what the most suitable regulatory grounds must be to guarantee the rights of the petitioner.

This "hermeneutic slip" used by the judges in the case of Ms. Mayr and which induced them to identify, in Directive 1976/207 (equal treatment at work) rather than Directive 1992/85 (*tout court* dismissals), the highest level of guarantee in favour of the petitioner, urges us to state that the Court grounded its judgement on a point of view of great pragmatism.

In short, the Court of Luxembourg placed the national judge under conditions of guaranteeing the highest and most profound level of protection for the petitioner, through a selective process of the regulatory material available to it; in doing so, it resolves a question that has never before been presented before Community judges or national judges.

A similar argument shows how the Court tends to use Directive 1976/207 "rhetorically", as if it were a kind of *Grundnorm* able to keep the entire framework of EU anti-discriminatory law working.

3. Community labour market and jurisprudence of the Court of Justice: beyond the principle of equality?

When I claim that the Court of Luxembourg makes rhetorical use of the principle of non-discrimination to guarantee a higher degree of legal protection for female workers during pregnancy, I mean that Directive 76/207 becomes strongly effective in its persuasiveness (Perelman, Olbrechts-Tyteca 1958).

At the moment in which legal guarantees for female workers are extended, hereby raising them to the same level of males, a "strong" principle of equality is confirmed from a symbolic point of view.

Of course, the most attentive policy pointed out a rather ambiguous relationship between the principles of non-discrimination and equality, since the two concepts do not perfectly coincide from a legal point of view (Martin 2006: 515-520).

Nevertheless, in this case I believe that the non-discrimination principle is used to ascertain "symbolic" equality between men and women, who, thus, are considered exactly identical as concerns their rights within the Community labour market. This "symbolic" equality, which becomes a bearer of the non-discrimination principle, is very convincing precisely because it tempts one to believe in perfect equality between men and women within society.

Thus, the non-discrimination principle tends to neutralise the gender differences, existing between men and women, and further enforce that neutral vision of the law that feminist legal culture has been criticising for such a long time.

In any case, one thing about this must be specified: directive 1976/207 tends to lend itself to different legal uses.

It was not by chance that, in a previous decision, the *Dekker* judgement C-177/88 of 8 November 1990, the Court of Justice used the criterion of equality of treatment, in order to award a guarantee to a pregnant woman who was not hired by her employee for this reason.

In fact, in this case the judges in Luxembourg stated that an employer is in direct contravention of the principle of equal treatment embodied in Articles 2(1) and 3(1) of Council Directive 1976/207/EEC of 9 February 1976 on the implementation of the principle of equal treatment for men and women as regards access to employment, vocational training and promotion, and working conditions if he refuses to enter into a contract of employment with a female candidate whom he considers to be suitable for the job if such refusal is based on the possible adverse consequences for him of employing a pregnant woman, owing to rules on unfitness for work adopted by the public authorities, which assimilate inability to work on account of pregnancy and confinement to inability to work on account of illness. The fact that no man applied for the job is irrelevant.

Nonetheless, one must emphasise that, in the *Dekker* case, unlike the *Sabine Mayr* case, the petitioner had not yet been hired by her employer and the reason for not being hired was the fact that the woman was already pregnant when the talks were held with the deciding committee.

In this regard, the Court of Justice declared that "… the reason given by the employer for refusing to appoint Mrs Dekker is basically that it could not have obtained reimbursement from the Risicofonds of the daily benefits which it would have had to pay her for the duration of her absence due to pregnancy, and yet at the same time it would have been obliged to employ a replacement" (point 11 of the judgement).

Despite this, the community judges protected Ms. Dekker, their argument being that pregnancy cannot be considered a hindrance in performing a job, as if it were an illness.

The petitioner was denied access to the job because her position, as a pregnant woman, was compared to that of an ill person who would be unable to perform the ordinary tasks of the job: moreover, the hiring of a pregnant woman would have meant further expenditures for the employer.

If one considers this previous decision made by the Court of Justice and reads it in light of the more recent *Sabine Mayr* case, in the opinion of the undersigned, the idea that directive 1976/207 tends to neutralise the gender differences within the labour market is reinforced.

In fact, in the *Dekker* judgement, the gender difference is also indicated as a pre-juridical fact: a woman is pregnant but she is applying for a job; the employer who is evaluating her résumé also takes her "physical situation" into account and, due specifically to her state of pregnancy, decides not to hire her.

Thus, the female difference lies on the thresholds of the working world and does not indicate either the advantage or disadvantage for the woman: pregnancy, as such, is an irrelevant condition by law, since the theory of equality once again prevails (More 1993: 48).

Hence, this judgement further reinforces the "male" model implied in the Community directive because, in the concrete case in question, Ms. Dekker was the only candidate for the job in the education centre; there were neither males nor females competing with her for the position.

Another confirmation of the fact that directive 1976/207 tends to neutralise the gender differences, both upon entering into and within the labour market, is found in another Community directive, no. 1979/7, the purpose of which is the gradual implementation of the principle of equality of treatment between men and women regarding social security.

This regulation actually defines its range of application as *ratione personae*, hereby referring, in article 2, to the concept of an "active population" operating within the Community labour market.

So, the jurisprudence of the Court of Luxembourg was able to reassert, in more than one circumstance, that this phrase had to be interpreted restrictively and that a person who carries out a non-remunerated job, which involves taking care of a person afflicted with physical problems or bearing a handicap, could not fall within the so-called "active population" (Forlati Picchio 1991: 430).

More specifically, in the case of *Züchner vs. Handelskrankenkasse* of 7 November 1996 (C-77/95), the Court of Justice stated that a woman who is taking care of her husband, i.e. carrying out a non-remunerated job, who has never filled a working position in the past or sought a job, could not be indemnified by the German social security department for the care she supplies to her paraplegic husband.

According to the judges in Luxembourg, in practice, the so-called "personal care job" that women have always done within their own homes can in no way be considered a *tout court* job and whoever does it, even through personal fondness, cannot be included in the "active working population"; thus, such a person cannot benefit from equality of treatment between men and women in matters of social security.

In short, for the nth time, this decision shows how only within the *purview* of directive 76/207 is it possible to recognise an equality of treatment between men and women: everything that does not fall within this *purview* and lies on the margins of the labour market or, in any case, does not fall within the cost/benefit economic scheme, cannot be considered work and, hence, does not benefit from the Community protection regulations concerning equality of treatment.

The neutralisation of what is particularly female (pregnancy, personal "care" work) becomes necessary: in this way, what is feminine cannot be acknowledged, if it is not "made masculine" and if it does not fall within a particular vision of production relations, that is, relations in which men and women are "standardised" and become interchangeable, whether by role or task.

Directive 76/207 upholds a strong "symbolic" impetus able to neutralise the wish to bring to light a sexual (or gender) vision of relationships between men and women, above all within the labour market.

This way, the dominant model in European legal culture, i.e. the male model, is confirmed with more force and persuasiveness.

This is why, based on reflections carried out in the foregoing pages concerning the case of Ms. Mayr, I believe that Italian feminist thought when making the "difference" its battle horse, runs the risk of seeing its own claims of recognition of the sex-oriented character of the law marginalised in the legal debate.

Therefore, I believe feminist thought will have to deal with this persuasive capacity of Directive 1976/207 to assure the same rights of male workers to female workers (whether pregnant or not).

What clearly surfaces from the analysis of this case law is the increasingly important role of the body within legal debates, both feminist and not (Iacub 2004).

Perhaps, starting from the repossession of the body by a female juridical person, in a conception radically different from what has been linked to the Anglo-Saxon idea of *habeas corpus* for centuries, it will be possible to outline a sexual vision of the law that can also impose a different symbolic order on regulatory provisions.

PART III

QUESTIONING IDENTITY AND DIVERSITY:
AN ENLARGED CONSTITUTIONAL CONVERSATION

Discrimination against Homosexuals and 'Integration by Reasonableness': Suggestions from the *Maruko* Case

Giorgio Repetto

Synopsis. This contribution focuses on the role played by anti-discrimination in the fashioning of GLBT claims in European law. On the basis of a review of *Maruko*, a case decided in April 2008 by the European Court of Justice, I propose a rethinking of the functions of anti-discrimination, toward a more comprehensive consideration of its judicial enforcement. In particular, my thesis is that the decision set out in *Maruko*, contrary to the opinion of several commentators, offers a viable solution to protect the rights of homosexuals without giving up the specificity of their claims. The analysis of the arguments used by the Court reveals a more general approach to anti-discrimination, in that the Court a) offers a reading of anti-discrimination which is aware of the intertwinement between its social and its economical dimensions, and b) contributes to an ideal of the dignity of homosexuals that is not limited to reproducing prevailing heterosexual paradigms.
Keywords: Anti-Discrimination, Homosexual Rights, Legal Reasoning, Human Dignity.

1. Deconstructing polarities: anti-discrimination between social and economical dimension

In a constantly increasing measure, the legal recognition of non-majoritarian sexual identities is reshaping the substance of well-established concepts and institutions. Family law, welfare rights and labour law, in particular, are the fields in which GLBT (*Gay Lesbian Bisexual Transgender*) claims have more evidently contributed, in the last decades, to calling into question some traditional structures of legal regulation. The challenge to the inherited understanding of notions like 'legal personality', 'marriage', 'parenthood', and 'grounds for dismissal' has revealed the potential for oppression in legal concepts, but also the capacity of legal instruments to foster a more sensible approach to sexuality issues.

In the European Union, the law and politics of recognizing weaker and under-represented sex (prevalently woman in rapport to man) has been centred upon the principle of anti-discrimination. Originally conceived as a means to the end of carrying the freedom of movement into action, this principle has gradually taken on a relevance all its own[1].

Since *Defrenne*[2], ECJ has progressively abandoned a mere functionalist approach, by making anti-discrimination into something quite similar to a constitutional principle of equality: general in its applications, not structurally limited by other principles contained in the Treaties, and based both on a formal ('direct') and a substantial ('indirect') conception. Indeed, anti-discrimination regards not only situations in which a certain category is under-represented *as such*, but also (although more problematically) all those situations in which the discriminatory potential of a measure – even though it disadvantages the members of a group – does not affect recognizable categories *a priori*. In the former case, the instrument called upon to ascertain whether a certain measure is discriminatory is comparative analysis ('a pregnancy-grounded dismissal is as such discriminatory in that it affects only women and not men'), whereas in the latter case it is necessary to contextualize the measure in the specificity of a given *milieu* ('female recruitment should be favored in light of historical, cultural and social burdens paid by women as to work chances') (Fredman 2002: 92). Direct discrimination, even if not exclusively, implies a judgement on individual situations, while indirect discrimination requires mainly a judgement on group dynamics, in terms of exclusion and inclusion.

This evolution, in spite of judicial oscillations and the critiques of scholars, has been strengthened by recent Directives establishing a general framework for equal treatment in employment and occupation, aimed at combating discrimination on the grounds of "religion or belief, disability, age or sexual orientation" (2000/78/EC) and of "race and ethnic origin" (2000/43/EC). Both Directives extend the factors protected against discriminatory measures and, at the same time, strengthen the capacity of anti-discrimination to embrace, thanks to its indirect effect, new forms of social exclusion.

This evolution, so briefly summarized here, shows that antidiscrimination in EU law now broadly transcends the liberal imperative, which goes no further than requiring likes to be treated alike. Whether this new relationship is marked only by the progressive fading of the economic functions of discrimination law (Prechal 2004: 548), is an assertion I critically deal with. Although the shift of anti-discrimination from a

---

[1] For further references on this evolution see Mancini and O'Leary 1999: 331.
[2] Case 149/77, *Defrenne v. Sabena (Defrenne No. 3)*, *European Court Reports* (ECR), 1978, p. 365.

purely economic instrument (as a *market integrating* factor) to a more comprehensive social-oriented principle (in terms of substantive rights accorded to under-represented categories) has its evident basis in EC law and policy (first of all in the *post*-Amsterdam provisions of EC Treaty) (More 1999: 535), it should not be overstated. The abandonment of the more blatant (neo) liberal rhetoric towards the end of the 80's has indeed not relegated anti-discrimination out of the economic realm, since its role – along with the increasing relevance of social policy – has evolved in the direction of granting greater access to the labour market. In other words: from market building to market participation (Bell 2002: 196) and job creation (Fredman 2002: 25).

In articulating the facets of the principle, and in extending its capacity to encompass more and more aspects of civil and social life, EU law made anti-discrimination the guiding imperative of a new relationship between the economic and the social, based upon the intertwinement of connected values and ideals.

The willingness of the Court to adopt a far-reaching consideration of both economic and social spillovers of sex discrimination directives has given rise to opposite criticism. On the one hand, its actions have been censured because of a timidity to set up rights and guarantees not fully detached from the economic aim of the Treaties (Bell 2002: 107); on the other hand, its concern with social issues, which occasionally has gone far beyond the word of the Treaties, has raised several critiques as to the legitimacy of its action *vis à vis* political actors (for further details see Van der Vleuten 2003: 177).

On the contrary, the background of my thesis is that the trap in which the Court is said to be caught may represent a virtuous model of adjudication, since human rights claims arising from EC law present *by their own nature* a two-fold dimension, a persistent mix of social and economical aspects, which it is the task of the Court, at the same time, to preserve and to enhance. In this light, the evolution of Luxembourg case law on sex discrimination can be seen as the expression of the changing strategies that, in EC law, have led to a certain idea of human dignity and human relationships.

The impossibility of drawing a line between the economic and the social field shifts the focus from the search for a straightforward enforcement by the ECJ of what is considered each time the 'true' nature of anti-discrimination, to the consideration of the argumentative patterns used by the Court to foster the interaction between the different 'souls' of this nature.

The fashioning of this relationship is indeed not a clear-cut product, but represents the evolving outcome of the different rhetoric that goes toward shaping concepts and institutions at the European level. Consequently, the attention to the way in which ECJ selects, excludes and builds up arguments in favour of a certain interpretation of anti-discrimination can be fruitfully invoked as the most viable instrument in getting rid of what I call 'holistic' approaches.

Moreover, it must be considered that the enforcing of man-woman anti-discrimination does not have the same history as anti-discrimination against homosexuals or disabled persons.

Based upon the ECJ's recent decision in *Maruko*[3], what will be discussed below is the place and the direction of discrimination against homosexuals in the linking of economic and social aspects.

2. *Maruko*'s background

In 2001, Tadao Maruko and his male partner entered a registered life partnership pursuant to the Paragraph 1 of the German *Gesetz über die eingetragene Lebenspartnerschaft* (hereinafter: LPartG), according to which

> '(1) Two persons of the same sex establish a partnership when they declare to each other, in person and in the presence of the other, that they wish to live together in partnership for life (as life partners). The declarations cannot be made conditionally or for a fixed period. Declarations are effective when they are made before the competent authority. ... '

German law grants life partnership only to people of the same sex, with some limitations not relevant in this case, whereas marriage is reserved for heterosexual couples.

Mr Maruko's partner, H.H., had been a theater costume designer and, in that capacity, had been continuously affiliated with the German Theatres Pension Institution ('*Versorgunsanstalt der deutschen Bühnen*', VddB) since 1959.

After his death, Mr Maruko applied in January 2005 to VddB for a widower's pension, but his claim was refused because, according to the Collective Agreement for German Theaters ('*Tarifordnung für die deutschen Theater*'), only 'the spouse' of the insured man or woman could

---

[3] Case C-267/06, *Tadao Maruko v. Versorgungsanstalt der deutschen Bühnen*, ECR, 2008, I, p. 1757.

enjoy such a benefit[4]. In the opinion of VddB, Mr Maruko was therefore, in his situation, not entitled to be provided with a survivor's pension. After an unsuccessful appeal, he brought an action before the Bavarian Administrative Tribunal in Munich.

According to Mr Maruko, the denial of VddB violated, in two concurring directions, the principle of equal treatment.

Under a first aspect, the refusal to grant him the pension infringed upon paragraph 46(4) of the German Social Security Code, which aimed at placing on an equal standard the rights enjoyed by partners and spouses as to old-age pension schemes:

> '(4) For the purposes of determining entitlement to a widow's or widower's pension, the establishment of a life partnership shall be treated as equivalent to a wedding, a life partnership as equivalent to a marriage, a surviving partner as equivalent to a widow or a widower, and a life partner as equivalent to a spouse. The termination or dissolution of a new partnership shall be regarded as equivalent, respectively, to the dissolution or annulment of a new marriage.'

Secondly, he argued that the denial made by VddB due to the lack of a nuptial tie, in the presence of the same substantive and normative conditions of a surviving spouse, represents an indirect discrimination grounded upon his sexual orientation, and is therefore prohibited by Directive 2000/78/EC[5].

Rights and duties provided by LPartG for same-sex partners reproduce many aspects of the mutual engagement of spouses, in that they cover several facets of the life in common, and particularly: the duty to mutual support and care for the duration of the relationship (par. 2); the duty to contribute to the common needs of the partnership, with the previsions that the partners, as to the maintenance obligations, are bound by the

---

[4] In the German version of the agreement, a survivor's pension is granted to a male person married to an insured woman ('*der Ehemann einer Versicherten oder Ruhegeldempfängerin*') or to a female person married to an insured man ('*die Ehefrau eines Versicherten oder Ruhegeldempfängers*').

[5] According to Art. 2(2)(b) of the Directive, 'indirect discrimination shall be taken to occur where an apparently neutral provision, criterion or practice would put persons having a particular religion or belief, a particular disability, a particular age, or a particular sexual orientation at a particular disadvantage compared with other persons unless: (i) that provision, criterion or practice is objectively justified by a legitimate aim and the means of achieving that aim are appropriate and necessary, or (ii) as regards persons with a particular disability, the employer or any person or organisation to whom this Directive applies, is obliged, under national legislation, to take appropriate measures in line with the principles contained in Article 5 in order to eliminate disadvantages entailed by such provision, criterion or practice'.

provisions of the Civil Code applicable to spouses (par. 5); the common subjection to the financial regime of common ownership of property acquired *ex post facto*, unless otherwise agreed (par. 6); each partner has to be regarded as a member of the other partner's family (par. 11); lastly, in the case of the partners' separation, each partner can be subject to a maintenance obligation (par. 16) and to an equal apportionment of pension entitlements with the other partner (par. 20).

Given all these reasons, Mr Maruko claimed therefore that his right not to be treated less favourably by reason of his sexual orientation had been infringed by VddB.

Consequently, among other questions[6], the referring tribunal requested a preliminary ruling from the Court of Justice on the following:

'3. Does Article 1 in conjunction with Article 2(2)(a) of Directive 2000/78 [which regulates direct discrimination] … preclude regulations governing a supplementary pension scheme under which a registered partner does not after the death of his partner receive survivor's benefits equivalent to those available to spouses, even though, like spouses, registered partners live in a union of mutual support and assistance formally entered into for life?'

In his opinion of September 6, 2007, Advocate General Ruiz-Jarabo Colomer adopts a threefold consideration in order to support the discriminatory nature of the national regulations[7].

First of all, he argues that the denial by VddB is not directly discriminatory, for 'there is no evidence that such a pension has been granted to other individuals in identical or analogous situations', with the consequence that it 'is not based on the sexual orientation of the insured'.

Secondly, for the purpose of ascertaining whether the denial is indirectly discriminatory, the AG focuses on the comparability of the effects of marriage and of legal partnership. Ruling out that the task of the Court is to develop a 'European matrimonial law', his efforts do not concentrate on access to marriage, but rather on the similarities between the two

---

[6] Of the five questions referred to ECJ by the Tribunal, only the third directly concerned the inquiry as to whether the denial of VddB constitutes a discrimination based on sexual orientation. The other questions, which fall outside the focus of this paper, regarded the applicability of Directive 2000/78/EC to the payments at stake provided by VddB (first and second question), the relevance of Recital 22 of the preamble to the same Directive, according to which it is 'without prejudice to national laws on marital status and the benefits dependent thereon' (fourth question), the temporal applicability of Article 141 EC (fifth question).

For more detailed comments see Bonini Baraldi 2008, Toggenburg 2008, Tobler and Waaldijk 2009.

[7] Para. 96-104 of the opinion.

situations at issue, which can only shed a light on the legitimacy of the measure.

Thirdly, having accepted the view of the referring Tribunal, according to which marriage and registered partnership in German Law attribute similar rights and obligations to the involved parties, the AG lastly recognizes that the refusal to grant a pension to Mr Maruko represents an indirect discrimination based on sexual orientation, contrary to Article 2(2)(b) of Directive 2000/78/EC.

The same conclusion is shared by the applicant and the Commission[8].

3. 'Out of the traps': the resources of reasonability

The Court's answer, at first glance, sounds surprisingly straight-forward.

The core of the decision, under this aspect, is that German Law, as referred by the national judge, places marriage and life partnership in a comparable situation. However, this comparability is not relevant as such, but only inasmuch it 'concerns the survivor's benefit at issue in the main proceedings'[9].

Consequently,

'72 If the referring court decides that surviving spouses and surviving life partners are in a comparable situation so far as concerns that survivor's benefit, legislation such as that at issue in the main proceedings must, as a consequence, be considered to constitute direct discrimination on grounds of sexual orientation, within the meaning of Articles 1 and 2(2)(a) of Directive 2000/78.'

Both the finding of a direct discrimination[10], instead of an indirect one (as submitted by the AG, the Commission and the applicant, but not by the referring Tribunal), and the decisive reliance on national law for the purpose of inquiring the discriminatory effect of the legislation, have raised several critiques by commentators.

Bonini Baraldi, for example, criticizes the decision of the Court to shift its focus from indirect to direct discrimination, since the latter limits the relevant aspects of the case to a limited internal analogy with marriage,

---

[8] Para. 63 of the decision.

[9] Para. 69 of the decision.

[10] According to Art. 2(2)(a) of the above-mentioned Directive 2000/78/CE, 'direct discrimination shall be taken to occur where one person is treated less favourably than another is, has been or would be treated in a comparable situation, on any of the grounds referred to in Article 1', among which there is sexual orientation.

whereas the former allows a critical evaluation of the rights and duties enshrined in the two régimes as a whole (Bonini Baraldi 2008: 663-664).

Toggenburg, on the other hand, although welcoming the result, argues that the decision would have been different if German Law had not provided life partners with the possibility to stipulate a registered partnership which grants rights and duties which are comparable with marriage[11].

Even though I share some doubts about the decision, these critical comments, in my opinion, tend in general to stress excessively the lack of aggressiveness of the ECJ, while not giving the right importance to the implication of the legal reasoning followed by the Court.

My thesis is indeed that the arguments used in this decision support an 'integration by reasonableness', according to which anti-discrimination can occasionally work not only as a 'catch-all' instrument, but also as a principle able to adapt itself to the overwhelming variety of social relations, while not losing its potential.

First of all, the innovations in *Maruko* appear quite evident if compared to its precedents.

In *Grant*[12], for example, the applicant was a woman who lived in stable but unregistered partnership with another woman. She claimed against her employer's decision not to benefit her partner with travel concessions otherwise accorded not only to the spouse of dependants, but also to non-married, heterosexual, partners with a meaningful relationship for at least two years. The Court, in a first step, ruled out that the employer had acted discriminatorily in relation to 'sex'. In a second step, having been called upon to decide whether discrimination on grounds of 'sex' even covered sexual orientation choices[13], the Court dismissed the application for two main reasons: a) the test elaborated in *P v. S* [14] in relation to trans-sexualism was not applicable in this case, since gender reassignment concerns the core of sex discrimination, whereas discrimination on the grounds of sexual orientation was outside the borders of the invoked right; b) in the majority of EC member states, a same-sex relationship is not considered as equivalent to a heterosexual relationship.

---

[11] Toggenburg 2008: 181, adds that 'this means that the member states frame the comparability between homo- and heterosexual situations and thereby indirectly decide upon the applicability of EU law'. This approach, according to this author, seriously threatens the enduring vitality of any *effét utile* in the matter of discrimination on grounds of sexual orientation.

[12] Case C-249/96, *Lisa Jacqueline Grant v. South West Trains*, ECR, 1998, I, p. 621.

[13] Directive 2000/78 was obviously not yet into force.

[14] Case C-13/94, *P v. S and Cornwall County Council*, ECR, 1996, I, p. 2143.

What must be highlighted in this case is the Court's choice to dismiss the application by ruling that the decision of the employer is not discriminatory, considering that the condition imposed 'is ... applied regardless of the sex of the worker concerned. Thus travel concessions are refused to a male worker if he is living with a person of the same sex, just as they are to a female worker if she is living with a person of the same sex'.

In so doing, the Court chose a comparator which is clearly unable to face situations that go beyond a straightforward symmetric male/female approach (Mancini and O'Leary 1999: 350). The formal and categorizing argument indeed reveals the difficulty of overcoming a rigid and dichotomic vision of gender discrimination, which remains fixed to a notion of 'sex' reduced to a merely biological divide[15].

In another famous case, *K.B.*[16], the Court was asked to rule on the pension scheme afforded by the UK National Health Service, which precluded the granting of a widower's pension to the partner of the applicant, R., who was born a woman and became a man after a gender reassignment operation. Since R. could not be registered as a man in the birth certificate, the couple was unable to marry, with the consequence that R., as K.B.'s partner, was not entitled to enjoy the survivor's pension.

While ruling out that the restriction to married couples of social benefits is *per se* discriminatory on the grounds of sex, the Court admits that the restriction is indirectly discriminatory, since marriage constitutes a necessary precondition for the grant of the invoked benefit[17].

However, the indirect nature of the discrimination, although justified in consideration of the limits of EC law in family issues, shows the Court's reluctance to give relevance to individual choices regarding sexual identity that is autonomous from a heterosexual paradigm. The claim of R. and K.B. has been entrapped into EC law insofar it concerns an institution like marriage, whose centrality is reinforced through its concession to a couple hosting a transsexual, because this does not call directly into question its heterosexual appearance.

In other words, the finding of indirect discrimination in *K.B.* sheds light on the mimetic capacity of 'sex' to encompass and normalize desires and relationships that do not fall entirely within heterosexual paradigms. A mechanic search for comparators, whether it leads to overestimating differences as in *Grant* or to obscuring the richness of diversity as in *K.B.*,

---

[15] For further references to similar 'comparison traps' see Prechal 2004: 544.
[16] Case C-117/01, *K.B. v. National Health Service Pensions Agency*, ECR, 2004, I, p. 541.
[17] Para 29-30.

ends up offering a 'normalized' vision of difference, which is unable to deal with the question of whether a given solution takes care of the specific claims invoked by non-majoritarian groups and subjects.

Even a comparative survey that is not limited to ascertaining formal or categorical similarities, but rather seeks for a 'fair' and 'reasonable' result, can occasionally lead to imposing ideas of normality or human dignity on sexual minorities which blurs theirs claims, since these are depicted each time as tolerated deviations to a unique standard.

From this standpoint, the solution set out in *Maruko* appears to be a viable way to prevent the opposing risks of *Grant* and of *K.B.*

An important aspect of the decision is the Court's refusal to submit the solution to the finding of a narrow comparator[18]. Thanks to the abandonment of the 'but for' test, *Maruko* defines sexual identity of homosexuals not just through a comparison with heterosexuals, but rather by giving it the chance to express itself in the different aspects of social life. Indeed, the question faced by the Court is not the comparability of two abstract, typical, situations (i.e. marriage and same-sex partnership), but only the comparability of concrete claims and issues, in this case 'so far as concerns that survivor's benefit'[19].

This approach reveals the capacity of legal reasoning to go beyond a straight group categorization, in that it emphasizes a non-essential notion of sexual difference, relying on a process of relational self-definition rather than on deviance from a unique norm (in the terms used by Young 1990: 170).

The reasonable solution of *Maruko* shows indeed the failure of the blindly mechanical way of conceiving of anti-discrimination, whether it is grounded in a negative and comparative analysis, or is supported by a bold value-driven approach.

Moreover, the Court acknowledges that the equalization between marriage and registered partnership afforded by national law is sufficient to focus its analysis on direct discrimination.

---

[18] Tobler and Waaldijk have correctly emphasized that *Maruko* constitutes an important step toward a more substantive approach to anti-discrimination, in that the Court seems to have abandoned a strict formal logic, shifting its focus from form to substance (Tobler and Waaldijk 2009: 739-740).

[19] Para. 73 of the decision. Adamietz and Schreier 2008: 196 argue that this approach is the opposite of that followed by German tribunals, which emphasize formal differences between marriage and registered partnership in order to dismiss discriminatory claims submitted by homosexuals.

As in *Nikoloudi*[20], direct discrimination occurs today when a given measure, though formally neutral, in consequence of a legislative provision, has the same exclusionary effect as a measure directly relying on a prohibited criterion[21].

Consequently, in relation to the second above-mentioned critique, even the doubts concerning the opportunity to link anti-discrimination in EC law to the previsions of national law can be answered in a more comprehensive way.

Although I admit that the conditional effect established in *Maruko* can pose a threat to the uniformity of EC law, it is just as undeniable that a similar approach strengthens the capacity of the ECJ to set up a process of loose harmonization of family law, based on the elaboration of better practices rather than of binding rules.

Particularly in relation to family law, a field in which member States traditionally guard their competences jealously, antidiscrimination cannot be overcharged with the task of promoting a judicial-driven harmonization[22]. Its virtues could rather be found even in the capacity to take national diversities into account, by elaborating rules and standards not aimed at substituting local regulations, but intended to accompany them in a progressive redefinition of rights and duties. In this evolution, the Court can play a significant role in furthering a system of protection which is based not only on the enactment of hard principles, but also on the finding of viable solutions that need to be elaborated and enforced through both formal and non-formal procedures (such as OMC) (Niccolai 2010).

---

[20] Case C-196/02, *Vasiliki Nikoloudi v. Organismos Tilepikinonion Ellados AE*, ECR, 2005, I, p. 1789, in which the Court stated that 'the ... exclusion of a possibility of appointment as an established member of staff by reference, ostensibly neutral as to the worker's sex, to a category of workers which, under national rules having the force of law, is composed exclusively of women constitutes direct discrimination on the grounds of sex (para. 36).

[21] After highlighting the similarities with *Nikoloudi*, Tobler and Waaldijk 2009: 740 argue that the finding of a direct discrimination in *Maruko* 'is not a result of the modern legal definition of direct discrimination under Directive 2000/78/CE'.

[22] In the past, the reluctance of ECJ to define family rights and status (see, for example, case 184/83, *Hofmann v. Barmer Ersatzkasse*, ECR, 1984, p. 3047 and case 59/85, *Holland v. Reed*, ECR, 1986, p. 1283) can be probably linked to the negative and weak use of comparative test used at the time by the Court. I thank Silvia Niccolai for this suggestion. For a critical evaluation of harmonization in family issues see Marella 2006.

4. Neither repression nor liberation: dignity and the variety of human desires

Beyond its wording, *Maruko* calls into question the traditional reading of antidiscrimination in ECJ case-law as an instrument which can alternatively reach economic *or* social goals. This case, in line with other Court precedents [23], seems indeed to deviate – for the arguments it uses and for the aim it achieves – both from a pure economic dimension and even from an exclusively social attitude.

The focus on direct discrimination shows that anti-discrimination, in the hands of the Court, is the tool through which economic integration is able, *by its own virtue*, to capture and give a viable solution to social claims. If the Court had chosen to find in *Maruko* an episode of indirect discrimination, this would have left the judges a space of adjudication detached from the dynamics of European law, for the Court would have been compelled to ground its judgement on external criteria, transcending as such the concreteness of the invoked claim[24]. Moreover, this solution would have confirmed the existence of an endemic conflict between the economic and social aims of antidiscrimination, since the goal of a more structural equalization between homosexuals and heterosexuals could have been achieved only by overcoming a plain consistency with EC systemic requirements.

Hence, the soundness of the solution can be found in that the Court has fully grounded in the system and in the proper constraints of Community law a decision whose substance is destined to widen and evolve in the ongoing debate on the rights of homosexuals both at the European and at the national levels.

Lastly, this decision sheds light on the contribution of anti-discrimination to shaping a new image of dignity concerning homosexuals.

Different ways to conceive of anti-discrimination reflect different ways to understand the fashioning of under-represented personal and group identities.

In relation to homosexuals, anti-discrimination is widely depicted as the instrument called upon to combat a far-reaching repression, whose potential appears evident if we only compare the constraints suffered by homosexuals in private, social and economic life with the ruling paradigm of heterosexual relationships. These emancipatory claims have often been

---

[23] I share here many conclusions developed by Niccolai 2009 and 2010 in relation to the case C-303/06, *Coleman v. Attridge Law*, ECR, 2008, p. 5603.
[24] As implicitly acknowledged by Bonini Baraldi 2008: 663.

associated with a vision of personal dignity that coincides with an ideal of sexual liberation. In this direction, the autonomous management of self-identity is the necessary precondition for establishing an institutional framework called upon to accompany the process of sexual self-definition. In the words of Anthony Giddens, democratization of the self and institutional reflexivity as to sexual claims involve each other (Giddens 1992: 28).

In my opinion, this current tends to overemphasize an excessively individual and rationalist vision of dignity. On the one hand, this opinion supports an idea of society that is intrinsically non-relational, since it is rather constituted by individuals who independently of one another deliberate on one's own identity and life projects. Sexuality, like every other social construct, is instead the evolving outcome of individual and social discourses, shaped both by horizontal relationships between and within groups and by basic social patterns like emancipation, protection and institution (Commaille 1998).

On the other hand, the liberation current ends up obscuring the deepest effects of regulative power on the structure of homosexual rights and duties. According to Foucault, sexuality is, rather than just the realm of intimacy, the form of knowledge produced by the same apparatus of power it aims to denounce (Foucault 1979). This analysis can be fruitfully invoked to give a deeper account to the ongoing divarication between the progressive recognition of rights to GLBT and the persisting centrality of heterosexual paradigms in social, political and economic life.

By this, recognition of rights for homosexuals seems the more effective, the wider is the acceptance of a notion of dignity rooted in the specificity and in the variety of human desires.

In doing this, the contribution of law, and particularly of antidiscrimination, can be that of challenging not only the formal machinery of rights, but even the symbolic horizons they bring, which continuously tend to reinforce and legitimate patterns of social exclusion.

Diversity as a Public Good? Cultural Identity in Legal Narratives[1]

Ilenia Ruggiu

Synopsis. This article explores some of the legal discourse regarding cultural identity in international, European and national law. From the analysis, important differences emerge. Generally, the recognition of cultural identity, especially in nation states, serves to compensate for forms of injustice, or to accommodate specific minorities within the state: it is a tool used to fight discrimination. On the contrary, today, at an international and European level and in a few "multicultural" states, distinctive identities are starting to be perceived as having autonomous value, that deserve protection not only in order to defend neglected and vulnerable groups, but because diversity represents a public good for the whole community. In this second perception, the coexistence of different identities becomes a new constitutional value in the construction of a civilized democracy. This article argues that this shift in constitutional narratives on cultural identity is positive and should be extended to other identities such as gender, in order to elaborate new visions of dignity. The connection between protection of identities and anti-discrimination has been extremely useful in re-establishing justice, but it also risks perpetuating power structures. Maintaining non-majority identities within anti-discrimination discourse impedes them from being seen in other lights and ways that the article tries to represent and visualize.
Keywords: Identity, Culture, Diversity, Power, Cultural Minorities, Aboriginal people

Introduction

After the Second World War, constitutionalism refused entirely the concept of cultural identity in its collective dimension, associating it with the "ethical state", and with the "blood and soil" myth[2]. For a long time

---

[1] Part of this paper was written while I was visiting the Department of Political Science at the University of Victoria, BC Canada. I would like to thank this institution for its hospitality, and particularly: Avigail Eisenberg, for the vibrant exchange of ideas; Taiaiake Alfred, Rita Dahmon, Matt James, Charles Horne, James Tully for the very useful interviews. Also thanks to the Intercultural Society of Duncan for introducing me to the culture of the Native people of Canada. The University of Cagliari supported the project.
[2] This closure is due both to historical and constitutional factors: the tragic consequences of Nazi exaltation of national identity; the individualistic approach that put the person (not the group) at the centre of constitutional universe; a certain interpretation of the equality

legal texts used only a restricted concept of culture, intended as specialized knowledge, acquirable through education, or as creative artistic work (Clavero 2009)[3]. This concept was different from the anthropological definition of culture that is at the core of multicultural debate today[4].

For the last thirty years, this trend has slowly changed and cultural identity has received increased attention, first in international law, then in national Constitutions, para-constitutional texts, and in European law[5] (Donders 2002; Eisenberg 2009). Is the recognition and protection of cultural identity at these different levels of government perceived in the same way? Is the conversation between them regarding, for example, concepts such as cultural rights, cultural defence, equality and diversity helping found a common legal tradition? Is law protecting cultural

---

principle that made theorizing positive actions difficult e.g. in favour of gender, or derogatory treatments in favour of groups e.g. cultural defence in courts.

[3] For example, the "right to participate in the cultural life of the community", stated in art. 27 of the Universal Declaration of Human rights 1948, was referred to this previous use of culture.

[4] I adopt a conventional definition of culture "as the set of distinctive spiritual, material, intellectual and emotional features of society or a social group" that "encompasses, in addition to art and literature, lifestyles, ways of living together, value systems, traditions and beliefs" (Preamble of UNESCO's *Universal Declaration on Cultural Diversity*, 2001). This legal definition reflects the anthropological definition of culture as a complex symbolic system composed of different elements and practices. At the end of the paper, this classical definition of culture is put into question by the idea of culture as a semiotic space in which communication occurs, and in which there are no fixed cultural practices.

[5] There are also other levels of government – outside of this analysis – that develop cultural discourses: regions and local governments. The revival of territorial cleavage has produced a new wave of federalism and regionalism often based on identity claims. There are three mains difference in regional claims that suggest keeping them separate from other cultural identities: 1) Regional diversity is, generally, not as strong as it can be in other minorities. The regions operate in a modernized State in which often the process of assimilation or of encountering of cultures has been accomplished. 2) Regional experiences of reclaiming identity often fit better into the post-materialist theorem (Inglehart 1977). According to this theory, identity politics are the consequence of a shift in values in post-war society: the fact that these societies have enjoyed a period of strong peace, widespread education, and the welfare State have changed the priority of values. The values in short supply become a sense of belonging, connection with the past, recovery of history, the environment, etc. – sorts of "luxury goods", that one can start to reach for when others basic needs have been satisfied. 3) In some regions identity claims mask financial claims. This makes the request less honest in the public sphere. This is for example, the case of the *Lega Nord* in Italy that has invented a "Celtic identity", according to which people of North Italy are different from those of the South, in an attempt to justify greater political autonomy and fiscal federalism.

identities because they are in a "state of injury" (Brown 1995) and a fight against discrimination is needed, or are other narratives emerging?

Keeping these questions on the horizon, my analysis proceeds as follows.

In the first part I provide an overview of the huge debate surrounding identity to summarize the theoretical roots from which legal discourses arises. Particular emphasis is given here to the interaction between personal identity and collective identities as explored by the five main theories: liberal, communitarian, cultural liberal, intersectional, and relational.

In the second part I focus on cultural identity and I illustrate how it is recognized by various legal texts. I explore in particular the difference and the changes in international law, European law, and nation states (selected in the area of Europe and North-South America). In international law cultural rights are described as minority rights (art. 27 of the *International Covenant on Civil and Political Rights* 1966), but also as rights of "everyone" (art. 15 of the *International Covenant on Economic, Social and Cultural Rights* 1966). Even if the connection to minorities is strong, cultural rights are acquiring the full status of human/universal/fundamental rights (Donders 2002 even with some reservations that lead the author to define cultural rights as the "Cinderella of the human rights family", 65). In nation states, cultural rights are not yet recognized everywhere and have, generally, the dimension of special/exceptional rights with uncertain positions in the rights and legal sources systems. I explore how both international, European, and sometimes national law have recently entered the constitutional conversation surrounding cultural rights with the idea that diversity is an important value for the majority as well, an idea that in some way subverts the concept of minority still dominant in mainstream cultural rights' rhetoric and narratives.

In the third part I concentrate on the importance of the legal conceptualization of diversity. Visualizing some examples of cultural interactions between native people in Canada and western society, it is possible to see how diversity fits perfectly into the idea of constitutional pluralism and how important it is to regenerate law. Through a narrative of diversity it is also possible to avoid some of the risks connected to anti-discrimination aims that surround identity politics. In fact, sometimes the discrimination paradigm, albeit unwillingly, helps perpetuate power structures and maintains a sense of vulnerability for minorities.

Ilenia Ruggiu

1. The debate on identity: an overview

This section tries to answer three preliminary questions: What does identity mean? When was it first introduced as a concept in the social sciences? What is the present status of the debate on identity?

1.1. DEFINITION OF IDENTITY: PERSONAL AND COLLECTIVE

Etymologically the word identity comes from the Latin *idem*, "the same", and shares the same root with words such as identify, identification, identity card, identical, etc. The word has been labelled with different adjectives: cultural, gender, class, sexual, age, religious, political, physical (e.g. able/disable), national identity, and more recently: cyborg, post-human, post-national, trans-national identity. All of them fit in a broader *summa divisio* that distinguishes between "personal" identity and "collective" identity.

According to a classic definition, personal identity expresses the core self that makes each of us unique, and the continuity of the personality; the condition or fact of being the same person throughout the various phases of existence[6].

Collective identity expresses the capacity to recognize oneself in a group, a community, with which the subject shares some characteristics. These characteristics of the group contribute in turn to building her/his own personal identity, and can be constitutive of the self.

The interactions between personal and collective identities can be considered the core of all identity studies that have articulated them in different ways (par. 1.3).

1.2. THE BEGINNINGS OF THE DEBATE.

There are two main answers to the question "when did identity studies start?"

---

[6] The concept of personal identity was deeply questioned throughout the 20th century, that is, by definition, the century of the crisis of the subject. After the discovery of the unconscious, the multiplication of personalities, the post-modern attacks on any fixed self, the dramatic revival of identity studies today seems almost nonsensical. But even if apparently contradictory, the identity debate is deeply rooted in the 20th century inheritance of the crisis of the subject. In fact today personal identity is no longer perceived as something that stands alone, but is generally the product of interactions with some form of collective identity.

If a continuity approach is adopted, the debate on identity started with the end of Cartesian's *cogito ergo sum*. The *cogito*, in fact, implicated a rationalist subject that could ontologically exist without any "other", without any connection to collective identities. In fact the source of its existence was inside its mental processes. It was Hegel's theory of recognition that broke with this approach and reclaimed the need for an "other" to build our personal identity, according to the dynamic described in the servant/master metaphor. This shift in philosophy put the sources of the self outside it, generating an interest in the ways in which it interacts with external identities.

If a discontinuous perspective is adopted, it was the psychologist Erikson who properly invented the concept of identity, when he coined the expression "identity crisis" in a study dedicated to adolescence (Erikson 1968). From psychology, the term spread to many other sciences: anthropology, sociology, social psychology, political science, and more recently law.

Constitutional law has been particularly sensitive to this debate given that the neglect or marginalisation of collective identities (gender, race, sex etc.) can represent an obstacle to the full achievement of substantial equality. At the same time constitutional law is founded on liberal-individualistic roots, and has serious difficulties in theorizing collective identities. This is the case of cultural identity explored in this paper.

It was international law that first gave recognition to cultural identity in 1966. In national law, the constitutional debate on culture started in 1971 in Canada[7] and was codified officially in the 1982 Constitution, considered the first multicultural constitution. Today more than 50 Constitutions around the world recognize cultural rights, especially for aboriginal people or for national minorities, but there is not yet a shared theory or *consensus* on cultural rights, and on the role of cultural differences in politics and courts of law.

1.3. INTERACTIONS BETWEEN PERSONAL AND COLLECTIVE IDENTITY

Five mainstream theories can be used to order the interactions between personal and collective identity: the liberal, the communitarian,

---

[7] It was the former Canadian premier Trudeau who, in 1971, coined the expression "multiculturalism", developing it from "biculturalism" in order to reflect that Canada was not only composed by two cultures (English and French-Quebecois) but that native people and immigrants also composed the cultural mosaic. The multicultural debate also started in Australia in 1974.

the cultural-liberal, the intersectional and the relational theory. All of them are relevant in better understanding the transformations in the way human dignity is perceived and the dynamics of discrimination. In fact identity has become, in the social sciences including law, what was once represented by the concept of "class": a category with which to analyze social groups, and to detect power structures in a more comprehensive way than those class permitted (Martin Alcoff 2003: 2).

Table 1. Liberal model

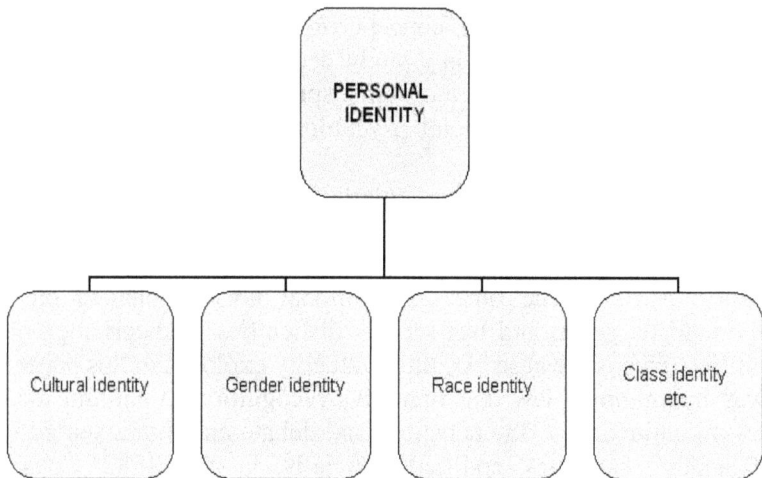

According to the liberal theory, the subject fully controls her/his own personal identity and, with complete freedom, chooses how to construct her/his self. No matter what the influences of different collective identities in which the subject is immersed are, she/he stands above all of them, controlling them with her/his will.

According to the liberal theory, discrimination can exist only against the single individual.

Consequentially, there is no space for cultural rights or group rights. Scared by the "blood and soil" mythology, the liberal theory wants a subject completely free by the State, but also by any group or community that can oppress him/her.

The task of constitutional law is to protect the individual with her/his subjective rights (civil, political, social rights). This model has been criticized for seeing the subject as an isolated and powerful Robinson Crusoe, without any connection with the external world and other people.

Table 2. Communitarian model

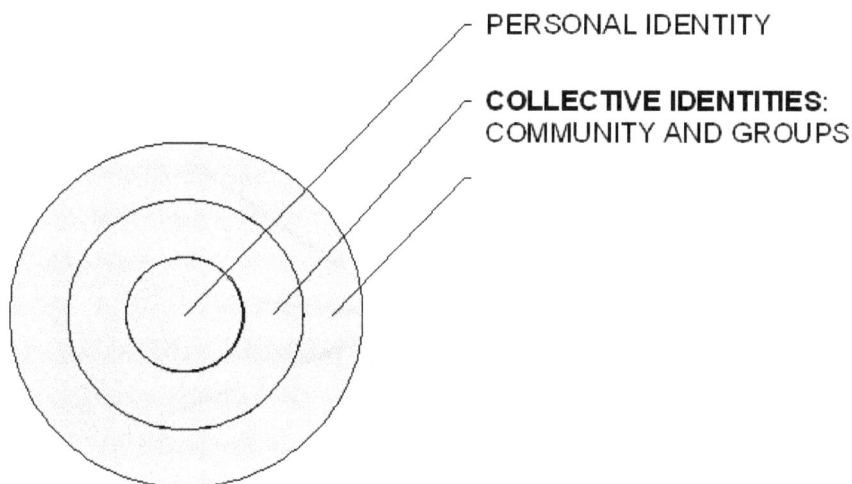

PERSONAL IDENTITY

COLLECTIVE IDENTITIES:
COMMUNITY AND GROUPS

According to the communitarian theory – on the contrary – the self is deeply shaped by the community in which it is inserted. Basically there is no difference between the individuals and the values that permeate their community.

If there is a lack of recognition, mis-recognition or an attempt to destroy that community, the personal identity of the subject is also automatically damaged.

Discrimination against a group is one of the most powerful tools of discrimination against individuals; the dignity of the self passes through the dignity attributed to the culture to which he/she belongs. Collective cultural rights are then required to protect the groups and indirectly the self.

This model has been criticized for not recognizing any margin of action and of freedom in the subject. In fact, communitarism does not consider that the self may feel constrained and oppressed by its own group and he/she may want leave (or change the culture of) the group.

Table 3. Cultural-Liberal model.

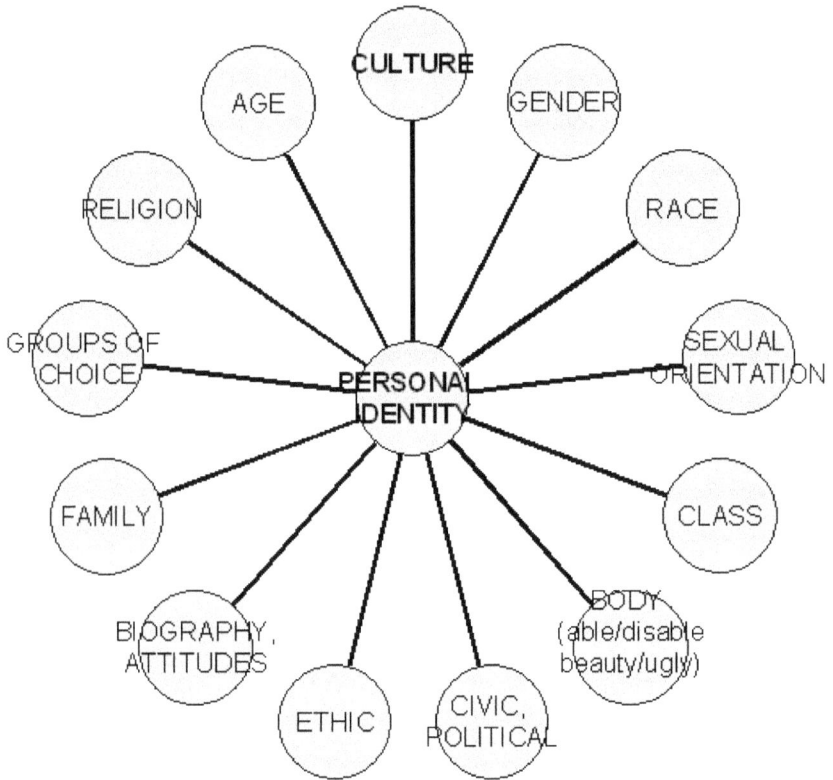

According to the cultural-liberal theory, the self is influenced by external groups, but also conserves some levels of autonomy (Robinson 2007). This theory is a synthesis of the two models described above. A subject's self-esteem could be compromised in the case of discrimination of one of the "pieces" of identity that are important in the construction of his/her personal identity. At the same time, the self can control which collective identity is given more importance (gender, race, nation etc.), and the interactions between the core self and external factors are more open. This model has been criticized for being too analytical in separating the different pieces that build personal identity, that are often more interrelated.

Table 4. Intersectional model.

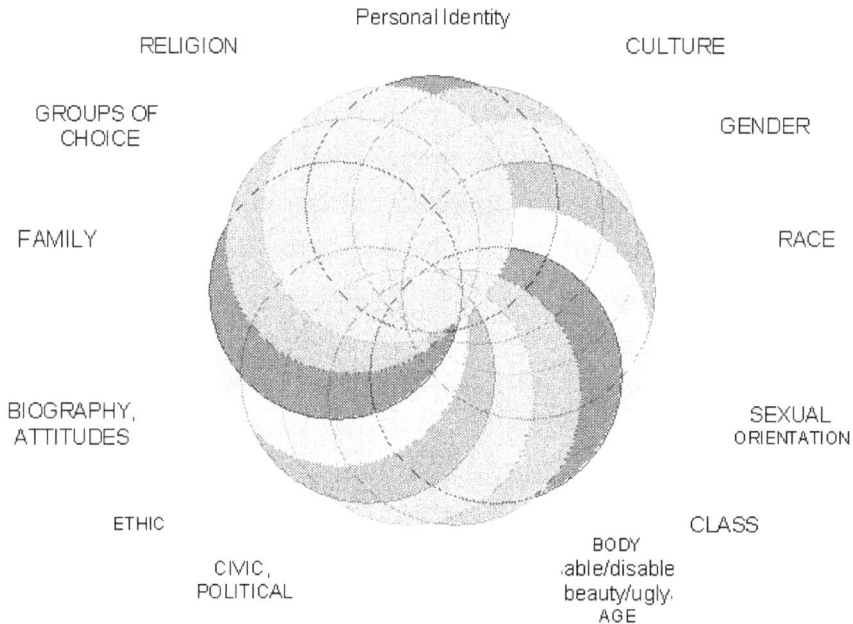

Personal Identity

RELIGION
CULTURE

GROUPS OF
CHOICE
GENDER

FAMILY
RACE

BIOGRAPHY,
ATTITUDES
SEXUAL
ORIENTATION

ETHIC
CLASS

CIVIC,
POLITICAL
BODY
able/disable
beauty/ugly,
AGE

According to the intersectional theory, there are no single pieces of different identities: they continually overlap, creating a complex, non-static, non-isolated interrelation that must be taken into account in order to better capture the problem of discrimination.

This theory was forged within black women's studies to demonstrate how gender identity could interact with race identity thus increasing the level of misrecognition (Crenshaw 1991). The theory was then extended to all fields of discrimination. Intersectionalism focuses its attention not only in cultural rights, but in politics of respect towards all different "pieces" of identity.

Ilenia Ruggiu

Table 5. Relational model

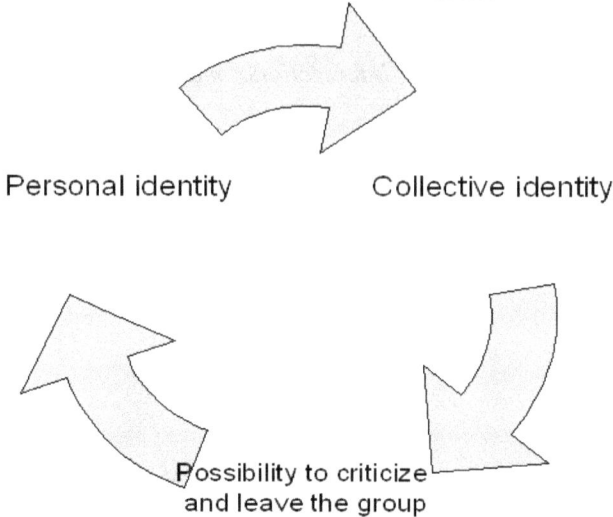

Personal identity   Collective identity

Possibility to criticize
and leave the group

According to the theory that can be called "relational" the distinction between personal and collective identity is not epistemologically correct. In fact groups are not external things independent of the subjects that constitute them. The subject is in constant, active relation to social positions rather then being entirely forged by them. In this model personal identity is seen basically as an agency – an agency that leaves open lots of possibilities for interaction between individuals and groups. For example, belonging to a minority could be considered and acted on by the subject as a reason for pride and strength, instead of shame, and this attitude can change other people's perspective thus reducing the risk of discrimination; or the subject can try to change the group's cultural practices, making criticisms and not applying the rules and behaviour of the majority of the group (internal dissent); or the subject can even decide to leave the group and assume a different collective identity. In general, in the relational model the group is not an "entity" impermeable to its members, or to other groups.

1.4. CRITICISMS OF IDENTITY

With regard to the third question posed at the beginning – what is the present status of the identity debate? – from one side, the category of identity appears very strong, and the five models described above are still followed, forming a shared dictionary between scholars. From the other side, scepticism regarding the epistemological validity of identity has increased. This section analyses some of the main criticisms (for further analysis see Dhamoon 2007).

One of the first attacks comes from Butler's statement that gender does not exist, it being only a question of performance (Butler 1990). This theory first referred to gender, but has been extended to other kinds of identities to affirm that the unfixed and fluid nature of any identity challenges the hard core of its definition: continuity. Identities appear "contradictory, partial, and strategic. With the hard-won recognition of their social and historical constitution, gender, race, and class cannot provide the basis for belief in 'essential' unity" (Haraway 1991: 155).

Notions of essentialist identities, (gendered, racial, ethnic, sexual, national, etc.) have also been challenged by other postmodern thinkers who have read them as narratives (Mohanty 2003). Introducing at best a Foucoultian approach, identities are no longer considered narratives that could help fight discrimination. On the contrary identity becomes a disciplinary tool that only perpetuates power structures. In fact individuals are predisposed to see themselves gendered, nationalized, race-defined, etc. instead of being free to relate to each other outside a fixed identity. There is more. When any of this collective identity is discriminated against, this situation blocks an emancipation discourse capable of looking to the future, because the subject cultivates a "wounded attachment" to an identity that results from a memory of pain and suffering (Brown 1995: 52-76).

Other criticisms of the category of identity claim we are entering a post-identity era based on the fact "that our culture has become so fragmented (ideologically and otherwise) so as not to allow for consensus about individual or community notions of identity"[8] (Rombes, Culik and Howard 1997).

According to other thinkers, the problem of identity lies in its academic use. The category is over-saturated with meanings and has ceased to have an epistemological function: if identity is everywhere it is nowhere (Brubaker and Cooper 2000).

Even if they do not declare themselves openly critical, other theories also indirectly put into question identity.

According to some scholars, the concept of identity itself may still be valid, but without all the traditional adjectives connected to it: cultural,

---

[8] But the same authors seem to recognize the validity of the category of cultural identity: "what might be termed a post-identity culture" is in the very end "a culture wherein these identities actually converse with each other" (Rombes, Culik and Howard 1997).

national, gender etc. In fact, new ways of identifying ourselves are arising, based on the feeling of global vulnerability (Brown 1995), or on post-human attitudes (Vint 2005) such as cyber identity. In this new description of identities, for example, national identity could disappear in favour of trans-national identity or in favour of post-national identity in which rather than the classic national elements (territory, language, religion, *ethnos*) other factors are crucial, such as the care for the environment, the sense of a common future, a commitment to diversity (see the European nation-building process).

Another indirect criticism of identity comes from the "personal nationalism" theory (Cohen 1996). According to this theory there is a great level of subjectivity and creativity in choosing single elements of a collective identity. For example national identity can mean different, and often opposite, things to different people. Similarly, the process that makes one feel like a woman, a transsexual, an aborigine, etc. can change personally. This high level of individual choice makes designating elaborate homogeneous characteristics to a group difficult.

Some scholars have stressed how identity is a sort of pick and mix business: lots of identities overlap in each of us and we can give different importance to each of them according to the context (Sen 2006)[9]. Others have observed how the process of identity building could be multiplied *ad infinitum* as new sub-identities arise every day. For example from the homosexual identity (GL) we passed to GLBT (gay, lesbian, bisexual, transsexual), then to queer, inter-sexual etc.[10]

Despite all this criticism, the category of identity is still used between scholars, and its use is increasing in legal lexicon.

1.5. CULTURAL IDENTITY

In this paper I focus on that kind of collective identity that is cultural identity. Critics of this concept are vocal also in this field, to the point of suggesting "multiculturalism without culture" (Phillips 2007). There is not yet any consensus around culture and cultural rights in law, and criticism of the possible reactionary effects of multiculturalism has been stressed

---

[9] According to other scholars, nevertheless, the fact that there are hierarchies of belonging do not put at risk the category of identity (Henderson 2007).
[10] National identities can be multiplied as well: e.g. even in the classical English/Scottish opposition, Scottish identity could be defined as north/south Scotland, urban/rural, or Edinburgh/Glaswegian, casting doubt even on the feasibility of speaking of Scotland as one identity.

(Eisenberg and Spinner-Halev 2005), but it is a matter of fact that the number of legal texts that make reference to cultural identity is constantly increasing.

The interest in cultural identity arises for two reasons: first, cultural identity is a field in which discrimination can occur regarding stereotyped or invisible cultural groups (Young 1990)[11]. Secondly, in this field we can see a slow shift in the perception of cultural identity by constitutional legal discourses, that could be summarized as: multiculturalism has been theorized in strict relation to the theory of recognition, as a tool to fight discrimination; today the protection of cultural identities reflects a new emerging value of diversity as something important not only for the specific minority protected but for the entire society. This shift deserves attention because, if it is confirmed and extended, it could be used to "rethink" all the other kinds of non-majority and non-dominant identities, including gender, and to re-elaborate the constitutional idea of dignity by making it more sensitive to elements of diversity and pluralism.

In order to better understand the constitutional aspects of the debate, in the following chapter I will start to show which are the constitutional consequences that depend on the moral source put at the base of recognition. Then I will give some examples of the codification of cultural identity.

2. Cultural identity in international, European, and national law

2.1 THE MORAL SOURCE OF CULTURAL IDENTITY, AND CONSTITUTIONAL CONSEQUENCES

It is understood that the category of cultural rights is still uncertain in constitutional theory. While the other three genres of rights – civil, political, and social – have full status of human and fundamental rights, cultural rights are not protected everywhere. The law recognizes cultural identity in different ways and intensity depending on the moral sources behind it, the legal value or good that the normative system wants to protect. The following table, that will soon be explained, tries to summarize the constitutional consequences according the moral source of cultural identity.

---

[11] Cultural Identity is a field of discrimination that regards stereotyped or invisible cultural groups. Following a shared classification there are three of these groups: national minorities, immigrants and indigenous people. The latter have gained an autonomous status within the national minorities (Kymlicka 1995).

Table 6.

Moral source, value to protect	Constitutional consequences
Personal identity, authenticity, human dignity	Cultural rights as human/universal right for everybody (international law)
Justice	Cultural rights not universal, but only for disadvantaged, invisible or stigmatized groups (international, European, national law)
Protection of minorities	Cultural rights for historical national minorities (European, national law)
Equality between citizens	Extension of equality principle to culture
Diversity of cultures as public good, human heritage	Constitutional principle of cultural diversity, universal cultural rights (European, international law)

If the moral source/legal good to protect is considered to be the strong relationship that cultural identity has with personal identity – according to the communitarian model or the theory of recognition (Taylor 1992; Honneth 1995) – the protection of cultural identity should be considered a constitutional task because culture is crucial for the individual, and the individual is the centre of the constitutional value system. "The right to culture is, thus, not only the right to identify with a group but the right to secure one's personality identity" (Margalit and Halbertal 1994). This "right to culture" consequentially must be universal and recognized for everybody, minorities and majority, without distinction with other constitutional rights. The reasons why cultural identity is important for personal identity can be different and have been explored by communitarians and cultural-liberal scholars. Preserving culture may be necessary to build a meaningful life (Robinson 2007) or to permit choices (Kymlicka 1995)[12] or to complete personal authenticity because cultural

---

[12] For an overview of the different positions of Kymlicka, from the idea of the instrumental role culture plays in people's ability to make meaningful choices and lead a self-directed existence, to the idea that culture is important for their secure and effortless belonging and their self-respect, and of the difficulty of moving between different cultures, see Courtois 2008.

identity is one of the sources of the self (Taylor 1992) that without recognition can suffer discrimination (Honneth 1995).

This approach that connects cultural identity with personal identity is partially followed by international law (e.g. art. 15 of the *International Covenant on Economic, Social and Cultural Rights* 1966; art. 20, 23, 29, 31 of the *Convention on the Rights of the Child*, New York, 1989, while art. 30 still contains a minority narrative). National law is still reluctant to fully adopt this approach.

A second moral source that could legitimate constitutional recognition of cultural identity is justice. Since the work of Iris Marion Young (Young 1990) *Justice's Culturalists* scholars (Benhabib 2002: 57[13]) have added culture as one of the fields in which injustices are perpetrated. Post-colonial studies particularly claim cultural recognition to compensate for injustices and discriminations suffered in the past.

Inside this approach we can find a group of scholars that slightly differ in their use of culture as a tool to promote justice and to fight discrimination. These scholars can be called *pragmatists* because they defend cultural claims with the consciousness that they are just a way to discuss other problems of distributive justice such as lost lands, poverty, natural resources exploitation etc. Cultural identity is used, in this context, as an instrumental political tool, as one of the many aspects of oppression, albeit not the main one (Macklem 2001[14]; Alfred 2005[15]; Markell 2005).

Nation states generally follow the cultural-justice approach. It permits the construction of cultural recognition as an "exception" accorded only to some minorities (e.g. ex colonies, aboriginal people) and denied to others (e.g. immigrants) toward which the state has not developed any obligation based on past discrimination; it does not subvert the principle of equality to which nation states are strongly attached and permits derogations only in certain conditions. This approach avoids also the problems connected with theorizing the new category of "cultural rights" because it permits saying that there is no need to put such rights at the same level as other universal/human or fundamental constitutional rights, and allows their classification as more restricted "minority rights", a kind of special rights.

Constitutional states are also comfortable with a possible third moral source of the recognition of cultural identity: the need to protect

---

[13] That observes: "claims to authenticity presuppose claims to justice".

[14] Macklem says that culture *per se* is not sufficient to justify aboriginal claims, and he uses three more elements: treaties, prior occupancy, prior sovereignty.

[15] The author stresses the importance of land-claims and the recovery of sovereignty as the main narrative that aboriginal people should utilise.

minorities. This is rooted in the DNA of constitutionalism based on the ideas of limiting power, and of protecting individuals – alone or as part of a minority – against majority rule. The constitutional consequence of this approach is to give recognition to national minorities within the state; these are minorities normally composed of people that are already citizens and that must be protected in front of the majority of the other citizens. There is no need to recognize a general right to cultural identity for everybody, such as immigrants.

A fourth moral source of cultural identity is identified in the equality between citizens, extended to the factor of culture (Eisenberg 2003). The constitutional consequence of this approach is a need to reformulate the constitutional principle of formal equality. Today, in fact, formal equality is affirmed regarding religion, nation, race, sex, gender, and often the "cultural" dimension is not present. A different discourse must be held regarding the principle of substantive equality: it already permits different treatment for different situations. In this sense perhaps it is sufficient to interpret the principle as evolving, extending it at a cultural level and permitting positive actions or derogatory treatments on a cultural basis (Tully 1995). In some senses, the fact that many national courts are using the cultural argument to make exceptions even in applying criminal law, could be considered as rooted in this constitutional framework.

A fifth moral source of cultural identity is found in the positive value that diversity has for the whole society. Anthropologists' ideas about the importance of preserving the ethno-sphere in order to have different ways of imagining the world and life have been translated into legal discourse especially by European law (see par. 2.3). Also at the international level there are soft law documents that reveal this shift in perception such as the UNESCO's *Universal Declaration on Cultural Diversity*, 2001, in which diversity is presented "as necessary for humankind as biodiversity is for nature", as "common heritage of humanity" (art. 1) and as a factor of development (art. 3)[16] and of creativity (art. 7)[17]. Very few constitutional states have explored this idea through the insertion of clauses in which multiculturalism is presented as "national heritage" (Canada and Brazil)

---

[16] According to the Declaration, cultural diversity "widens the range of options open to everyone; it is one of the roots of development, understood not simply in terms of economic growth, but also as a means to achieve a more satisfactory intellectual, emotional, moral and spiritual existence".
[17] Art. 7: "Creation draws on the roots of cultural tradition, but flourishes in contact with other cultures. For this reason, heritage in all its forms must be preserved, enhanced and handed on to future generations as a record of human experience and aspirations, so as to foster creativity in all its diversity and to inspire genuine dialogue among cultures".

or in which the ideas that "equality between all cultures" (Ecuador) and the "enrichment" of society (Guyana) are affirmed. The constitutional consequences of this approach would be: the disappearance from constitutions of the concept of cultural minorities in favour of the recognition of a broader principle of diversity in which all cultures (within the nation, but also brought from outside by immigrants) are equalized; the recognition of cultural rights as full human rights and universal[18]; the development of cultural politics not only to preserve, but also to promote cultural diversity.

Given this general background, in the following two sections I will explore the different perceptions regarding cultural identity in nation states and in the European context.

2.2. APPROACHES TO IDENTITY IN CONSTITUTIONAL STATES. CULTURAL RIGHTS AS MINORITY RIGHTS

As part of a broader project that aims to explore all of the world's nations, in this paper I analyze the presence of words such as identity, culture, multiculturalism, cultural minorities in the Constitutions of North and South American States (37 states with USA counting as one), and in the European Union area (27 states). Quantitatively the results are surprising: more than 50 Constitutions include these terms. Qualitatively, the recognition of cultural identity assumes, in the constitutional states analysed, two dimensions. The first is the building and reinforcing of national identity: national language, symbols (flags, feasts, etc.), national cultural heritage. The second is the protection of cultural minorities, that represents a second cultural order, normally pre-existing to the state in the same territory. Only in six Constitutions is there a third dimension: an echo of diversity as a public good through a reference to multiculturalism or inter-culturalism or pluri-culturalism[19].

---

[18] Art. 5 of UNESCO's 2001 Declaration states: "Cultural rights are an integral part of human rights, which are universal, indivisible and interdependent. The flourishing of creative diversity requires the full implementation of cultural rights as defined in Article 27 of the Universal Declaration of Human Rights and in Articles 13 and 15 of the International Covenant on Economic, Social and Cultural Rights. All persons have therefore the right to express themselves and to create and disseminate their work in the language of their choice, and particularly in their mother tongue; all persons are entitled to quality education and training that fully respect their cultural identity; and all persons have the right to participate in the cultural life of their choice and conduct their own cultural practices, subject to respect for human rights and fundamental freedoms".

[19] They are: Argentina, Brazil, Canada, Ecuador, Guyana, Mexico.

The countries of South America[20] have experienced the most significant constitutional reforms in order to recognize cultural identity. They refer to indigenous identity and reflect the above mentioned cultural-justice model (par. 2.1). Being the most recent to have been reformed (often precisely to give recognition to aboriginal cultural claims), some South American Constitutions incorporate the international idea of diversity as a factor that enriches the whole society.

In the North American area, the leading country in developing a cultural constitutional discourse is Canada. Here the reference to multiculturalism seems to equalize all cultures, and to see diversity as a public good (art. 27 of the 1982 Constitution: "multicultural heritage of Canadians"). A separate discourse must be held regarding the recognition of rights of aboriginal people: these are not based only on cultural difference, but on treaty rights (art. 35). The peculiar situation of aboriginal people in Canada, based on the fact that they were never conquered, creates a mix between a cultural and sovereignty discourse in order to legitimate various practices and ways of life.

Eastern European[21] constitutions represent a case of strong nation-building that go as far as protecting the identity of citizens abroad, but also contain different clauses to protect minorities. These clauses always refer to national minorities. Kosovo's Constitution is the most accurate in developing a cultural framework, for the existing minorities and with a general proclamation of a principle of equality between cultures and the idea that all communities deserve protection as "an integral part of the heritage of Kosovo".

In western European constitutions such cultural language is less present[22]. They seem to be neutral and indifferent to nation-building – with the

---

[20] The Constitutions in which words such as identity, culture, or multiculturalism are present are: Argentina (art. 75), Belize 1981 (preamble), Bolivia 1995 (art. 171), Brazil 1988 (art. 216, 221, 242), Canada 1982 (art. 25, 35, 27), Columbia 1991 (art. 7, 8), Chile 1980-2003 (art. 19) Costa Rica 1949-1999 (art. 76-89), Cuba (art. 39), Ecuador 1998 (art. 49, 62, 63, 64, 65, 66, 84), El Salvador 1983-2000 (art. 53, 62), Guatemala 1985-1993 (art. 57-65), Guyana 1980-1996 (art. 35), Honduras 1985-2005 (art. 153, 171), Mexico 1917-2001 (art. 2), Nicaragua 1987-1995 (art. 89-91), Panama 1972-1994 (art. 76-86), Paraguay 1992 (art. 25, 62, 73), Peru (art. 2, 17), Venezuela (art. 15, 98-111, 119, 121). Suriname and Uruguay make a general reference to national culture.

[21] The Eastern European Constitutions in which words such as identity, culture, or multiculturalism are present are: Albania (art. 4), Bulgaria (art. 6, 23, 54), Bosnia Herzegovina, Croatia (preamble; art. 15), Kosovo (art. 57-59), Poland (art. 6, 35, 73), Slovakia (preamble, art. 34, 44), Slovenia (art. 5, 61, 64), Czech Republic (preamble), Romania (art. 6, 7).

[22] Italy (art. 6), Spain (art. 1), Germany, France (art. 2), Switzerland (art. 69, 70).

exception of France which is the only Constitution that recognizes the national language, French, as official – but in practice there is a "banal nationalism" spread through everyday political and cultural life (Billing 1995) as the state controls many aspects of cultural reproduction. There is protection of named national minorities, but in general the recognition is limited to selected cultural elements (e.g. linguistic minorities)[23].

The European constitutions that recognize cultural rights do not however give them the full status of universal/human/fundamental rights. In this sense the majority of constitutional states still remain attached to the idea of nation as a compact group with minorities as exceptions to protect[24]. To summarize what emerges from nation states' constitutions we have to stress how the recognition is mostly based on some specific minority, named in the constitutions and pertaining to the nation's territory. In this scheme immigrants are always excluded, reflecting an attitude also described in Gianluca Bascherini's contribution in this book. The constitutional technique used is the recognition of specific "cultural rights" and not the statement of a "principle" of diversity. Cultural rights are often seen as in conflict with individual rights, and generally succumb before them (Eisenberg 1994).

2.3. APPROACHES TO IDENTITY IN EUROPE. FROM THE PROTECTION OF MINORITIES TO THE IDEA OF DIVERSITY AS PUBLIC VALUE

Moving from Constitutional States to the European Union, the two dimensions of cultural identity (national and minority identities) reappear (Van Ham 2001), but with deep differences.
Grimm's critique that Europe would never be legitimate until it had a *demos* urged the search for a European identity that could unify dispersed peoples. But other European narrative issues have slowly emerged and the attempt to build a European identity has become very different from the classical process of nation-building according to "political romanticism".

---

[23] The Italian Constitution has since 1948 (art. 6) protected linguistic minorities, and many Eastern European States have recently included similar provisions. This means that the cultural elements pre-selected by the Constitution are limited to language. On this ground, the Italian law 482/1999 refused the protection of Roma and Sinti languages with the justification they do not have a territorial link to any part of Italy.

[24] Among the many reasons that prevet States fully recognising diversity is the conflict between cultural and social rights. Some authors have observed how a high degree of diversity could compromise the welfare state because people are more inclined to share their wealth with people that are similar to them than with strangers (Alesina and Gaesler 2004). This thesis has also been criticized (Banting and Kymlicka 2006).

The EU could have chosen to insist on only one cultural identity (e.g. choosing English as common language or Christianity as the root religion), or even on a civic identity (values), professing itself to be culturally neutral. On the contrary European identity also incorporates cultural differences and is being constructed as a multicultural project. This multicultural project embraces both member states' cultures, and other cultural minorities.

The Preamble of the EC Treaty uses the plural: "foundations of an ever closer union among the *peoples* of Europe", that breaks the relationship between *ethnos* and *demos.*

Art. 151 of the EC Treaty demonstrates even better this multicultural project as extended to national and regional diversity: "The Community shall contribute to the flowering of the cultures of the Member States, while respecting their national and regional diversity and at the same time bringing the common cultural heritage to the fore". The equal recognition of the member states is accompanied by an anti-discrimination discourse (EC Treaty, art. 12).

Europe also uses the classic concept of *cultural minorities*

The European Charter of Regional and Minority languages of 1992 which was followed in 1994 by the *Framework Convention for the Protection of National Minorities* are examples of this approach. The *Charter of Fundamental Rights* (Nice 2000) includes, in chapter III, two articles on non-discrimination and on cultural, religious and linguistic diversity.

These legal texts are mainly based on the perception of diversity as something vulnerable (Brown 1995), rather than as a benefit. But they also contain the idea of diversity as a value per se, as something vital for democratic society. This new legal narrative emerges in the broader European context: alongside an anti-discrimination discourse (cultures must be equal and discrimination on the grounds of culture must not exist), there is a diversity discourse in which cultural differences are no longer perceived as a problem, but rather as a public good.

An example of this European approach can also be seen in the judgments' reasoning. There is a concern for anti-discrimination, but also a concern for the preservation of diversity as a source of wealth for the whole society. In the words of the European Court of Human Rights, there is "an emerging international consensus amongst the Contracting States of the Council of Europe recognising the special needs of minorities and an obligation to protect their security, identity and lifestyle... *not only for the purpose of safeguarding the interests of the minorities themselves but to preserve a cultural diversity of value to the whole community*" [25].

The European approach to diversity is more uniform then the national approach that selects which minorities are given recognition: all cultures are recognized, not only the ones that win their fight for recognition. Within this framework, it remains uncertain what is the situation of non-EU citizens that have migrated to Europe. A coherent development of the cultural diversity principle should imply that the value of diversity depends on the contribution of all cultures, not only on those that have citizenship. Nevertheless, the strong divide between Europeans' and non-Europeans' rights that Gianluca Bascherini notes in his contribution comes back in the selection of which minorities are recognized. The diversity that Europe celebrates is a diversity within Europe. Europe's multiculturalism is strictly a "European multiculturalism". It includes all the peoples "of Europe"; all the nations and also nations without State that are territorially based in Europe. This exclusion of migrants by way of the diversity framework of Europe is similar to the process that Silvia Niccolai demonstrates regarding the contribution of migrants' care work in fostering the rights of European women.

To summarize the results of this analysis, the legal narratives on cultural identity have deep differences. States strictly control the dynamics of recognition limiting it to the minorities they choose. Meanwhile European and international law is forging a general principle of diversity that could work as a general clause of recognition for every cultural group on the assumption that diversity is a good *per se*. This approach is actually only fully followed at international level, as Europe still seems tied to a Eurocentric approach. There are some changes in the State's perception of cultural diversity, which is starting to be seen as a value in the very few "multicultural" clauses.

After the analysis of the legal narratives on identity and diversity further reflection is needed. In fact this statement "diversity is a public good" made at supra-national level could seem to some apodictic or even naive. Why should diversity be considered a public good, a new constitutional value? Does the anthropologic idea of ethno-sphere deserve to be translated into law despite its potentiality to generate conflicts? Why does

---

[25] The case 27238/95 *Chapman v. the United Kingdom,* ECHR, 18 January 2001, regards a Gypsy that wanted to establish her caravan on land she owned but was refused by the city council because it risked compromising the aesthetic of the landscape. The ECHR recognized a general cultural right to nomadic life, a "right to live in a Gypsy way", but negated the violation of art. 8 in this case.

the idea of human dignity need a consideration of diversity? What are the advantages of introducing a diversity approach in constitutional conversations and in legal reasoning?

3. Beyond the identity-power connection

Identity studies have been strictly connected to power studies. With the exception of post-materialism (Inglehart 1977 criticized in James 2006) that gives an "aesthetic" explanation of the renewed interest in cultural diversity, all the other movements that have studied cultural differences declare that they want to reveal structures of power. "Culture" has become the substitute for "class" in fights against hierarchies, and all "identity politics" are generally constituted by marginalized groups whose numbers are continuously growing (Gutman 2003). Constitutional discourses, as we have seen, also connect the recognition of cultural identity to anti-discrimination aims. The recognition of different cultural identities is actually a powerful tool for the politics of respect and regarding anti-discrimination for neglected groups.

This reason alone would be sufficient to justify a general clause of recognition for all the cultures operating in the constitutional public sphere, instead of requiring a "fight for recognition" from every minority culture. Anyway, the fact of keeping within the anti-discrimination paradigm misses some other benefits of cultural diversity. For example it misses that the "majority" also have something to gain.

Let's try to explain this with some visual examples.

The pictures that follow have been taken during a research held in British Columbia, Canada. According to Cervati (2009a), Law can benefit in defining its changing values not only by written texts, but also by any other form of language such as visual language.

The different meaning and perspectives that can be developed in front of the same entity, are strongly evoked in these pictures that compare the views and perceptions of nature, territory and art in Native people and settlers.

As we will see, radically different views are not fated to collide: they can intermingle, transforming each other. And Law can help this process.

3.1. WHAT CAN YOU SEE HERE?

1. Nu na thca's territory, Vancouver Island, Tofino, Long beach, BC Canada.

2. Vancouver Island, BC Canada.

3. Cowichean river, Duncan, BC Canada.

A forest? Water?

Many of the Europeans that arrived in what is now called British Columbia, Canada, saw trees to cut, and rivers in which to find gold.

4. Mural, Chemanius, Vancouver Island, BC Canada

The native people that the Europeans called Indians, that still live there, see this:

5. "Reflections" by Darlene Gait, One Moon Art Gallery (www.onemoon.ca), Esquimalt Reserve, Victoria, BC Canada

6. "Legends" by Darlene Gait, One Moon Art Gallery, (www.onemoon.ca), Esquimalt Reserve, Victoria, BC Canada

7. "Letting go" by Darlene Gait, One Moon Art Gallery, (www.onemoon.ca),
Esquimalt Reserve, Victoria, BC Canada

They see an ancestral, spiritual territory, in which animals, humans and nature are "all connected". A land that is only borrowed from future generations. No property, according to the principle: "We cannot own the Land; the Land owns us". In the water, they see the blood of the Mother Earth; in the plants, their cousins.

The dialogue with indigenous identity has deeply influenced the global environment movement that imported many of its ideas from Indian spirituality and their animistic relationship with nature.

The law itself has been then regenerated by the contact with native culture. Concepts such as "environmental rights" have been created as result of a cultural interchange.

Also the "rights for future generations" have been inspired to western law by the native practice of taking decisions looking at the consequence of that decision for the next three or seven generations.

Let's see another example of different perspectives between majority and minority.

What can you see here?

8. Eagle Totem, Quw'utsun' Cultural and Conference Centre, Duncan, BC Canada

9. Long house, Royal Museum, Victoria, BC Canada

10. Long house, Tofino, BC Canada

Perhaps you see a strong, expressive primitive art.

Traditional American West Coast native art is bi-dimensional and the figures are static. There is no action, no movement. The founding myths of a native nation are generally narrated in totems put in front of the long houses. The rules of the iconography were solid, established and they excluded action and perspective.

Bill Reid, an artist from the Haida indigenous nation (now Queen Charlotte Island, British Columbia), after having experimented and study different artistic styles, came back to his community to rediscover native art. At the same time, the cultural contact with Western tradition had transformed his view of the world. He could not see the world as before this contact. He applied Renaissance ideas to Haida traditional art. These are the results:

11, 12, 13. The Raven and the First Men by Bill Reid (Haida), 1980. Courtesy
UBC Museum of Anthropology, Vancouver, Canada. Photo: Bill McLennan.

The traditional characters of the indigenous myths – eagle, raven, killer
whale, thunderbird, frog, salmon, etc. – start to move and act; the figures
become naturalistic and plastic. In Bill Reid's sculpture, Raven, the
mythical birth, arrives on the land just emerged after a flood and finds
mankind in a trembling shell. The hand of the man trying to exit the shell
expresses the effort of a first, slow movement – probably the first
movement registered in the Haida people's art. The dialogue between
traditional indigenous and western canons renews and inspires the
indigenous art movement.
Contact with different identities can change our horizons of meaning, our
view of the world. Integrating diversity into the public sphere, as a
common value, as a new constitutional principle, thus freeing diversity
from the narrow, even if useful, space of minority rights, could have two
very important results: fighting discrimination by integrating more
identities on an equal ground with a general clause of recognition for
every culture, in this way normalizing diversity; and increasing the
opportunity to build and enrich our personal identities.

3.2. CULTURES AS SEMIOTIC SPACES THROUGH WHICH LAW CAN REGENERATE
ITSELF

The examples given above allow us to see some aspects of cultural identity that are missed when keeping to a strictly anti-discriminatory discourse. Identity politics were raised to fight power and oppression, but legal discourses can also fall into a hierarchy despite their best intentions.
For example, "identity politics" in the American debate has been accused of imprisoning people in pre-determined roles, thus losing their potential for emancipation. As Giorgio Repetto observes, the recognition of transsexual identity does not avoid the influence of the heterosexual paradigm. At the same time, the recognition of cultural identity does not avoid the perception of the majority paradigm: the minority remains a minority, not a bearer of another way of life capable to put in question that of the majority. The principle of diversity is more consistent with what Silvia Niccolai writes in this book regarding the fact that "what a normal and worthy life is considered to be" should be kept as open as possible to permit the full realization of human dignity.
In this sense, even the creation of the new taxonomy of "cultural rights" for some minorities can consolidate power structures. Is it not, in some ways, an attempt to refuse a constitutional framework in which all the cultures are equivalent? Is it not a way of perceiving only "others" as bearers of culture, while the majority remains unconscious of also carrying cultural baggage[26]?
The concept of minority seems too narrow because "relegating" diversity to that minority (only those that have won their fight for recognition) does not appreciate the consequences for the rest of the society. The minority stays in its protected and isolated constitutional space, with its own set of "cultural rights" guaranteed, but without any recognition of its potential to change our view of the world. The insertion of a "cultural diversity principle" seems more coherent with the new idea of dignity for different reasons. First this principle serves in admitting that minorities are important not only for themselves, but for society. Secondly, this principle is also able to operate as a general clause of recognition, putting all cultures at the same level, instead of according recognition only to cultures able to affirm themselves in the public sphere (e.g. national

---

[26] An anthropological criticism to this attitude in western culture is well described in a famous paper "Body rituals among the Nacirema" (Miner 1956) in which the author describes the Nacirema (American spelt in reverse) as if they were a remote tribe under research.

minorities), and leaving others, weaker or more marginalized even to fight for recognition (e.g. immigrants) on the margins. Thirdly a constitutional principle of diversity is more coherent with the post-modern condition according to which the self has become de-centered and in need of the 'other' in order to discover itself.

If this approach to diversity is confirmed and if a common legal tradition arises, the theory of recognition that today is the most important philosophical justification of identity politics would also need a "revision". This theory is something that is strictly connected to an intimate need for the other, and is surely less solipsistic than the Cartesian *cogito*. Nevertheless this need for the other is, in some sense, affirmed for narcissistic reasons: I need the other in order to have a healthy and stable identity, the theory of recognition seems to say. The emerging value of diversity seems to reflect another existential need. I need the other in order to go outside myself, I need the other in order to regenerate myself, to see things that I cannot see while isolated in my cultural space, to see things and perspectives that, perhaps, make my life more meaningful.

Incorporating diversity in the constitutional value system makes culture be perceived, instead of as a fixed set of elements (language, dress, ceremonies, etc.) that need protection through cultural rights, as a semiotic space in which society, and consequentially law, can be regenerated with new meanings. These new meanings are extracted through an exercise of decentralization, putting the self in the place of the other and starting to see things through the eyes of others. The insertion of new meanings in the legal universe, the capacity of enriching the judicial interpretation of facts, and the constitutional conversation about what a dignified and meaningful life is, are all elements that fit into the idea of constitutional pluralism. Constitutionalism is used to distinguishing between pluralism and multiculturalism, stating that pluralism expresses different views inside the same society's expression of a unique vision of the world, while multiculturalism expresses different views that come from outside society and pertain to a completely different vision of the world (Zagrebelsky 2009: 200). In this sense the views that come from outside need to be submitted to a "stricter scrutiny" of compatibility with the constitutional values. This distinction is too narrow and, in my opinion, constitutional pluralism should include cultural pluralism in order to embrace new opportunities for law. In fact, constitutional pluralism has in some sense suffered a process of "domestication" insofar as it has been reduced to political pluralism: this reduction worked quite well in a context in which political visions were very different, but today the homologation of ideologies and the post-modern death of great political narratives has emptied the strength of political pluralism. In this context a revitalization of our legal system could come from cultural pluralism.

There are different ways to regenerate the law. One is inserted in a pathology of law that needs to be disobeyed and infringed; a second one could be more physiological and could be accomplished by the constitutional interiorization of the principle of diversity. Both are based on the idea that rules are open to the outside, and "the outside can reflexively fold back into the rules so that it can regenerate and transform them" (Bankowski 2001). Pluralism has been disciplined and reduced to political pluralism[27], but the possibility to think of completely new ways of life is kept alive by other cultures that have the potential to actually enrich our horizon of meaning. This is true also when dealing with difficult cases[28].

The normative situation that emerges from the analysis of statutory legal texts (par. 2.2 and 2.3) reveals how cultural recognition is fixed within a minority centred, protective, anti-discrimination discourse. But other fields of the legal system (part of the already quoted international and European law) reveal how pluralism of meanings is at the core of the constitutional attention to culture. This is the case of judicial interpretation in courts, and cultural defence (Foblets and Dundes Renteln 2009; Basile 2008). Scholars have already stressed how courts that use cultural arguments do not resolve cases as a clash between individual versus collective rights, but they concentrate more on discovering wheter

---

[27] I do not consider the question of ethical pluralism in this paper e.g. different positions regarding abortion, euthanasia, artificial procreation etc. In my opinion the strength of this conflicts weakens Zagrebelsky's distinction between pluralism and multiculturalism, demonstrating how in the same culture a different vision of the world can exist.

[28] The above described examples regarding Indigenous Nations could be accused of being too optimistic, and not capable of resolving hard cases that other kinds of cultural contact can generate such as genital mutilation or the use of burka or veil as a symbol of the oppression of women, etc. As Bascherini notes in his chapter to this book "openness to the reasons of others and to transformations" does not always mean "completely disfiguring ourselves". So I am not arguing that these cases must be resolved through a relativistic approach but I think that an anthropological perspective based on the attitude "what can you see here?" could help in better resolving the hard cases. Let's take the example of "barbaric rituals" (Gilman 1999: 57-64) such as the sexual mutilation of women. Firstly the suggested approach permits reading the behaviour of the parents not as directed to the voluntary damage of the child. Secondly contact with this practice can have a regenerating effect in perceiving other practices of our society. For example it helps to see plastic surgery from a different perspective, as a practice that expresses the same activity of controlling a woman's body. Thirdly this approach could suggest that a resolution such as the one found in Canada is possible regarding a symbolic mutilation practiced in hospitals, without any consequences for the child's body.

behaviours are identity-related (Eisenberg 1994: 9). I would add to this convincing argument that what motivates courts in using cultural arguments is the need to give space, in legal reasoning, to the different perspectives in front of the same situation that could arise from individuals belonging to different cultures or groups. Cultural defence is in fact also practiced in courts in those states where there is no recognition of any kind of cultural rights (e.g. Italy)[29] and it is, precisely, based on the need that law has to accommodate different ways of seeing things. This openness does not always avoid misunderstanding cultures through very well known phenomena such as reification[30] and allochronism[31], but in times in which political pluralism has been disciplined, attention to others cultures is increasing in importance as one of the few ways by which to regenerate law through a new semantic of actions, perspectives and behaviour.

---

[29] Corte di Cassazione, decision n. 44516/2008, November 28th, in which the charge against a Gypsy woman for begging with her child was reduced using the argument that this is a cultural practice of the Gypsy community (Cherchi 2009; Niccolai and Ruggiu 2009).

[30] The word reification was coined by Georg Lukacs to explain the extension of capitalist goods exchange mentality to all aspects of human life. In cultural studies the word is used to express the aptitude of seeing the other as an object, with a set of fixed cultural elements, and without the capacity to relate and interact with the outside world (Honneth 2007). A similar concept is included in the phenomena of essentializing a group that in legal reasoning produces the category of "frozen rights": rights conceded to aboriginal people on the condition that they respect the set of traditions they followed in the pre-contact period (for example they can fish but not sell the fish, because before contact with European they did not have commercial traditions, R. v. Van der Peet (1996) 2 SCR 507).

[31] Allochronism, from the greek "other time", is a term coined by the anthropologist Joahnnes Fabian to express the "denial of coevalness" that the observer, who was moving in a present, dynamic time, had with respect to the observed, perceived as fixed in a timeless past (Fabian 1983: 32). Allochronism is ubiquitous with a person/people in another time, especially in the past, and was very frequently used in colonial anthropology.

Immigration, Family Life and EU Citizenship: Challenges to the Concept of Human Dignity

Gianluca Bascherini

Synopsis. This paper focuses on immigrants' right to respect for family life, and more generally on the relationship between immigration and family life in Europe. These issues reveal interesting and often neglected connections between individual, social, cultural and political rights and at the same time have proved to be an arena for multiple cleavages of discrimination. Growing socio-cultural diversity in Europe, which is to some extent due to the migration flows tells us that if the rights involved in the relationship between migrations and family life are to be effective, they must not be considered as gender-neutral, or culture-neutral. In fact, these relationships reflect different cultures and views about family, work, and gendering of social roles and of relationships among individuals and groups, between parents and children, and between institutions and normative codes in the religious and public spheres. With regard to this, the paper briefly examines some recent developments involving immigrant's right to family life that have characterized the rulings of the European Court of Human Rights and of the European Court of Justice. In fact, these rulings may shed some light on important current trends in the construction of EU citizenship and on the EU mechanisms of *multilevel* protection of rights: trends which directly affect many sensitive problems of discrimination. Finally, the paper focuses on the challenges posed by immigration regarding key concepts such as human dignity, EU citizenship and the EU process of integration.
Keywords: Immigration, Family Life, EU Citizenship, European Court of Human Rights, European Court of Justice, Multilevel Protection of Rights, Human Dignity.

1. Introduction: immigration and family life

In talking about discrimination, an interesting perspective is provided by the legislative provisions and decisions regarding immigrants' right to family life. The fundamental right to family life is a right that enables the individual to become a person; it is a right that concerns the very first occasions to develop one's personality in a social context. Growing socio-cultural diversity in Europe, which is to some extent due to the number of migrants reaching Europe, tells us that if the right to family life is to be effective, it must not be considered as gender- or culture-neutral. In fact, family life reflects different cultures and views about family, work, and gendering of social roles and of the relationships among individuals and groups, between parents and children, and between institutions and normative codes in the religious and public spheres.

Family has proved to be a major instrument of eligibility to welfare benefits because "being a family member means also being entitled in the eyes of the State, public administration, society, and the public sphere" (Marella 2006: 95). On the other hand, the lack of an essential social buffer such as family is in itself a key to understanding the precarious condition of immigrants, especially during the early phases of migration. The right of immigrants to a family life, in fact, entitles them to major welfare rights, and therefore shows that the access to these rights plays a pivotal role in terms of promoting both social integration and individual freedom. The opportunities to access education, health care, housing and employment for immigrants in general, and for immigrant women in particular, constitute in fact an important support for the self determination of individuals and for the possibility for one person to make choices that differ from those of their families and communities of origin. The right of immigrants to family life reveals therefore interesting – and often neglected – connections between individual, social, cultural and political rights and at the same time has proved to be an arena for multiple cleavages of discrimination: gender, race, citizenship, and also, as is particularly evident in the Italian scenario, discrimination related to the kind of family life that one decides to build (based on marriage or *de facto* heterosexual or homosexual relationships)[1].

In recent years, family re-unification has become a major channel of immigration, due to the fact that the presence of immigrants has become increasingly stable, while entry for work reasons has become more and more difficult. At the same time, the increasing presence of settled immigrants means that the expulsion of first or second generation immigrants who commit crimes – or who simply reside in Europe 'irregularly' – produces particularly grave consequences for their family life and unity.

The theme of immigrant family life in Europe then leads to another area, touched on by Silvia Niccolai in her work, which concerns the relationship between immigration and the lives of European families. This

---

[1] A recent example regarding the family life of a non-EU citizen is seen in the ruling of the Italian *Corte di Cassazione*, n. 6441 of 17 March 2009, that rejected the request of a New Zealander man, already holder of a Permit of Stay for study, who had asked the Livorno Police Office to change the title to a Permit of Stay for family motives, based on the recognition of the *de facto* relationship with an Italian man by the relevant New Zealand authorities.

is particularly relevant in countries like Italy where, along with a drastic contraction in the public welfare offer, the role that immigrants, particularly women from non EU countries, have in caring for EU families is in fact an increasingly important one. The presence of these workers is part of the transformation of European life, be it 'productive' or 'reproductive', in turn transforming the gendering and structure of both forms of work[2].

The migration and family life of immigrants – such as the relationships, economic and otherwise, that develop between immigrants (predominantly women) and European families in the area of care work, which we will return to shortly – raise what are in some ways similar questions to those that regard female labour, gender policies, and the principle of anti-discrimination. In particular, the family life of immigrants urges us to rethink the relationships between market and society, on both the real and the symbolic levels; it proposes reflection upon the transformations of labour and upon repositioning the boundary between productive and reproductive labour; and it raises questions on the cornerstones of European anti-discrimination law, starting from the prohibition against sex and nationality based discrimination.

However, unlike what occurred in the European space for gender policies, thanks to the role played by the anti-discrimination principle within them, in the case of immigrants and their families the relationships between market and society operate towards a direction of exclusion, or at least one highly discriminatory with respect to EU citizens and, where applicable, their non-EU citizen relatives. That specifically European idea of dignity discussed by Silvia Niccolai in her report – an idea of dignity

---

[2] See in this book the contribution of Silvia Niccolai, at page 61, which underlines that today care "demonstrates a plausible sexed (or gendered) orientation, given that those who buy care are mostly EU women and those who sell it are mostly non EU women thus establishing a bridge. This, far from entailing a merely monetary exchange, is for both also an opportunity of citizenship, self-realization and a dignified life". In any case a rethinking of the confine between productive and reproductive work in Europe – that demonstrates how the specifics of care work, and the vast range of gender and citizenship relationships that characterise such work – clearly shows "that a very strong connection exists, between the European system's development potentialities and the perspective for social inclusion of the so called 'migrants' [and] that a link exists between European Employment Policies and European Migration Policies. As a matter of fact, this is a link very rarely considered. This lack of attention demonstrates how abstract and unrealistic [...] the European mainstream reading is of the market economy, people's needs, relationship between production and reproduction". See also, for a sociological analysis of care and domestic work from an international perspective, Lutz 2008 and Ehrenreich and A. R. Hochschild (eds.) 2003.

that invests heavily in the capacity of the market to perform as a socially inclusive player and is characterised by the rejection of "the idea that different social roles pertain to men and women, ordered along the divide between productive and reproductive work"[3]- doesn't seem to apply to immigrants and their families. The condition of third country national workers in fact remains disconnected from the possibilities of circulation and from the inclusive and participatory claims that national and European Community Law accord the European workers. Instead, there remains the force of the regulatory claims that legal systems attempt to exercise over immigrant labour, seeking to bend it univocally to the needs of the host country, and the weakening – in the case of foreign workers – of the claims for liberation and inclusion that characterize the European constitutionalism after the Second World War with regard to labour and citizenship. In the case of immigrants, labour is disconnected from the sphere of political participation and ends up to very prerequisite of residence: neither does it free immigrants to circulate on a par with citizens, nor does it convey dignity, respect, or recognition.

The importance that family re-unification has taken on as an immigration channel, the centrality of family life as a means of social integration and the social dynamics created through the existence of long-term immigrants raise important questions in front of the courts and give rise to the various attempts to regulate this issue both on a national and international level. With regard to this, I shall briefly examine recent developments involving family life that have characterized the decisions of the European Court of Human Rights (henceforth ECHR) and of the European Court of Justice (henceforth ECJ). I believe in fact that they may shed some light on important current trends in the construction of EU citizenship and on the European mechanisms of multilevel protection of rights: trends that directly affect many sensitive problems of discrimination.

2. Family life in Strasbourg...

In the ECHR case-law the ruling *Abdulaziz, Cabales, Balkandali* of 1985 has constituted a leading case both in terms of family re-unification of immigrants and sexual discrimination. The ruling maintained that the provision in British immigration law that differentiated the possibility of family reunification depending on the gender of the immigrant applicant

---

[3] *Ibidem*, at page 36.

already resident in the country, was discriminatory on the grounds of gender. Moreover, it was this ruling in which the ECHR for the first time stated that differences of treatment on the ground of gender are admissible only if they are founded on "very weighty reasons"[4]

The ECHR doesn't recognize the right of a third country national to either access or to non expulsion from the nation of residency for reasons related to family life[5]. Between the eighties and the nineties the ECHR -referring to a factual notion of family, aimed at protecting actual bonds which exist among the persons concerned, over and above their legal status - extrapolated from the right to respect for private and family life (art. 8 of the Convention for the Protection of Human Rights and Fundamental Freedoms, henceforth, the "Convention") some important limitations to State prerogatives concerning the access and expulsion of third country nationals.

---

[4] In considering art. 8, the Court has pointed out that as far as the positive obligations inherent in an effective "respect" for family life, "the notion of "respect" is not clear-cut". Furthermore, the judges underlined that "this is an area in which the Contracting Parties enjoy a wide margin of appreciation in determining the steps to be taken to ensure compliance with the Convention with due regard to the needs and resources of the community and of individuals ... In particular, in the area now under consideration, the extent of a State's obligation to admit to its territory relatives of settled immigrants will vary according to the particular circumstances of the persons involved. Moreover, the Court cannot ignore that the present case is concerned not only with family life but also with immigration and that, as a matter of well-established international law and subject to its treaty obligations, a State has the right to control the entry of non-nationals into its territory" (para. 67). As to the the allegation that the provisions in question amount to discrimination to the ground of sex as defined in articles 14 and 8, the Court has recognised that concerns about immigration control and protection of the domestic labour market may be considered as legitimate causes for different treatment, but "this does not in itself establish the legitimacy of the difference made in the 1980 Rules as to the possibility for male and female immigrants settled in the United Kingdom to obtain permission for, on the one hand, their non-national wives or fiancées and, on the other hand, their non-national husbands or fiancés to enter or remain in the country". So while undoubtedly "the Contracting States enjoy a certain "margin of appreciation" in assessing whether and to what extent differences in otherwise similar situations justify a different treatment", it is also true that "the scope of this margin will vary according to the circumstances, the subject-matter and its background" and that "the advancement of the equality of the sexes is today a major goal in the member States of the Council of Europe. This means that very weighty reasons would have to be advanced before a difference of treatment on the ground of sex could be regarded as compatible with the Convention" (para. 78).

[5] It is worth mentioning that many contracting States place limitations to the expulsion of foreigners for reasons connected to their family life and that the Parliamentary Assembly of the Council of Europe has adopted Recommendation 1504 (2001) on the non-expulsion of long-term immigrants.

The Strasbourg judges indeed recognized that the exclusion of a foreigner from the place where his or her family members reside, could interfere with the rights protected by art. 8 of the Convention; this interference, in order to be admissible, must be *"in accordance with the law"*, must have a legitimate objective and must be viewed as *"necessary in a democratic society"* and therefore proportional to the objective. During this period the ECHR developed on a comparative basis a set of common rules on this issue, aimed mainly at avoiding provisions which would hamper the integration processes of long-resident immigrants[6].

---

[6] The defense of family unity offered by the ECHR depends nonetheless on the positive or negative obligations which come from that protection for contracting States.

In the first case (for re-unification), the ECHR orientation is restrictive and recognizes the prerogative of State controls on immigration, and that immigration for family re-unification depends on the specific conditions in which the people involved find themselves (the ECHR pays particular attention to cases in which minors are involved) and that art. 8 of the Convention does not require contracting States to respect the choices of families regarding their place of residence (in ECHR case law regarding the theme of re-unification for minor children see for example - for a negative opinion - Case 23218/94, *Gül v. Switzerland*, 19/2/1996 and Case 21702/93, *Ahmut v. the Netherlands*, 28/11/1996, among decisions in which similar situations found violations of art. 8 see Case 31465/96, *Sen v. the Netherlands*, 21/12/2001 and Case 60665/00, *Tuquabo-Tekle and Others v. the Netherlands*, 1/3/2006).

The ECHR has a more lenient approach when considering the legitimacy of refusal to the issue of a residence permit to subjects who have already created (illegally) a family life in the country of residence. In those cases, the denial of a residence permit impacts on family relationships which have already been established and, although the ECHR establishes that the contracting States have not complied with its positive obligations, it follows an approach closer to decisions regarding provisions for expulsion. See for instance Case 44328/98 *Solomon v. the Netherlands*, 5/9/2000, where the Court outlines the criteria necessary for consideration of whether the rejection of a request for residence permit constitutes a breach of art. 8 of the Convention. According to these criteria, "Whether removal or exclusion of a family member from a Contracting State is incompatible with the requirements of Article 8 will depend on a number of factors: the extent to which family life is effectively ruptured, the extent of the ties in the Contracting State, whether there are insurmountable obstacles in the way of the family living in the country of origin of one or more of them, whether there are factors of immigration control (eg. history of breaches of immigration law) or considerations of public order weighing in favour of exclusion".

Greater protection for family reunification characterizes the ECHR decisions on the legitimacy of an expulsion decision which involves the negative obligations of contracting States to avoid impinging on existing family life. Similarly, the ECHR has confirmed several times that internal legislation must provide protective measures against arbitrary interference by public authorities and this is a key point as the ECHR has always denied application of art. 6 of the Convention for expulsion procedures (see for instance Case 50963/99, *Al-Nashif v. Bulgaria*, 20/6/2002 espec. para. 117-119 e 124-126). Equally relevant is the fact that the ECHR, when evaluating if an expulsion is "necessary in a

As is well known, from the second half of the 1990s onwards, some European countries have adopted reforms that gradually restrict the possibility for non-European citizens of family reunification, and these reforms have been essentially legitimated by their constitutional courts, despite their impact on the right to family life[7].

These trends have contributed to a partial *revirement* of the ECHR decisions in this area, mainly linked either to a changed perception on the part of this Court of the State's need for public order, or to the progressive Europeanization of immigration policies. Thus, since the late 1990s, the ECHR has become increasingly sensitive to the need for the States to control migration flows, giving more and more importance - in balancing these State needs against migrants' right to family unity - to issues such as: how serious were the crimes committed by the applicants, who are often second generation immigrants; whether links with the country of origin have or haven't been kept; whether the family ties in question were officially registered or only de facto. State restrictions to the right of family re-unification were thus often justified by the Court on the basis of the non marital nature of family relationships. Among the most recent decisions that best demonstrate this revised approach I would like to recall for instance the Case 46410/99, *Üner v. the Netherlands*, 18/10/2006, which shows the already mentioned attention that the judges in Strasbourg have recently given to State prerogatives in this area and that use the

---

democratic society", has reserved ample room for consideration of whether the measure adopted is proportional to the aim it intends to pursue. As far as the criteria which orient evaluations of the Court, see Case 54273/00, *Boultif v. Switzerland*, 2/8/2001, where the judges have stated that "In assessing the relevant criteria in such a case, the Court will consider the nature and seriousness of the offence committed by the applicant; the duration of the applicant's stay in the country from which he is going to be expelled; the time which has elapsed since the commission of the offence and the applicant's conduct during that period; the nationalities of the various persons concerned; the applicant's family situation, such as the length of the marriage; other factors revealing whether the couple lead a real and genuine family life; whether the spouse knew about the offence at the time when he or she entered into a family relationship; and whether there are children in the marriage and, if so, their age. Not least, the Court will also consider the seriousness of the difficulties which the spouse would be likely to encounter in the applicant's country of origin, although the mere fact that a person might face certain difficulties in accompanying her or his spouse cannot in itself preclude expulsion" (para. 48). On the ECHR case law on family life see e.g. Andriantsimbazovina 2002 and Bascherini 2007.

[7] Here I am thinking for instance of the Italian situation after the adoption of the "Bossi-Fini" law (2002) and of the French scenario after the laws "Sarkozy 1" (2003) and "Sarkozy 2" (2006). However, similar restrictions had already been introduced in other European countries that are traditional destinations of immigration flows, such as the UK, the Netherlands and Germany. See Bascherini 2008: 89-93.

margin of appreciation and the comparative argument to justify views of migrants' rights to family life which are more restrictive than previous EHCR case law[8]. At the same time, it must not be neglected that, in this decision, the Court made explicit "two criteria which may already be implicit in those identified in theBoultif judgment: the best interests and well-being of the children, in particular the seriousness of the difficulties which any children of the applicant are likely to encounter in the country to which the applicant is to be expelled; and the solidity of social, cultural and family ties with the host country and with the country of destination" (para. 58).

It isn't possible here to thoroughly analyse the overall path of the related decisions concerning the family life of migrants. I am more interested in recalling the important role it has played in the development of laws and decisions in Europe, both at the national and community level; the contribution it has made to a revamped and deeper public debate on the question of the integration of immigrants; the demand to more attentively asses changes in the presence of immigrants and to make the countries of immigration more aware of the structural nature of such a presence and of the changes it involves. To some extent, this also involves challenging the prevailing vision of migration flows, which is strictly utilitarian. In addition, while it is easy to highlight the swings in this case law and the different rigor with which, in accordance with its vocation, it evaluates the extent to which contracting States respect their positive and negative obligations, it is also true that this case law is on the whole open, sensitive to the new issues which immigration creates, and willing to safeguard family relationships and the interests of those most exposed to the consequences of measures which impinge on or break family unity[9].

---

[8] The joint dissenting opinion of judges Costa, Zupančič and Türmen and their concluding wish – "we would have liked to see this dynamic approach to case-law tending towards increased protection for foreign nationals (even criminals) rather than towards increased penalties which target them specifically" (para. 18) – provides a very clear summary of the doubts raised by this ruling, because of its favourable views about State decisions on expulsions, and because of its lack of attention to the experiences and needs related to the family life of the persons concerned.

[9] In the recent ECHR case law, see e.g., Case 1820/08, *Omojudi v. the United Kingdom*, 24/11/2009, in which the Court has condemned the United Kingdom for a violation of Article 8 of the Convention. In this decision – attaching "considerable weight to the solidity of the applicant's family ties in the United Kingdom and the difficulties that his family would face were they to return to Nigeria" (para. 46) – the Strasbourg judges have stressed in fact that, to be "necessary in a democratic society", a deportation of a third country national who commit crimes must be proportionate to the safeguard of its social and family ties.

3. ... and in Luxembourg

Moving on to the ECJ's decisions with regards to family life[10], it is important to note that these decisions, even though they are linked to those of the ECHR, differ from them in many aspects.

Indeed, these decisions show how the ECJ has moved further and further away from its original economic focus, towards an approach that is more focused on fundamental rights. Art. 8 of the Convention and the related ECHR decisions have played an important role in this process. Again, if we examine the changes in these decisions, we can identify two major phases, and the turning point between the two is represented by the proclamation of the Charter of Fundamental Rights of the European Union and by the adoption of some recent directives on the subject: the previously cited directive 2004/38, on the right of citizens of the Union to move and reside freely within the Member States, and directive 2003/86 on the right to family re-unification, which directly addresses the family life of immigrants[11]. At the same time it is important to remember the different margins of action within which the decisions of the judges of Luxembourg can move when they find themselves facing problems regarding the family life of EU citizens and their non-EU citizen relatives as opposed to the problems of families composed exclusively of third country nationals. In the first case, freedom of circulation is evidenced as

---

[10] It is important to remember that it was EC law that developed the institution of family re-unification (See articles 10 and 11 of Regulation (EEC) N. 1612/68 of the Council of 15 October 1968 on freedom of movement for workers within the EC, later modified by European Parliament and Council Directive N. 2004/38 of 29 April 2004 on the right of citizens of the Union to move and reside freely within the Member States) and established specific limits on expulsion (see in particular Council Directive 64/221/EEC of 25 February 1964 on the co-ordination of special measures concerning the movement and residence of foreign nationals which are justified on the grounds of public policy, public security or public health, and Council Directive 68/360/EEC of 15 October 1968 on the abolition of restrictions on movement and residence within the Community for workers of Member States and their families). In addition it must not be neglected the process of 'comunitarization' of policies on migration, which was developed starting with the Treaty of Maastricht and most significantly the Treaty of Amsterdam, moved the organs of the European Union and the ECJ to intervene on questions regarding family life of non-EC citizens.

[11] The tortuous proceedings for the adoption of this directive, the fact that Denmark, Ireland and the U.K. did not participate and the gaps the directives reveal between the principles it proclaims and its feeble contents, highlight the different concepts of family life which circulate in the European space, as well as the convergence of closure that characterizes national law in the matter of family life of immigrants. For details on the adoption and contents of this directive, see Sirianni 2006: 34-37.

a principle and a founding right of the creation of the EC, while in the second case, the question revolves around immigration and the margins of control which member States exercise on immigration.

In the first phase, what was considered essential was the link between family life and freedom of circulation: in other words, the channel through which the question of family life entered the sphere of competence of the ECJ was the freedom of circulation of European workers. In addition, in this phase, there was a development in the way in which ECJ case law in relation to art. 8 of the Convention and related ECHR case law interpreted the traditional and restrictive notion of family which had characterized the initial EC measures on that issue. At the same time, in order to efficiently guarantee an economic right such as workers' free circulation, the ECJ found itself intervening on matters, such as the theme of family life, on which it had no competence, and -as a consequence- it had to examine the possibility of distinguishing clearly between economic and civil rights or rather, between the economic dimensions and personal and social dimensions of rights connected to family life[12].

In a second phase, this link between family life and freedom of circulation became increasingly loose, and was finally replaced by the reference to the wider protections deriving from European citizenship: in this phase, European citizenship became increasingly focused on matters of residency and less on nationality. Emblematic of this shift is for instance the *Baumbast* decision, concerning an EU citizen, where the link between European citizenship and protection of family life is manifest[13]. On the

---

[12] The following decisions are emblematic of the dynamics and the connections between family life and freedom of movement: Case 249/86, *Commission of the European Communities v Federal Republic of Germany*, ECR 1989, p. 01263; Case 65/98, *Safet Eyüp v Landesgeschäftsstelle des Arbeitsmarktservice Vorarlberg*, ECR 2000, p. I-04747; Case 60/00, *Mary Carpenter v Secretary of State for the Home Department*, ECR 2002, p. I-06279; Cases 482/01 and 493/01, *Georgios Orfanopoulos and Others* and *Raffaele Oliveri v Land Baden-Württemberg*, ECR I-05257; Case 459/99, *Mouvement contre le racisme, l'antisémitisme et la xénophobie ASBL (MRAX) v Belgian State*, ECR 2002 p. I-06591.

[13] The basis for this change in case law by the Luxembourg Court can be found, rather than in the very brief arguments expounded in the Court decision (see para. 50, where the Court simply stresses that "freedom of movement for workers, requires, for such freedom to be guaranteed in compliance with the principles of liberty and dignity, the best possible conditions for the integration of the Community worker's family in the society of the host Member State"), in the Opinion of Advocate General Geelhoed, which highlights the need to update the interpretation of legal provisions, in view of the fact that working conditions have changed and so have family relations, while the court is more and more frequently asked to settle matters concerning non-EU nationals "Regulation No 1612/68 dates back to a time when family relationships were relatively stable ... The traditional family of course

other hand, as far as the direct condition of non-EU immigrants and of their families is concerned, an interesting position is expressed in Case 540/03, *Parliament v. Council* (ECR 2006, I-5769), on the directive 2003/86, where the ECJ dismissed the demand for annulment of the European Parliament but, relying on the jurisprudential instruments forged by the ECHR and on the best interest of the child, restricted the margin of appreciation and specified the positive duties that rest on the State in this regard.

The *Carpenter* decision for instance, is emblematic of the passage between the first and the second phase[14], and of recourse to art. 8 of the Convention in ECJ case law on family life, and also constitute an interesting example of the complementary nature of the means of protection of different national and European courts. In addition, this ruling, contemporaneously adopted with the promulgation of the Charter of Nice, upholds a more decisive commitment by the ECJ to protect fundamental rights and a certain convergence of approaches by the judges of Luxembourg and those in Strasbourg on questions regarding family life. The case regards a Filipino woman who is married to a British citizen. Served with an expulsion order, Mrs. Carpenter admits that she has no right of her own to reside in any Member State but claims that her rights derive from those enjoyed by Mr. Carpenter to provide services and to travel within the European Union. Mrs Carpenter, therefore, appealed against the deportation order with an argument for her right to stay based on her support of the professional activities of her husband -in that she took care of his children while he travelled around the EU for business- which is founded on the fundamental right to the free circulation of services recognised in art. 49 EC of the Council Directive 73/148/EEC. The judges in Luxemburg put forward that the case did not rest entirely on the Community Dispositions cited, tending to concentrate more on the woman's right to family life. The Court acknowledged the relationship between family life and freedom of circulation, and that in this case the

---

continues to exist but has become much less dominant amongst the forms of cohabitation in the Western world. Family relationships and forms of cohabitation have become less stable and more varied ... An additional factor is that families in which the spouses are of different nationalities or where children of other nationalities are present are occurring more and more frequently, precisely as a result of the increasing mobility of persons. These families may include nationals of non-Member States" (para. 23).

[14] See also, more recently: Case 1/05, *Yunying Jia v. Migrationsverket*, ECR 2007, I-1; Case 127/08, *Metock and Others v Minister for Justice, Equality and Law Reform*, not yet reported; Case 291/05, *Minister voor Vreemdelingenzaken en Integratie v R.N.G. Eind*, ECR 2007, I-10719.

provision of the former facilitated the latter, and in its decision chose to concentrate on the right to family life contained in Article 8 of the Convention, and to the relative Strasbourg case-law (para. 39) and its connection with freedom of circulation, thus guaranteeing with a new intensity the right to family life for non-EU citizens[15].

Also on these ECJ decisions , it isn't possible in this context to reconstruct the whole process (see, e.g., Ninatti 2007 and Tryfonidou 2009). I would like just to underline two points.

Firstly, until the end of the nineties, the Strasbourg Court was the icebreaker in the protection of immigrants' right to family life. Now the most interesting dynamics and openings come from the judges of Luxembourg, particularly as regards non-EU citizen relatives of European citizens. This seems an interesting element, not for the purpose of defining a hierarchy of the European courts, of finding out which is the most 'constitutional' of the courts, but for the purpose of studying the European processes of multilevel protection of rights not from a rigid and systematic perspective, but rather from a perspective that pays attention to the real ongoing processes and to the concrete interests at stake. Decision 540/03 shows us an ECJ that, pressed by the European Parliament and building on the contributions of ECHR decisions, has engaged the EU in a deeper discourse about fundamental rights, while at the same time engaging national judges in a court-to-court dialogue, encouraging them to redress the *defaillances* of national legislation, the scope of which was also restricted by the Court itself, using rights-based arguments. Decision 540/03 also shows that the ECJ is acting more and more as a judge of fundamental rights and confirms the "bursting in of the rhetoric of balancing in ECJ decisions", due mainly to the "growing pressure of the fundamental rights' discourse on the economic dynamics of the free market" (Vespaziani 2007: 545).

Secondly, I would like to call attention to the ambiguities which can be concealed within the calls for EC citizenship as a general rule for non-discrimination in the area of family life, as to the risks that these ambiguities may create another vector for discrimination and exclusion. In

---

[15] See *supra* Niccolai at pages 65-66 on *Carpenter* ruling as paradigm of a "change in the tenor of the demands of justice which reach the Court" and of the "importance that non-EU women's work has towards the functioning of the European social and economic model". Carpenter, therefore, as an example of the "demands for recognition that demonstrate the new dislocation of work and care in Europe today, and signal a common sense in change in which care work start to discover its own dignity, and thereby, while claiming recognition for its importance also for prduction, it can thus emancipate itself from a symbolic subordination toward the latter".

fact, these calls strengthen the protection of the right to a family life for EU citizens and their non-EU citizen relatives, reducing the importance of the economic roots of such a right for these persons, re-evaluating the criteria for residence and therefore de-linking protection for family life (but we could say the same for all social rights and in part for political rights) from nationality and the conditions of the worker, and, lastly, increasing the protection of 'mixed' family units which constitute an important element in intercultural relationships and integration.

The picture changes when we come to the right to family life for non-EU nationals, at least for those families that do not include EU citizens. In fact, although it is true that, in recent EU case law, State prerogatives on the control of immigration tend to be restricted with the aim of defending fundamental rights linked to family life, it is also true that in those decisions, regain importance the economic motives to protect family rights in the EC area and the prerogatives of state control and management of migratory flows.

In this way, a clear distinction is created in the protection of family life in the EC area, and this distinction includes both the principles and the values on which the recognition of those rights stand, and both the form and concrete content of protections which characterize the notion of family life when referred to EU citizens as opposed to non-EU citizens. While protection of the rights of families which include Europeans are no longer rooted in nationality and employment status, for non-EU families, the trend is to strengthen the bond between nationality, employment status and the protection of these rights, in a perspective of exclusion. Consider on the one hand the 'double penalty' (imprisonment and expulsion) which strikes a non-EU citizen who commits a serious crime[16] and, on the other hand, the different extension in terms of degree of relationship and form of cohabitation which for the purposes of re-unification, characterizes the EU citizen vs. the non-EU citizen and the different social rights recognized for the members of the two families[17].

---

[16] In the majority of the member States of the Council of Europe, second-generation immigrants may be deported by the authorities on the ground that they have been convicted of a criminal offence. Eight member States have provided in their laws that second-generation immigrants cannot be deported on the basis of their criminal record or activities: Austria, Belgium, France, Hungary, Iceland, Norway, Portugal and Sweden. Apart from Iceland and Norway, this protection is not confined to those who were actually born in the host country but also applies to foreigners who arrived during childhood (varying from before the age of three in Austria to before the age of fifteen in Sweden).

[17] Tryfonidou 2009: 648-652 underlines two other problems in the ECJ "*liberal approach*" characterizing cases such as *Carpenter*, *Eind* and *Metock*. First, this approach could give

4. Family life of immigrants in the EU space, from citizenship to discrimination

The picture sketched and, in particular, its recent developments are cause for pessimism: immigration is changing from a question of public order to one of national in/security. The militarization of the control of entry into the EU space produces victims[18] but does not reduce the percentage of illegal entries and unregistered migrants, while the politics of integration reveal greater evidence of their fragility and their use as tools of short term national interest. The European picture on the subject is nevertheless highly dynamic, open to different outcomes. We will have to examine very carefully the consequences that might emerge, in the area of multilevel protection of the right to family life of non EU citizens, from the adoption of the Charter of Fundamental Rights of the European Union and, in terms of procedures, from the introduction of an urgent preliminary ruling procedure for dealing with cases related to the area of freedom, security and justice. And while so far the Luxembourg court has intervened only in cases of families that included EU nationals, it is possible that in the future claims to a direct application of the provisions included in directive 2003/86 may be submitted to that court.

In any event, so far I think we can say that immigration seems to constitute an *Unheimlich* (Freud 1919) of European citizenship: something that is somehow very familiar to it, and at the same time is set aside and silenced. And this perturbing aspect relates to the possibility of circulation of workers and their families, which isn't only at the base of the European construction, but has also contributed to giving a certain social dimension to European citizenship. In this context, migration poses important political challenges to the European integration process and to the kind of citizenship that is being defined within that space. Especially if

rise to a problem of reverse discrimination; in fact, since the Court may have decided to extend EC human rights protection to all *moving* Union citizens, or, in other words, to all Union citizens who can point to a link with more than one Member State, Union citizens who fail to satisfy those linking requirements will continue to be excluded from that protection. Secondly, "the feasibility of this new approach in light of the possibility of the Treaty of Lisbon coming into force and its effect of making the EU Charter of Fundamental Rights binding, appears to be questionable, since the scope of application of the Charter is obviously narrower than the scope of application of EC human rights protection under this new principle and, in fact, may even be narrower than the current scope of EC human rights protection as developed in the Court's case-law". See also Jacobs 2007.

[18] From 1988 to 30 September 2009 14,835 immigrants are documented to have died while trying to enter Europe (source: Fortress Europe).

the aim is that of promoting an idea of citizenship capable of tackling the ethnic and gender discrimination that has historically marked national citizenship development.

Immigrants are central to the transformations in European citizenship. There are risks but also potentialities; the rights-based claims advanced by migrants on the issue of citizenship seem to confirm that citizenship is still a vibrant notion, as long as it is approached from a historical perspective, rather than as an absolute notion, and, last but not least, as long as it responds to the challenges posed by these movements of people (Benhabib 2004: especially 171-182 and 209-211). Problems tied to the family life of immigrants and, more broadly, to the relations between immigration and (EU and non-EU) family life, require in other words a rethinking of the key concepts of the current discussion on the EU constitution regarding citizenship and rights, beginning from the concept of human dignity: a concept that in mainstream discourse is treated as a typical product of 'Western' civilization and encapsulated in a rigid dogma in order to create an unchangeable normative principle. Various contributions in this book make reference to the articulation of new interpretations of dignity, that have been elaborated and encouraged by European anti-discrimination law and some of these emphasise the importance of enlarging the paradigm of dignity with respect to culture and the needs of immigrants in the Community space[19].

Human dignity and other similar clauses can open important perspectives in the development of European constitutional rights and constitutional law if their significance and contents are broadened by identifying the axiological foundation in the dialectic of "becoming" and trying at the same time, to paraphrase the title of the book written by D. Chakrabarty,

---

[19] In the conclusion to his chapter Giorgio Repetto (p. 149) notes that in the Maruko case a notion of dignity concerning homosexuals "rooted in the specificity and in the variety of human desires" and that "the contribution of law, and particularly of anti-discrimination, can be that of challenging not only the formal machinery of rights, but even the symbolic horizons they bring, which continuously tend to reinforce and legitimate patterns of social exclusion". In Silvia Niccolai's contribution, already cited, this re-reading of the concept of dignity is connected to the transformations taking place in Europe of the relationships between productive and reproductive work, and between the market and society. For Ilenia Ruggiu this new dimension, specifically European, can also be linked to affirmation within European discourse on cultural identities and minority rights of a cultural diversity principle that sees in diversity a "public good"- capable of enriching the constitutional conversation by introducing "new meanings in juridical universe" (p. 182) through the problematization of the points of view – that go outside of the typical prospects expressed by the ordinances of EU states – which see in diversity an exception to the general of protecting only those minority groups seen as "weak" or "disadvantaged".

to "provincialize human dignity" (Chakrabarty 2000) – in other words, to search not for a conceptual equivalent but an approximation that avoids rigid readings of those cultures and deepening ethical contents, interior dynamics of attitudes and the relational contexts of opening. This is an idea of dignity taken from a "modern humanism" (Said 2004), that avoids the shallows of the political correctness of multiculturalism and the eddies of fetishising the idea of diversity; that banks on importing democracy and not exporting it. It is an idea that works towards an enlargement of the visual outside of that narrow minded euro-centric view, and that attempts to favour a direct understanding of those realities, returning to cultivate the connection between rights and the other social and human sciences and keeping in mind that the work of a 'comparatist' moves constantly within the tension between *same* and *different* (Legrand 2003).

In this light there is little to be gained by rigid dogmatisation (Nussbaum 2000: 19, speaks of an intuition of human dignity): dignity is allowed to fulfil its function when we think of it as the horizon of deliberative research in which jurists play an important role. Jurists, as interpreters of the values of coexistence, are called to challenge cultural closure, opening a debate on EU constitutional values as a starting point for the comprehension of current matters and identifying values which can be shared within and among communities which are ethically, culturally and socially diverse; exploring the contradictions and conflicts which characterize diverse experiences and the relationships between these experiences without neglecting the changes which characterize them. Cultural and juridical pluralism is crucial to the processes of European integration and should induce jurists to compare different juridical solutions and different argumentative and dogmatic perspectives. It should induce jurists, in other words, to be more open to a comparison which is not aimed at diminishing the complexity and differences between juridical cultures but which creates reciprocal respect, pays attention to changes and is characterized by an open-minded and factual approach (Cervati 2009b: 237 ff. and 250 f.).

Questions linked to the family life of immigrants do not merely claim inclusion in the "world as it already was, but a transformation of it, and firstly of its interpretative and linguistic keys, of the processes of assigning value, recognizing needs, and naming experience" (Niccolai 2010: par. 2). From this perspective there could be an enlargement of the juridical dynamics regarding dignity to include the claims and conflicts that come from the immigrant component of the European population. Such a process could come from a critical rethinking of the antinomic narration of dignity, which is specifically European. This would be an idea of dignity that opposes the "ancient" idea of dignity (moralizing, aristocratic and unequal; a dignity of saints, cavaliers and gentlemen, based on the actions and the virtues of a single individual) with a "modern" dignity of Kantian origins (liberating, egalitarian, and genetic: a sort of nutshell of a human being considered in isolation and abstractly, but in reality much more concretely described as European, male, white, well off and mainstream, safe from economic hardship or social isolation). Today this "modern" conception of dignity no longer seems adequate; it no longer responds to the demands of justice that are presented, because the claim for dignity today does not regard only an isolated or individualistically abstract subject, but regards at the same time collective needs and choices. Today the migration and family life of immigrants require investment in an idea of dignity that can be translated into a "relationship ethic" capable of putting into discussion those traditional attributes of intangibility, absoluteness and rigidity, and capable therefore of taking into account the specific historical context in which they take place, along with the actual players and contents, yet capable at the same time of conserving the attention to the individuality and the egalitarian spirit that have characterised its developments in the constitutionalism after the Second World War. It is an idea of dignity that works against forms of reification of the human being[20] and focuses attention on the quality of relationships, especially in the situations "at the limit" (situations that generally regard the body of the individual, but not only, as is clearly demonstrated by questions regarding immigration, can also regard the 'social body'); an idea that promotes a recognition that means openness to the reasons of others and to transformations, but without completely disfiguring ourselves (Pech 2001: 91)[21].

---

[20] In the area of immigration, this idea of dignity has induced various courts to prohibit the repatriation of immigrant women that risk undergoing genital mutilation in their country of origin. V. ad es. T.A. Lyon, 12 .6. 1996, and, more recently House of Lords, 19. 10. 2006, *Secretary of State for the Home Department v. K. Fornah.*

[21] On the theme of recognition, worthwhile inspiration for reflection on the relationships that today tie the elaboration of the concept of dignity, migratory dynamics and the role that jurists are called upon to play in the process can be found in the writings of Ricoeur 2005 and Honneth 1995.

Works Cited

Adamietz, L. and Schreier, M. (2008) 'Antidiskriminierungsrichtlinie: Witwerrente eines eingetragenen Lebenspartners?', *Europäisches Wirtschafts- und Steuerrecht*, 5: 195.

Andriantsimbazovina, J. (2002) 'Le mantien du lien familial des étrangers', in Sudre F. (ed.), *Le droit au respect de la vie familiale au sens de la Convention européenne des droits de l'homme* (Bruxelles: Bruylant).

Agustín, L.M. (2007) *Sex at the Margins* (London & New York: Zed Books).

Alesina, A., Glaeser, E. (2004) *Fighting Poverty in the Us and Europe: A World of Difference* (Oxford: Oxford University Press).

Alfred, T. (2005) *Wasáse: Indigenous Pathways of Action And Freedom* (Peterborough: Broadview Press).

Alter, K.J. and Vargas, J. (2000) 'Explaining Variations in the Use of Litigation Strategies', *Comparative Political Studies*, vol. 33, n. 4: 452.

Andall, J. (2000) *Gender Migration and Domestic Service. The Politics of Black Women in Italy* (Aldershot: Ashgate).

Anderson, B. (1983) *Imagined Communities: Reflections on the Origin and Spread of Nationalism* (London: Verso).

Baer, S. (2009) 'Il diritto all'uguaglianza nella Carta dei Diritti Fondamentali dell'Unione europea', in Rossilli M. R. (ed.), *I diritti delle donne nell'Unione Europea. Cittadine Migranti Schiave* (Roma: Ediesse).

Bagni, S. (2008) 'L'argomento comparatistico nel dibattito parlamentare sulla procreazione assistita', *Politica del diritto*, XXXIX, no. 4: 635.

Bankowski, Z. (2001) 'Law, Love and Legality', *International Journal of the Semiotics of Law*, 14: 199.

Banting, K. and Kymlicka, W. (eds.), (2006), *Multiculturalism and the Welfare State. Recognition and Redistribution in Contemporary Democracies* (Oxford: Oxford University Press).

Barbera, M. (2002) 'Not the Same. The Judicial Role in the Community Anti-Discrimination Law Context', *Industrial Law Review*: 82.

Barbera, M. (2003a) 'Eguaglianza e differenza nella nuova stagione del diritto antidiscriminatorio comunitario', *Diritto del Lavoro e delle Relazioni industriali,* No. 3-4: 399.

Barbera, M. (2003b) 'The Unsolved Conflict: Reshaping Family Work and Market Work in the EU Legal Order', in Hervey, T. and Kenner, J. (eds.), *Economic and Social Rights under the EU Charter of Fundamental Rights. A Legal Perspective* (Oxford, Portland Oregon : Hart).

Barbera, M. (2007) 'Il nuovo diritto antidiscriminatorio: innovazione e continuità', in M. Barbera (ed.), *Il nuovo diritto antidiscriminatorio* (Milano: Giuffrè).

Barnard, C. (ed.), (2007a) *The Fundamental of EU Law Revisited. Assessing the Impact of the Constitutional Debate* (Oxford: Oxford University Press, Academy of European Law, European University Institute).

Barnard, C. (2007b) 'Introduction. The Constitutional Treaty, the Constitutional Debate and the Constitutional Process', in Barnard, C. (ed.), *The Fundamental of EU Law Revisited. Assessing the Impact of the Constitutional Debate* (Oxford: Oxford University Press, Academy of European Law, European University Institute).

Bascherini, G. (2007) *Immigrazione e diritti fondamentali. L'esperienza italiana tra storia costituzionale e prospettive europee* (Napoli: Jovene).

Bascherini, G. (2008) 'Las políticas migratorias en Europa: una visión comparada', *Revista de Derecho Constitucional Europeo*, 10: 49.

Bascherini, G. (2009) '*Ex Oblivione Malum*. Appunti per uno studio sul diritto coloniale italiano', *Rivista critica del diritto privato*, 2/XXVII: 245.

Basile, F. (2008) *Immigrazione e reati "culturalmente motivati". Il diritto penale nelle società multiculturali europee* (Milano: Cuem).

Beck, G. (2007) 'The State of EC Anti Sex Discrimination Law and the Judgment in Cadman, or how the legal can become political', *European Law Review*, 32(4): 549.

Bell, M. (2002) *Anti-Discrimination Law and the European Union* (Oxford: Oxford University Press).

Benhabib S. (2002) *The Claims of Culture* (Princeton: Princeton University Press).

Benhabib, S. (2004) *The Rights of Others. Aliens, Residents and Citizen* (Cambridge: Cambridge University Press).

Berkovitch, N. (1999) *From Motherhood to Citizenship. Women's Rights and International Organizations* (Baltimore and London: Johns Hopkins University Press).

Billing, M. (1995) *Banal Nationalism* (London: Sage).

Bock, G. and Thane, P. (eds.), (1992) *Maternity and Gender Policies: Women and the Rise of European Welfare States, 1880s-1950s* (London: Routledge).

Bock, G. (2000) *Frauen in der Geschichte Europas. Vom Mittelalter bis zur Gegenwart* (München: Beck).

Bonini Baraldi, M. (2008) 'La pensione di reversibilità al convivente dello stesso sesso: prima applicazione della direttiva 2000/78/CE in materia di discriminazione basata sull'orientamento sessuale', *Famiglia e diritto*, 7: 660.

Brown, W. (1995) *States of Injury. Power and Freedom in Late Modernity* (Princeton: Princeton University Press).

Brubaker, R. and Cooper, F. (2000) 'Beyond "Identity"', *Theory and Society*, 29/1, February: 1.

Burri, S. and McColgan, A. (2008) 'Sex-Segregated Services', European Network of legal experts in the field of gender equality, European Commission, Directorate-General for Employment, Social Affairs and Equal Opportunities, Unit EMPL/G/2 (http://ec.europa.eu/social/BlobServlet?docId=1773&langId=en).

Burri, S. and McColgan, A. (2009) 'Sex Discrimination in the Access to and Supply of Goods and Services and the Transposition of Directive 2004/113/EC', European Network of legal experts in the field of gender equality, European Commission, Directorate-General for Employment, Social Affairs and Equal Opportunities, Unit EMPL/G/2 (http://ec.europa.eu/social/main.jsp?catId=732& langId=en).

Butler, J. (1990) *Gender Trouble: Feminism and the Subversion of Identity* (New York/London: Routledge).

Caiani, L. (1957) *I giudizi di valore nell'interpretazione giuridica* (Padova: Cedam).

Caracciolo Di Torella, E. (2005) 'The Goods and Services Directive: limitations and opportunities', *Feminist Legal Studies*, 13: 337.

Caton, F.L. (1999) 'Feeling Romantic-Thinking Postmodern: Notes on Postcolonial Identity', *Post Identity*, 2/2: 22.

Cavarero, A. (1987) 'Per una teoria della differenza sessuale' in Diotima (ed.), *Il pensiero della differenza sessuale* (Milano: La Tartaruga).

Cavarero, A. and Restaino, F. (eds.), (2002) *Le filosofie femministe* (Milano: Bruno Mondadori).

Ceccherini, E. (ed.), (2008) *La tutela della dignità dell'uomo* (Napoli: Editoriale Scientifica).

Centini, M. (2007) 'La tutela contro gli atti di discriminazione: la dignità umana tra il principio di parità di trattamento ed il divieto di discriminazioni soggettive', *Giurisprudenza costituzionale*, 3: 2405.

Cerrone, F. (2009) 'Alessandro Giuliani: un'idea di ragione critica, dialettica e controversiale per il diritto', *Archivio di diritto e storia costituzionali*, (http://www.dircost.unito.it/dizionario/pdf/Cerrone-AlessandroGiuliani.pdf) and *Sociologia (*forthcoming 2010).

Cervati A.A. (2009a) *Per uno studio comparativo del diritto costituzionale* (Torino: Giappichelli).

Cervati, A.A. (2009b), 'Integrazione europea e valori costituzionali comuni', in Cervati, A.A., *Per uno studio comparativo del diritto costituzionale* (Torino: Giappichelli).

Chakrabarty, D. (2000) *Provincializing Europe. Postcolonial Thought and Historical Difference* (Princeton: Princeton University Press).

Cherchi, R. (2009) 'I diritti dello straniero', in Cherchi, R. and Loy, G. (eds.), *Rom e Sinti in Italia. Tra stereotipi e diritti negati* (Roma: Ediesse).

Cichowski, R. (2001) 'Judicial Rulemaking and the Institutionalization of European Sex Equality Policy' in Stone, A., Sandholtz, W., and Fligstein, N., (eds.) *The Institutionalization of Europe* (Oxford: Oxford University Press).

Cigarini, L. (1995) *La politica del desiderio* (Parma: Nuove Pratiche).

Cigarini, L. (2008), 'Un'altra narrazione', in Buttarelli, A. and Giardini, F. (eds.), *Il pensiero dell'esperienza* (Milano: Baldini Castoldi Dalai).

Ciliberti, R. (2001), 'Il diritto tra sviluppo della tecnologia biologica e problematiche etiche', *Materiali per una storia della cultura giuridica*, XXI, no. 2: 463.

Clavero, B. (2009) 'Why Are Only Indigenous Peoples Internationally Entitled to a Specific Right to Their Own Culture?', Lecture at the Columbia University, 21st January 2009 (http://clavero.derechosindigenas.org).

Cohen, A.P. (1996) 'Personal Nationalism: A Scottish View of Some Rites, Rights, and Wrongs', *American Ethnologist*, 23(4): 802.

Collier, R.B. and Collier, D. (1991) *Shaping the Political Arena. Critical Junctures, the Labor Movement, and Regime Dynamics in Latin America* (Princeton: Princeton University Press).

Collins, D. (1975) *The European Communities: the Social Policy of the First Phase* (London: Martin Robertson).

Commaille, J. (1998) 'Une sociologie politique du droit de la famille. Des référentiels en tension: émancipation, institution, protection' in J. Pousson-Petit (ed.), *Liber amicorum Marie-Thérèse Meulders Klein. Droit comparé des persons et de la famille* (Bruxelles: Bruylant).

Costello, C. (2003), 'Gender Equalities and the Charter of Fundamental Rigths of the European Union', in Hervey T. and Kenner J. (eds.), *Economic and Social Rights under the EU Charter of Fundamental Rights. A Legal Perspective* (Oxford, Portland Oregon: Hart).

Courtois, S. (2008) 'A Liberal Defence of the Intrinsic Value of Cultures' *Contemporary Political Theory* 7: 31.

Craig, P. and de Búrca, G. (eds.), (2008) *EU Law. Text, cases, and materials* (Oxford: Oxford University Press).

Crenshaw, K.W. (1991) 'Mapping the Margins: Intersectionality, Identity Politics, and Violence Against Women of Color', *Stanford Law Review*, 43, July: 1241.

Crompton, R. (2006) *Employment and the Family. The Reconfiguration of Work and Family Life in Conteporary Societies* (Cambrigde: Cambridge University Press).

Davis, A.Y. (2003) *Are prisons obsolete?* (New York: Seven Stories).

De Witte, B. (2005), 'The Trajectory of Fundamental Social Rights in the European Union', in De Búrca, G. and De Witte, B. (eds.), *Social Rights in Europe* (Oxford: Oxford University Press).

Deakin, S. and Browne, J. (2003), 'Social Rights and Market Order: Adapting the Capability Approach', in Hervey, T. and Kenner, J. (eds.), *Economic and Social Rights under the EU Charter of Fundamental Rights. A Legal Perspective* (Oxford, Portland Oregon: Hart).

De La Porte, C., and Pochet, P. (eds.), (2002) *Building Social Europe through the Open Method of Co-ordination* (Brussels: Peter Lang).

Dhamoon, R. (2007), 'The Politics of Cultural Contestation' in Arneil, B., Deveaux, M., Dhamoon, R., and Eisenberg, A. (eds.) *Sexual Justice/Cultural Justice: Critical Perspectives in Political Theory and Practice* (London: Routledge).

Donners, Y.M. (2002) *Towards a Right to Cultural Identity?* (Antwerpen, Oxford, New York: Intersentia).

Dorsen, N., Rosenfeld, M., Sajó, A., and Baer, S. (2003) *Comparative Constitutionalism* (St. Paul: West).

Ehrenreich, B. and Hochschild, A. R. (2003) *Global Women. Nannies, Maids and Sex Workers in the New Economy* (London: Granta).

Eisenberg, A. and Spinne-Halev, J. (eds.), (2005) *Minorities within Minorities. Equality, Right and Diversity* (Cambridge: Cambridge University Press).

Eisenberg, A. (1994), 'The Politics of Individual and Group Difference in Canadian Jurisprudence' *Canadian Journal of Political Science/Revue Canadienne De Science Politique*, 27/1: 3.

Eisenberg, A. (2003) 'Difference and Equality: Three Approaches to Cultural and Sexual Difference', *Journal of Political Philosophy*, 11 (1): 41.

Eisenberg, A. (2009) *Reasons of Identity. A Normative Guide to the Political and Legal Assessment of Identity Claims* (Oxford: Oxford University Press).

Ellis, E. (1998) *EC Sex Equality Law* (Oxford: Clarendon Press).

Ellis, E. (2005) *EU Anti-Discrimination Law* (Oxford: Oxford University Press).

Erikson, E.H. (1968), *Identity: Youth and Crisis*, (London: Faber & Faber).

European Commission (2006) *Roadmap for equality between women and men* (2006-2010) (http://ec.europa.eu/social/main.jsp?catId=738&langId=en& pubId=12&furtherPubs=yes).

Fabian, J. (1983) *Time and the Other. How Anthropology Makes Its Object* (New York: Columbia University Press).

Florio, S. (2009), 'I diritti delle donne e il ruolo del Sindacato Europeo', in Rossilli, M.R (ed.), *I diritti delle donne nell'Unione Europea. Cittadine Migranti Schiave* (Roma: Ediesse).

Foblets, M.C. and Dundes Renteln, A. (eds.), (2009) *Multicultural Jurisprudence. Comparative Perspectives on the Cultural Defense*, (Oxford, Portland Oregon: Hart).

Forlati Picchio, L. (1991) 'Il lavoro delle donne nella normativa internazionale', *Rivista internazionale dei diritti dell'uomo*, no. 2: 429.

Foucault, M. (1979) *History of Sexuality vol. I: An Introduction* (London: Allen Lane).

Fraser, N. (2009). 'Feminism, Capitalism and the Cunning of History' *New Left Review* 56 (Mar/Apr): 97.

Fredman, S. (2001) 'Equality: A New Generation?', *Industrial Law Journal* 30: 145.

Fredman, S. (2002) *Discrimination Law* (Oxford: Oxford University Press, Clarendon Law Series).

Fredman, S. (2006) 'Transformation or Dilution: Fundamental Rights in the EU Social Space', *European Law Journal* 12: 41.

Fredman, S. (2008) *Human Rights Transformed. Positive Rights and Positive Duties* (Oxford: Oxford University Press).

Freixes Sanjuáb, T. (1999) 'Constitución, Tratado de Ámsterdam e igualdad entre hombres y mujeres', in *Consolidación de derechos y garantías: los grandes retos de los derechos humanos en el siglo XXI* (Madrid: CGPJ).

Freud, S. (1999) 'Das Unheimliche' (1919) in ID., *Gesammelte Werke* vol. XII (Frankfurt am Main: Fischer).

Frevert, U. (1985) 'Fürsorgliche Belagerung: Hygienebewegung und Arbeiterfrauen im 19. und frühen 20. Jahrhundert', *Geschichte und Gesellschaft* 11: 420.

Giddens, A. (1992) *The Transformation of Intimacy. Sexuality, Love and Eroticism in Modern Societies* (Cambridge: Polity Press).

Gilman L. (1999) 'Barbaric rituals', in J. Cohen (ed.) *Is multiculturalsim bad for women? Susan Moller Okin with respondents*, (Princeton: Princeton University Press).

Giuliani, A. (1966), *La controversia. Contributo alla logica giuridica* (Pavia: Tipografia del libro).

Gómez-Sánchez, Y. (2005), 'Dignidad y Ordinamiento Comunitario', *Revista de Derecho Constitutional Europeo*, n. 4 (http://www.ugr.es/~redce).

Gonzáles Rivas, J.J. (2003) *La Constitución española de 1978: Estudios sistemático y jurisprudencial* (Madrid: Civitas).

Guaglione, L. (2007) 'Le discriminazioni basate sul genere', in Barbera, M. (ed.), *Il nuovo diritto antidiscriminatorio* (Milano: Giuffrè).

Guariello, F. (2007) 'Il ruolo delle istituzioni e della società civile', in Barbera, M. (ed.), *Il nuovo diritto antidiscriminatorio* (Milano: Giuffrè).

Gutmann, A. (2003) *Identity in Democracy* (Princeton: Princeton University Press).

Haas, P.M. (1992). 'Introduction: epistemic communities and international policy coordination', *International Organization* 46(1): 1.

Häberle, P. (1998) *Verfassungslehre als Kulturwissenschaft* (Berlin: Duncker&Humblot).

Häberle, P. (2003) 'La dignità umana come fondamento della comunità statale', in Häberle, P., *Cultura dei diritti e diritti della cultura nella storia costituzionale europea. Saggi* (Milano: Giuffrè).

Habermas, J. (2004) *Il futuro della natura umana. I rischi di una genetica liberale* (Torino: Einaudi).

Hantrais, L. (1995) *Social Policy in the European Union* (Basingstoke: Macmillan).

Haratsch, A., Koenig, C. and Pechstein, M. (eds.), (2006) *Europarecht, 5. völlig neu bearb. Aufl.* (Tübingen: Mohr Siebeck).

Haraway, D.J. (1991) *Simians, Cyborgs, and Women: The Reinvention of Nature* (New York: Routledge).

Hardt, M. and Negri, A. (2004) *Multitude* (London: Penguin Books).

Heintz, B. and Schnabel, A., (2006) 'Verfassungen als Spiegel globaler Normen? Eine quantitative Analyse der Gleichberechtigungsartikel in nationalen Verfassungen', *Kölner Zeitschrift für Soziologie und Sozialpsychologie*, 58, n. 4: 685.

Henderson, A. (2007) *Hierarchies of Belonging. National Identity and Political Culture in Scotland and Quebec* (Montreal and Kingston: McGill-Queen's University Press).

Hobsbawm, E.J. (1990) *Nations and Nationalisms since 1870. Programme, myth, reality* (Cambridge: Cambridge University Press).

Hochschild, A.R. (2000) 'Chains of Love', *The Guardian*, 8 March.

Honneth, A. (1995) *The Struggle for Recognition: The Moral Grammar of Social Conflicts* (Cambridge: Polity Press).

Honneth, A. (2007), *Reificazione. Uno studio in chiave di teoria del riconoscimento* (Roma: Meltemi).

Hooghe, L. and Marks, G. (2001) *Multi-Level Governance and European Integration* (Lanham: Rowman and Littlefield).

Hoskyns, C. (1996) *Integrating Gender. Women, Law and Politics in the European Union* (London:Verso).

Hoskyns, C., Niccolai, S. and Stewart, A. (2009) 'Disability Discrimination by Association: Social and Legal Implications of the ECJ Ruling in *Coleman*', Paper given at *Complexity, Conflicts and Justice* Conference in Onati, Spain, International Institute of the Sociology of Law, 7-10 July.

Hoskyns, C. and Rai, S.M. (2007) 'Recasting the Global Political Economy: Counting Women's Unpaid Work', *New Political Economy* 12(3): 297.

Iacub, M. (2004) *L'empire du ventre: pour une autre histoire de la maternité* (Paris: Fayard).

Inglehart, R. (1977) *The Silent Revolution: Changing Values and Political Styles Among Western Publics* (Princeton: Princeton University Press).

Jacobs, F. G. (2007) 'Citizenship of the European Union – A Legal Analysis', *European Law Journal*, 13: 591.

James, M. (2006) *Misrecognized Materialists. Social Movements in Canadian Constitutional Politics* (Vancouver-Toronto: Ubc Press).

Jepperson, R.L. (1991) 'Institutions, Institutional Effects, and Institutionalism', in Powell, W.W. and Di Maggio, P. (eds.), *The New Institutionalism in Organizational Analysis* (Chicago: University of Chicago Press).

Joerges, C. (2004) 'What is left of the European Economic Constitution?', *European Law Review:* 461.

Kessler-Harris, A., Lewis, J. and Wikander, U. (1995) 'Introduction', in Wikander, U., Kessler-Harris, A. and Lewis, J., *Protecting women: Labor Legislation in Europe, the United States, and Australia, 1880-1920* (Campaign: University of Illinois Press).

Kilpatrick, C. (2001) 'Gender Equality: A Fundamental Dialogue' in Sciarra, S. (ed.), Labour Law in the Courts. National Judges and the European Court of Justice (Oxford: Hart).

Kronsell, A. (2005) 'Gender, Power and European Integration Theory', *Journal of European Public Policy* 12(6): 1022.

Kymlicka, W. (1995) *Multicultural Citizenship: A Liberal Theory of Minority Rights* (Oxford: Clarendon Press).

La Rocca, D. (2007) 'Le discriminazioni nei contratti di scambio di beni e servizi', in Barbera, M. (ed.) *Il nuovo diritto antidiscriminatorio* (Milano: Giuffrè).

LeBaron, G. (2007), 'The "New Constitutionalism" and Social Reproduction: Capitalism, Enclosures and Everyday Life', Draft paper prepared for presentation at the British International Studies Association conference at Cambridge University, December 17-19, 2007.

Legrand, P. (2003) 'The same and the different', in Legrand, P. and Munday, R. (eds.), *Comparative Legal Studies: Traditions and Transitions* (Cambridge: Cambridge University Press).

Lewis, J. (ed.), (1993) *Women and Social Policies in Europe: Work, Family and the State* (Aldershot: Edward Elgar).

Lewis, J. and Giullari, S. (2005) 'The adult worker model family, gender equality and care: the search for new policy principles and the possibilities and problems of a capabilities approach', *Economy and Society* 34: 76.

Lewis, J. and Rose, S.O. (1995) 'Let England Blush. Protective Labor Legislation, 1820-1914', in Wikander U., Kessler-Harris A. and Lewis J., *Protecting women: Labor Legislation in Europe, the United States, and Australia, 1880-1920* (Campaign: University of Illinois Press).

Libreria delle donne di Milano (eds.), (1987) *Non credere di avere dei diritti. La generazione della libertà femminile nell'idea e nelle vicende di un gruppo di donne* (Torino: Rosenberg & Sellier).

Lubin, C. and Winslow, A. (1990) *Social justice for women. The International Labor Organization and Women* (Durham and London: Duke University Press).

Lutz, H. (ed.), (2008a) *Migration and Domestic Work. A European Perspective on a Global Theme* (London: Ashgate).

Lutz, H. (2008b), 'Introduction', in Lutz H. (ed.), *Migration and Domestic Work. A European Perspective on a Global Theme* (London: Ashgate).

Macklem, P. (2001) *Indigenous Difference and the Constitution of Canada* (Toronto: University Of Toronto Press).

Mancini, G.F. and O'Leary, S. (1999) 'The new frontiers of sex equality law in the European Union', *European Law Review*, 24: 331.

Marella, M.R. (2006) 'The Non-Subversive Function of European Private Law: the Case of Harmonisation of Family Law', *European Law Journal*, 12: 78.

Margalit, A. and Halbertal, M. (1994) 'Liberalism and the Right to Culture', *Social Research*, 61-3: 491.

Marinelli, A. (2008), 'La cura come unità di misura nella costruzione del territorio', in Cosentino, V. and Longobardi, G. (eds.), *La vita alla radice dell'economia* (Verona: Quaderni del Maeg).

Markell, P. (2005) *Bound By Recognition* (Princeton: Princeton University Press).

Marshall, T.H. (1950), *Citizenship and Social Class* (London: Pluto Press reprinted 1987).

Martìn Alcoff, L. (2003) 'Introduction. Identities: Modern and Postmodern', Martìn Alcoff, L. and Mendieto, E. (eds.), *Identities. Race, Class, Gender And Nationality* (Oxford: Blackwell).

Martin, D. (2006) *Égalité et non-discrimination dans la jurisprudence communautaire. Étude critique à la lumière d'une approche comparatiste* (Bruxelles: Bruylant).

Masselot, A. and Caracciolo di Torella, E. (2001) 'Pregancy, Maternity and the Organisation of Family Life: and Attempt to Classify the Case Law of the Court of Justice', *E.L. Rev.*, 26(3): 239.

Mazey, S. (1998) 'The European Union and Women's Rights - From the Europeanization of National Agendas to the Nationalization of a European Agenda', *Journal of European Public Policy* 5(1): 131.

McGlynn, C. (2000) 'Ideologies of Motherhood in European Community Sex Equality Law', *E.L. Rev.*, n. 6: 29.

McGlynn, C. (2001) 'Reclaiming a Feminist Vision: the Reconciliation of Paid Work and Family Life in EU Law and Policy', *Columbia Journal of EU Law:* 241.

McGlynn, C. (2007) 'Families and European Union Law', in Probert, R. (ed.) *Family Life and the Law. Under One Roof* (London: Ashgate).

Meenan, H. (ed.), (2007) *Equality Law in an Enlarged European Union. Understanding the Article 13 Directives* (Cambridge: Cambridge University Press).

Miner, H.M. (1956) 'Body Ritual among the Nacirema', *American Anthropologist* 58:3: 503.

Moffat, G. (2007) 'Work-Life Balance and Employment Law: Cultural Change or Mission Impossible?', in Probert, R. (ed.) *Family Life and the Law. Under One Roof* (London: Ashgate).

Mohanty, S.P. (2003), 'The Epistemic Status of Cultural Identity', in Martìn Alcoff, L. and Mendieto, E. (eds.), *Identities. Race, Class, Gender And Nationality* (Oxford: Blackwell).

Montalti, M. (2009), 'La tutela del genere nell'ordinamento comunitario', in Rossilli, M.R (ed.), *I diritti delle donne nell'Unione Europea. Cittadine Migranti Schiave* (Roma: Ediesse).

Mootz, F.J. (2006) *Rhetorical Knowledge in Legal Practice and Critical Legal Theory* (Tuscaloosa: The University of Alabama Press).

More, G. (1999) 'The Principle of Equal Treatment: From Market Unifier to Fundamental Right?' in Craig, P. and De Búrca, G. (eds.) *The Evolution of EU Law* (Oxford: Oxford University Press).

More, G.C. (1993) '«Equal treatment» of the sexes in European Community Law: what does «equal» mean?', *Feminist Legal Studies*, Vol. 1, no. 1: 45.

Münch, R. (2008a) *Die Konstruktion der europäischen Gesellschaft. Zur Dialektik von transnationaler Integration und nationaler Desintegration* (Frankfurt am Main/New York: Campus).

Münch, R. (2008b), Constructing a European Society', *European Law Journal*, 14: 519.

Muraro, L. (1991) *L'ordine simbolico della madre* (Roma: Editori Riuniti).

Negri, A. (2005) *La differenza italiana* (Roma: Nottetempo).

Niccolai, S. and Ruggiu, I. (2009) 'Se un bambino va con la mamma a mendicare: qualche riflessione sull'"argomento culturale" e le responsabilità della giurisdizione', in Brunelli, G., Pugiotto, A., Veronesi, P. (eds.), *Scritti in onore di Lorenza Carlassare* (Napoli: Jovene).

Niccolai, S. (2006) 'I rapporti di genere nella costruzione costituzionale europea. Spunti a partire dal metodo aperto di coordinamento', *Politica del diritto,* XXXVII, no. 4: 573.

Niccolai, S. (2008) 'Framing the Lisbon Strategy in the History of European Policies on Gender: a Postmodernist Vision of Human Dignità in the Making', in Jesién, L. (ed.), *European Union Policies in the Making* (Kraków: Tischner University Press).

Niccolai, S. (2009) 'Derecho Antidiscriminatorio, Nuevos Valores de Convivencia y Argumentación Constitucional. Commentario a la sentencia 'Coleman vs Attrige Law' del Tribunal de Justicia de la Unión Europea', *Revista de Derecho Constitucional Europeo,* n. 11: 437.

Niccolai, S. (2010) 'Trasformazioni del senso del lavoro e della cura e argomentazione costituzionale. A margine di una controversia di discriminazione per handicap', forthcoming in A. Cerri et al. (eds.), *Scritti in onore di Angel Antonio Cervati.*

Ninatti, S. (2007) 'Il diritto alla vita familiare all'esame della Corte di Giustizia', in M. Cartabia (ed.), *I diritti in azione* (Bologna: il Mulino).

Numhauser-Henning, A (2007) 'EU sex equality law post Amsterdam', in Meenan, H. (ed.), *Equality Law in an Enlarged European Union. Understanding the Article 13 Directives* (Cambridge: Cambridge University Press).

Nussbaum, M. (2000) *Women and Human Development. The Capabilities Approach* (Cambridge: Cambridge University Press).

Olivito, E. (2002) 'Azioni positive e rappresentanza femminile: problematiche generali e prospettive di rilancio', *Politica del diritto*, XXXIII, no. 2: 237.

Orloff, A.S. (1993) 'Gender and the Social Rights of Citizenship: The Comparative Analysis of Gender Relations and Welfare States', *American Sociological Review* 58, 3: 303.

Pateman, C. (1988) *The Sexual Contract* (Stanford: Stanford University Press).

Pech, T. (2001) 'La dignité humaine. Du droit à l'éthique de la relation', *Justices*, May: 90.

Perelman, C. (1980), *Justice, Law and Argument. Essays on Moral and Legal Reasoning* (Dordrecht: Reidel).

Perelman, C. and Olbrechts-Tyteca, L. (1958), *Traité de l'argumentation: la nouvelle rhétorique* (Paris: Presses Universitaires de France).

Perrons, D. (2003) 'Gender Mainstreaming in European Union Policy. Why Now?' paper to ESCR Gender Mainstreaming Seminar, Leeds, October.

Phillips, A. (2007) *Multiculturalism Without Culture* (Princeton: Princeton University Press).

Pizzorusso, A. (1982) *Lezioni di diritto pubblico* (Bologna-Roma: Zanichelli-Il Foro Italiano).

Polanyi, K. (1944) *The Great Transformation* (New York: Holt, Rinehart & Winston).

Pollicino, O. (2005) *Discriminazione sulla base del sesso e trattamento preferenziale nel diritto comunitario* (Milano: Giuffré).

Praetorius, I. (2008) 'Il mondo come ambiente domestico', in Cosentino, V. and Longobardi, G. (eds.), *La vita alla radice dell'economia* (Verona: Quaderni del Maeg).

Prechal, S. (2004) 'Equality of Treatment, Non-Discrimination and Social Policy: Achievement in Three Themes', *Common Market Law Review*, 41: 533.

Repetto, G. (2009a) 'Il metodo comparativo in Vico e il diritto costituzionale europeo', *Rivista critica del diritto privato,* 2/XXVII: 295.

Repetto, G. (2009b) 'I diritti all'identità sessuale e il ruolo della morale pubblica', in Vespaziani, A. (ed.), *Diritti fondamentali europei. Casi e problemi di diritto costituzionale comparato* (Torino: Giappichelli).

Ricoeur, P. (2005) *The Course of Recognition* (Cambridge: Harvard University Press).

Robinson, A.M. (2007) *Multiculturalism and the Foundations of Meaningful Life: Reconciling Autonomy, Identity, and Community* (Vancouver-Toronto: Ubc Press).

Rogowski, R. (2008) 'Governance of the European Social Model: the Case of Flexicurity', *Intereconomics* (Mar/Apr): 82.

Rombes, N., Culik, H., Howard, J.A. (1997) 'Otherwise: An Editorial Welcome', *Post Identity*, 1/1: 5.

Rossilli, M.R. (2009) 'Introduzione', in Rossilli, M.R (ed.), *I diritti delle donne nell'Unione Europea. Cittadine Migranti Schiave* (Roma: Ediesse).

Rubery, J. (2005), 'Reflections on Gender Mainstreaming: An example of feminist economics in Action?', *Feminist Economics*, 11/3: 1.

Ruggie, J. (1982) 'International Regimes, Transactions and Change: Embedded Liberalism in the Post-war Economic Order', *International organisation* 36(2): 379.

Ruggiu, I. (2006) 'Comparazione (diritto costituzionale)', in S. Cassese (ed.), *Dizionario di diritto pubblico* (Milano: Giuffré).

Sacksofky, U. and Rodríguez Ruiz, B. (2005), 'Gender in the German Constitution' in Rubio Marin, R. and Baines, B. (eds.), *The Gender of Constitutional Jurisprudence* (Cambridge New York: Cambridge University Press).

Said, E. (2004) *Humanism and Democratic Criticism* (New York: Columbia University Press).

Schefold, D. (2008) 'Il rispetto della dignità umana nella giurisprudenza costituzionale tedesca', in Ceccherini, E. (ed.), (2008) *La tutela della dignità dell'uomo* (Napoli: Editoriale Scientifica).

214

Schefold, D. (2007) 'La dignità umana. Aspetti e problemi della giurisprudenza costituzionale tedesca', in Panunzio, S.P. (ed.), *I diritti fondamentali e le Corti in Europa* (Napoli: Jovene).

Schiek, D. (2002) 'A New Framework on Equal Treatment of Persons in EC Law?', *European Law Journal*, vol. 8 n. 2: 290.

Schiek, D. and Chege, V. (eds.), (2009) *European Union Non-Discrimination Law: Comparative Perspectives on Multidimensional Equality Law* (London/New York: Routledge).

Schmitt, S., (1995) 'All These Forms of Women's Work Which Endanger Public Health and Public Welfare: Protective Labour Legislation for Women in Germany, 1878-1914', in Wikander U., Kessler-Harris A., Lewis J, *Protecting women: Labor Legislation in Europe, the United States, and Australia, 1880-1920,* (Campaign: University of Illinois Press).

Schon, D. and Rein, M. (1994) *Frame Reflection - Towards the Resolution of Intractible Policy Controversies* (New York: Basic Books).

Schwenken, H. (2005) 'Domestic Slavery versus Workers' Rights. Political Mobilizations of Migrant Domestic Workers in the European Union', Working Paper 116/January, The Center for Comparative Immigration Studies, University of California, San Diego (www.ccis-ucsd.org/publications/wrkg116.pdf).

Sciarra, S. (2005) 'Fundamental Labour Rights after the Lisbon Agenda', in De Búrca, G., and De Witte, B. (eds.), *Social Rights in Europe* (Oxford: Oxford University Press).

Scott, J.W. (1988) 'L'ouvrière! Mot impie, sordide …: Women Workers in the Discourse of French Political Economy, 1840-1860' in Scott, J. (ed.), *Gender and the Politics of History* (New York: Columbia University Press).

Scott, J.W. (1993) 'The Woman Worker', in Fraisse G. and Perrot M. (eds.), *A History of Women in the West. IV. Emerging Feminism from Revolution to World War* (Cambridge: The Belknap Press of Harvard University Press).

Scott, J.W. (1996) *Only Paradoxes to Offer. French Feminists and the Rights of Man* (Cambridge: Harvard University Press).

Scott, W.R. and Meyer, J.W. (1994) *Institutional Environments and Organization. Structural Complexity and Individualism* (Thousand Oaks, London, New Delhi: Sage).

Sen, A. (2006) *Identity and Violence: The Illusion of Destiny* (New York/London: Ww Norton & Company).

Shaw, J. (2000) 'Importing Gender: the Challenge of Feminism and the Analysis of the EU Legal Order', *Journal of European Public Policy*: 406.

Shaw, J. (2002) 'The European Union and Gender Mainstreaming: Constitutionally Embedded or Comprehensively Marginalised?', *Journal of European Public Policy*: 213.

Shaw, J., Hunt, J. and Wallace, C. (2007) 'EU Citizens in the Internal Market', *Dies. The Economic and Social Law of the European Union*, (Basingstoke: Palgrave Macmillan).

Sirianni, G. (2006) *Il diritto degli stranieri all'unità familiare* (Milano: Giuffré).

Somek, A. (1999) 'A Constitution for Anti-Discrimination. Exploring the Vanguard Moment of Community Law', *European Law Journal*, vol. 5 n. 3: 243.

Sorhab, J.A. (1994) 'Women and Social Security: the Limits of EEC Equality Law', *Social Welfare and Family Law*: 1.

Stratigaki, M. (2004) 'The Co-option of Gender Concepts in EU Policies - the Case of Reconciliation of Work and Family', *Social Politics* 11(1): 30.

Stratigaki, M. (2005) 'Gender Mainstreaming versus Positive Action: An On-going Conflict in the EU Gender Equality Policy', *European Journal of Women's Studies* 12(2): 165.

Taylor, C. (1992) *Multiculturalism and the Politics of Recognition* (Princeton: Princeton University Press).

Tega, D. (2008) 'Discriminazione e diritto antidiscriminatorio: considerazioni istituzionali (a partire dal diritto costituzionale italiano)' in T. Casadei (ed.), *Lessico delle discriminazioni: tra società, diritto e istituzioni* (Reggio Emilia: Diabasis).

Thelen, K. (2003) 'How Institutions Evolve: Insight from Comparative-Historical Analysis', in Mahoney, J. and Rüschemeyer, D. (eds.), *Comparative Historical Analysis in the Social Sciences* (Cambridge: Cambridge University Press): 208-240.

Thelen, K., (2002) 'The Explanatory Power of Historical Institutionalism', in Mayntz, R. (ed.), *Akteure – Mechanismen – Modelle: Zur Theoriefähigkeit makrosozialer Analysen* (Frankfurt am Main/New York: Campus).

Thompson, E.P. (1967) 'Time, Work, Discipline and Industrial Capitalism', *Past and Present*: 56.

Tobler, C. and Waaldijk, K. (2009) 'Annotation of ECJ, Case C-267/06, *Tadao Maruko v. Versorgungsanstalt der deutschen Bühnen*', *Common Market Law Review*, 46: 723.

Toggenburg, G.N. (2008) '«LGBT» go Luxembourg: on the stance of Lesbian Gay Bisexual and Transgender Rights before the European Court of Justice', *European Law Reporter*, 5: 174.

Tridimas, T. (2006), *The General Principles of EU Law* (Second Edition) (Oxford: Oxford EC Law Library).

Trucco, L. (2008) 'Le tutele comunitarie nei confronti delle lavoratrici alla prova della fecondazione *in vitro*', *Giurisprudenza italiana,* no. 10: 2143.

Tryfonidou, A. (2009), 'Family Reunification of (Migrant) Union Citizens: Towards a More Liberal Approach', *European Law Journal*, 15: 634.

Tully, J. (1995) *Strange Multiplicity. Constitutionalism in an Age of Diversity* (Cambridge: Cambridge University Press).

Van der Vleuten, A. (2007) *The Price of Gender Equality: Member States and Governance in the European Union* (Aldershot: Ashgate).

Van Ham, P. (2001) *European Integration and the Postmodern Condition: Governance, Democracy, Identity* (London/New York: Routledge).

Verloo, M. (ed.), (2007) *Multiple Meanings of Gender Equality - a Critical Frame Analysis of Gender Policies in Europe* (Budapest: CEU Press).

Vespasiani, A. (2004) 'La dottrina costituzionale europea nell'era post ontologica del diritto comparato', *Rivista di diritto pubblico comparato ed europeo:* 547.

Vespaziani, A. (2007) 'Tre metafore del costituzionalismo europeo: molteplicità dei livelli, tono costituzionale e ponderazione', in F. Cerrone e M. Volpi (eds.), *Sergio Panunzio. Profilo intellettuale di un giurista* (Napoli: Jovene).

Villa, P. (2009), 'La Strategia Europea per l'Occupazione e le pari opportunità tra uomini e donne', in Rossilli M.R (ed), *I diritti delle donne nell'Unione Europea. Cittadine Migranti Schiave* (Roma: Ediesse).

Vint, S. (2005) 'Theorising the Global: The Limits of Posthuman Subjectivity and Collective Agency in Joan Slonczewski's Brain Plague', *Post Identity*, 4/2.

Weil, S. (1949) *L'enracinement* (It. Translation 1990, Roma: SE Editore).

Wikander, U. (1995) 'Some Kept the Flag of Feminist Demands Waving: Debates at International Congresses on Protecting Women's Workers', in Wikander U., Kessler-Harris A. and Lewis J., *Protecting women: Labor Legislation in Europe, the United States, and Australia, 1880-1920* (Campaign: University of Illinois Press).

Wikander, U., Kessler-Harris, A. and Lewis, J. (eds.) (1995) *Protecting women: labor legislation in Europe, the United States, and Australia, 1880-1920,* (Campaign: University of Illinois Press).

Williams, C. (1989) *Gender Differences at Work. Women and Men in Nontraditional Occupations* (Berkeley: University of California Press).

Wobbe, T. (2003), 'From Protecting to Promoting: Evolving EU Sex Equality Norms in a Organisational Field', *European Law Journal*: 88.

Wobbe, T., (2009a) "Vom 'nation-building' zum 'market-building'. Der Wandel von Vergesellschaftsformen im europäischen Integrationsprozess", in *Mittelweg 36*, 18, 2009, Heft 3, 3-16 (http://www.eurozine.com/pdf/2009-06-23-wobbe-de.pdf).

Wobbe, T. (2009) 'Die Wettbewerbsfähigkeit als Selbstbeschreibung der Europäischen Union', in Scherzberg A., Wegner G. and Wobbe T. (eds.), *Dimensionen des Wettbewerbs – Europäische Integration zwischen Eigendynamik und politischer Gestaltung* (Tübingen: Mohr).

Wobbe, T. and Biermann, I. (2007) 'Die Metamorphosen der Gleichheit in der Europäischen Union. Genese und Institutionalisierung von Gleichberechtigungsnormen im supranationalen und globalen Kontext', *Kölner Zeitschrift für Soziologie und Sozialpsychologie* 59: 565.

Wobbe, T. and Biermann, I. (2009) *Von Rom nach Amsterdam: Die Metamorphosen des Geschlechts in der Europäischen Union* (Wiesbaden: VS Verlag für Sozialwissenschaften).

Young, I.M. (1990) *Justice and the Politics of Difference* (Princeton: Princeton University Press).

Zabrebelsky, G. (2008), *La legge e la sua giustizia* (Bologna: Il Mulino).

Other European Press Academic Publishing Publications:

International Politics and Economics

Roberto Di Quirico	*Building on Borrowed Bricks*
Ilkka Saarilahti	*40 vuotta Euroopan Union Budjetointia Yleisen taloisarvion kehitys vuosina 1968-2008*
Ilkka Saarilahti	*Les procèdures budgètaires de l'Union europèenne de 2004 à 2008*
Antonio De Chiara	*Multinationals Corporations*
Roberto di Quirico	*Europeanisation and Democratisation*
Jan van der Harst	*The Atlantic Priority*
Baroncelli -Varvesi	*Europe in Progress*
Xiaojie Xu Petro	*Petro Dragon's Rise*
Minoru Nakano	*New Japanese Political Economy and Political Reform*
Ryuji Mukae	*Japan's Refugee Policy: to be of the World*

European Press Academic Publishing (EPAP)
Publications on:
http://www.e-p-a-p.com
http://www.europeanpress.eu
orders@e-p-a-p.com

Printed in June 2010
by Digital Team- Fano
Italy

www.ingramcontent.com/pod-product-compliance
Lightning Source LLC
Chambersburg PA
CBHW060556220326
41598CB00024B/3117